Endorsements for *LASTING Transformation*

"*LASTING Transformation* is truly a gift to the world. Abby Rosen has translated her years of experience as a psychologist into a guidebook that brings its readers along a healing journey that addresses/enlightens both the heart and the soul. I'd wager that it's impossible to really read this book without being changed by it.

"Abby Rosen, a master of her trade, shares her secrets freely with the world in *LASTING Transformation*. This book is a holy offering; the fruit of a life dedicated to helping people heal their soul-wounds, find their joy, live their truth, and deepen their connection with the Divine source of all. Abby draws wisdom from all the stepping-stones along her journey and weaves it into a practical guide for self-improvement that bears the mark of a true master—it is gentle yet deep, modest yet profound."

—Sarah Yehudit Schneider, author of *Kabbalistic Writings on the Nature of Masculine and Feminine* and *You Are What You Hate;* founding director of A Still Small Voice: Correspondence Teachings in Jewish Wisdom.

"Abby Rosen brought into her book experiences from decades of psychotherapeutic work with clients and from her years of spiritual practice. Written in a clear, easily understandable style and strewn with humorous cartoons, *LASTING Transformation* is a manual that will guide its readers through the challenges of everyday life, as well as the ups and downs of the spiritual journey."

—Stanislav Grof, MD, author of *Psychology of the Future, The Cosmic Game, The Ultimate Journey,* and *When the Impossible Happens*

"This book is written from the heart. Abby Rosen's practical exercises and information give the reader many helpful tools to encourage and support change."

—Sharon Salzberg, cofounder of Insight Meditation Society; author of *The Kindness Handbook, Faith,* and *Voices of Insight*

"Both a visionary guide to the whole-some life and a step-by-step map of how to get there."

—Sam Keen, author of *Fire in the Belly: On Being a Man*

LASTING
Transformation
A Guide to Navigating Life's Journey

ABBY ROSEN, PhD

BALBOA.
PRESS

a Division of Hay House

ISBN: 978-1-4525-0006-5 (sc)
ISBN: 978-1-4525-0007-2 (hc)
ISBN: 978-1-4525-0008-9 (e)

Balboa Press books may be ordered through booksellers or by contacting:

Balboa Press
A Division of Hay House
1663 Liberty Drive
Bloomington, IN 47403
www.balboapress.com
1-(877) 407-4847

Printed in the United States of America

Balboa Press rev. date: 6/14/2010

CREDITS:
Cover painting by Barry Nemett
Cover design and layout by Laini Nemett, Lauren Allen, Chandra Rose
Creative Consultants: Alan Bower, Pamela McNay
Design Consultants: Jenn Handy, Amanda Koumoutsos
Design of interior layout: Katie Schneider, Robin Lasek
Editors: Diana Drew, Pythia Peay, Sheryl Sieracki
Illustration cartoons by Anne-Marie Esson
Photograph by Connie Reider
Stylist: Tommy Price
Timing Specialist: Dale O'Brien,
(see Acknowledgments/Credits for their contact information)

Dedication

This book is dedicated in loving memory to my parents, Rose and Dan Rosen, for whom I am eternally grateful. Even though you are no longer physically present, your unconditional love, values, guidance, and caring are ever present in all you have touched. To Mom, for your wisdom, grace, support, and always seeing the best in everyone. To Dad, for the love that radiated from your eyes, your giving nature, your community service, and your sense of humor. May all you have shared flow through me in the following pages, to make the blessing you have been in my life, a blessing for others.

Contents

Foreword.. ix

Introduction: An Overview of the Road Map...........................xi

Stage One: Life-Lesson Therapy

1. Uncovering the Cover-up...3
    In Practice: Getting to Know Your Cover-ups 19

2. Transforming Soul Holes into Whole Souls 25
    In Practice: Transforming Soul Holes into Whole Souls 35

3. Our Vulnerability Is Our Strength 37
    In Practice: The "Checking-In" Process.................................. 48

4. Vulnerability Is the Key to Intimacy............................. 51
    In Practice: Using the Formula for Conscious Communication.... 63

5. For Men, Mainly 65
    In Practice: Learning to Recognize Anxiety 78

6. The Higher Purpose of Relationships 83
    In Practice: Getting to Know Your Primary and Disowned Selves 96

7. How Behavioral Change and Transformation Happen 99
    In Practice: Behavioral Change and Transformation Experiment....... 111

Stage Two: Soul-Wisdom Therapy

8. Grow a Conscious Self—Know Your Inner Self...................... 117
    In Practice: Disidentification and Self-Identification 126

9. Communicating with the Source: The Power of Meditation 129
    In Practice: Developing a Meditation Practice 143

10. Accessing Our Intuition 145
    In Practice: Listening to Your Intuitive Wisdom........................156

11. The Gift of Faith.. 159

    In Practice: Transpersonal Inspiration and Psychological
    Mountain Climbing...169

12. Repairing Our World: From Self-Serving to the Serving Self... 173

    In Practice: Finding Right Livelihood and Discovering
    Your Serving Self.. 188

A Summary of the Journey: Life's Rules of the Road 191

The Inspiration for This Book and an Inspiration for Our Lives ..195

Acknowledgments 199

Bibliography and Resources 205

Glossary...211

Appendices

    Appendix A – Voice Dialogue: Discovering Our Selves................219

    Appendix B – List of Subpersonalities or Selves......................... 223

    Appendix C – Guided Visualization to Communicate with
                    Your Inner Child 225

    Appendix D – Inner Critic Self-Test... 229

    Appendix E – Primary and Disowned Selves............................. 233

    Appendix F – Meditation Practices 235

    Appendix G – Additional Resources on Meditation.................... 243

About the Author 247

About InnerSource, A Center for Psychotherapy and Healing..... 249

Foreword

Fine wine must be aged properly. It cannot be rushed, but must wait, fermenting in the proper way and for the proper amount of time. Only then can we experience that wonderful sense of well-being as we inhale the exquisite aroma and sip the first delicious sip. Although we are not true wine connoisseurs, it was this image that came to us as we thought about Abby Rosen and this fully matured book, *LASTING Transformation*.

We have known Abby Rosen for a very long time. She brings to the transformational table a long and varied life of fermentation. She has always been a worldly person, grounded in the material realities of living and family and work and business. On the other side, she has been, from early in her life, a woman of spirit—always searching for the deeper meaning, the higher intelligence, and finding ways to access this other dimension of consciousness. She is also a senior Voice Dialogue teacher and facilitator, and this has provided an important contribution to the development of her overall philosophy of life and healing and her approach to the transformational process.

It is quite natural for this book to emerge out of Abby's long experience as a psycho-spiritual therapist and teacher as well as her experience as a woman of the world. It is perfect timing—just the right amount of maturation—in many different ways. From the depths of her unconscious came the message that the wine was ready. The title of the book came to her in a dream, and she refers to this experience in the Introduction to the book as a "download from the Universe." That is how it works for people who have allowed themselves to gradually ripen in these spheres and experiences that combine the worlds of earth and spirit. They don't need to chase after wisdom any longer; it seems to emerge more and more in the form of "downloads from the Universe."

The book itself is actually two different books, woven into a single tapestry of earth and spirit. Stage One refers to what Abby calls "Life-Lesson Therapy." Stage Two refers to "Soul-Wisdom Therapy." The book is very personal and, at the same time, an objective and practical manual for moving along one's own transformational path. It seems very important to us that people understand the inseparable nature of learning practically about living life in a physical body on the planet earth while, at the same time, reaching out and embracing the transpersonal selves that thirst for union with spiritual realities. All of us are struggling with these opposites, sometimes more successfully than other times. Living between opposites of all kinds is very hard work, and we need all the help we can get, especially when it comes to the challenge of embracing heaven and earth.

So we welcome Abby Rosen's book, and we are pleased that the complex process of fermentation is at an end. It is now time for everyone to taste the fruits of a life well lived and a book well written.

> Sidra Stone, PhD, and Hal Stone, PhD, Albion, California
> Cocreators of "Voice Dialogue, Relationship, and the Psychology
> of Selves"; authors of *Embracing Our Selves, Embracing Your
> Inner Critic, Partnering*, and other consciousness tools

Introduction:
An Overview of the Road Map

I awoke one morning to neon shimmering letters in front of my eyes. At first, I had no idea what was going on—nothing like this had ever happened to me before. The shimmering letters spelled out L A S T I N G Transformation. *A few moments elapsed and then it struck me—this was the title for the book I had been working on. It was a download from the Universe! Then, with its inimitable sense of wise humor, I was told that it was an acronym for* **L**ife-**L**esson **A**nd **S**oul-Wisdom **T**herapy for **I**nner **G**rowth & **T**ransformation.

This book takes the reader on a journey to experience this process of transformation, which can result in positive, powerful change—a change that is irreversible. We will focus on tools that transform those behavioral patterns that create obstacles in our relationships and in our lives.

They say you learn your biggest life lessons from your most difficult experiences.

What a stupid system!

For such an important journey, you would think we would have gotten a road map to show us how to navigate it more easily. *LASTING Transformation* is such a road map. When life situations cause us stress, there are tools we can use to move into a place of greater awareness, resulting in a more conscious response.

A lifetime is a sacred journey we need to travel mindfully if we are to live lives filled with joy, love, and meaning, connected to ourselves, our Source, and the significant others in our lives. Life's journey provides us with many opportunities for self-knowledge, self-love, and deep personal transformation. The road map outlined in this book provides the reader with specific guidance for this sacred journey.

Why don't more people embark on this journey? The main reason is the guidance on how to find the path of self-awareness and transformation is not readily accessible, it is not yet mainstream in our society. One of the goals of this book is to awaken people to the idea that there is a path, and then to give them the tools, resources, and guidance necessary to embark on this journey. Another reason that many people don't take this road less traveled is that it is hard work and the rewards aren't instantaneous. However, the results we can achieve are exquisitely worth the effort.

Like most transformational journeys, this one has stages:

- **Stage One: Life-Lesson Therapy** focuses on reversing negative patterns of behavior that cause pain and problems in relationships. During this first stage the work centers on strengthening our sense of self and refining our personality, made up of our body, feelings, and mind. These chapters are based on a proven formula for communicating clearly with ourselves and others as we learn our life lessons. In the process, we gain a more profound understanding of how relationships work, and we develop the skills to move from behavioral change to lasting transformation. As we become more self-aware, self-loving, and able to navigate in our relationships in a healthy and conscious way, we enter the next stage of the journey.

- **Stage Two: Soul-Wisdom Therapy** involves learning techniques for listening within, which open us to experience the deeper spiritual realms of consciousness—those that are home to the soul and to that inner source of wisdom within each of us—the Inner Self. This "Self"-awareness helps us develop soul-wisdom, which, in turn, often evokes a desire to be of service in helping to repair our world.

LASTING Transformation offers a comprehensive approach that leads us on a step-by-step journey through these stages. The twelve chapters that follow are each divided into two parts. The first presents a theoretical framework, interlaced with client examples drawn from my experience as a practicing psychologist. These examples clarify the principles under discussion. Identifying characteristics of each client have been changed to protect their privacy. The first part of each chapter concludes with an "Experiences" subsection relating to the theme of that chapter. These experiences are designed to give us a deeper understanding of the evolution of consciousness by which different people have moved from awareness to behavioral change to transformation.

WOW! This transformation stuff really works!

The second part of each chapter, "In Practice," provides personal guidance and exercises that enable us to integrate a deep experience of the principles described in part one. The skills developed in the "In Practice" sections build on those taught in each chapter. All are designed to give us tools that can be life-changing. This is a proven process of therapy, which I have successfully used with many clients to promote self-awareness, personal growth, spiritual awakening, and lasting transformation. For those who don't have access to counseling, or would like to supplement their counseling, this book will help serve as a valuable resource. If you read something that interests you, there may be more information listed in the Bibliography or in the Appendices.

This book is a transpersonal guidebook. The term *transpersonal*, coined by Abraham Maslow, PhD, and Stanislav Grof, MD, refers to a human being as more than the personality. According to Maslow, we are able to transcend the personality and experience the higher spiritual planes of consciousness beyond the personality. *LASTING Transformation* gives you the tools to reach these higher planes.

Transpersonal Psychology is the psychological modality that goes beyond traditional and humanistic psychology and incorporates the spiritual dimension of personal growth. This alignment of the mind, body, and spirit creates a sense of wholeness that can result in lasting transformation. In addition, as we work toward such personal wholeness, our relationships tend to expand to include a deep concern for each other and the planet.

Today, more than ever, there is a desperate need to repair our world. In order for society to change, and to minimize conflict by managing how we deal with the stress in our world, we need to transform how we conduct our relationships, not only with ourselves and with each other, but also with our communities, with other societies, and with the earth itself. May this book be a guide for you on your journey toward this lasting transformation.

Stage One:
Life-Lesson Therapy

Barry Nemett, *Sculpted Head of Child,* 2009. Graphite on paper, 9×5 in.

1

Uncovering the Cover-up

What the caterpillar calls the end of the world, the master calls a butterfly.
——Richard Bach, *Illusions*

Michael grew up with an alcoholic father who would become enraged when he was drunk. If one of his children tried to hide his alcohol or take it away, he would kick that child out of the house. At one point he actually went after one of Michael's brothers with a kitchen knife. Michael learned to protect himself by covering up his feelings, so that he wouldn't be vulnerable. Instead of feeling hurt by his father's rage, he shut down that part of himself. To regain control, whenever Michael would experience feelings like fear, hurt, anxiety, sadness, loss of control, or being personally threatened in any way, he would get angry. After all, he had learned to protect himself from a master teacher, his father. These defense mechanisms—of shutting down emotionally whenever he felt exposed, and raging at others, both of which he learned to do growing up with his father—became destructive to Michael's relationships as an adult. His anger and need for control would intensify whenever he felt vulnerable. This was responsible, in large part, for the failure of his three marriages. Ironically, the cover-up that Michael created to protect himself was itself the cause of his failure to have the kind of love he so yearned for in his life.

The Cover-up

The culture we live in and the family we are raised in often inadvertently teach us a cover-up that can affect our lives, often producing devastating results. What is this cover-up? It is the process of covering over and negating

3

how, at our most essential level, we are vulnerable. If we find that it's not safe to express our feelings openly or have our needs met early in life, then, like Michael, we develop a system of defense mechanisms to protect, hide, and cover over our hearts.

A baby is totally dependent on its caregivers for survival, nurturance, and love. If a baby's needs for food, water, protection from the elements, and touch are not met, the baby dies. If the needs for affection, love, support, guidance, and healthy mirroring are not met, a part of the baby's emotional makeup dies or becomes disowned; that is, healthy emotions are covered over with an unhealthy expression of feelings to make sure the child isn't hurt even more, or, worse, abandoned. These may include protections like withdrawing or trying to become invisible. A history of hurt from abuse, neglect, or abandonment, which makes a child fearful, lonely, or feel out of control, may cause his or her core sensitivity to go into hiding. If the child doesn't feel safe, then a process begins in which the vulnerable feelings are protected by behavioral, emotional, psychological, spiritual, and relational patterns.

Some children develop other unhealthy ways to express their feelings. These antisocial behaviors are set up to protect them, making sure they don't get hurt or abandoned. So, instead of expressing hurt, sadness, anxiety, or any other vulnerable feeling, children like Michael learn to rage, put up walls, be tough, oppositional, or sarcastic. Some of us put others down to make ourselves feel better, becoming critical, controlling, and domineering. Abuse of alcohol and drugs is also a defense mechanism often used to numb painful feelings.

As children, some of us protect ourselves and gain approval by doing what we think others want us to do. We might have been acknowledged and praised whenever we exhibited behavior that pleased others by "being good." However, this can also be an unhealthy expression of feelings, because as you will see in the Client Experience that ends the first part of this chapter, the behaviors that we develop to cover up our core sensitivity can themselves create painful wounds. If we grew up in dysfunctional families, these mechanisms may have helped us survive as children, but not without lasting negative consequences.

In many instances, the role models we had in our early years taught us these ways of relating to people. If we didn't like how our role models acted, or we were hurt by their actions, we may have developed patterns of behavior that were just the opposite of those we saw. However, as we grow into adulthood, these mechanisms become the habitual ways we relate to the world; oftentimes, we are unaware of the damaging effects of our actions and how these patterns limit our choices and our relationships. These patterns tend to get in the way of meeting our authentic needs because they don't reflect our true self. In therapy, I can tell how traumatic an upbringing clients have had by how strong their defenses are. How healthy people are generally depends on how accessible their core sensitivity is.

Uncovering the Cover-up: Learning Our Life Lessons

As Michael experienced, many of the behavior patterns we develop as children to protect us from hurt may end up causing us the very pain they were set up to avoid once we reach adulthood. For instance, perhaps when we were young we built a wall around ourselves to protect us from our parents' constant battles as their marriage disintegrated. Years later, our spouse claims we're remote and don't express our feelings. The wall that protected us as a child is now keeping out the very love that we want. With the past exerting such a strong hold on the present, it's no wonder that 60 percent of American marriages end in divorce.

According to the National Institute of Mental Health, dysthymic disorder, or depression, affects approximately 1.5 percent of the U.S. population age eighteen and older in a given year. This figure translates to about 3.3 million American adults. The median age of onset of dysthymic disorder is thirty one years. Approximately forty million American adults ages eighteen and older have an anxiety disorder. One of the major causes behind these sobering statistics is the disconnection from, and cover-up of, our true thoughts and feelings.

Stage One of this book is about learning our life lessons—the lessons that our life experiences are showing us that we need to learn. When we find ourselves engaging in one failed relationship after another, or expressing ourselves in ways that wind up hurting ourselves or others, we need to change those negative behavior patterns. If we recognize that these life experiences are here to teach us, and then change our behaviors accordingly, we are able to learn our life lessons.

Consider Michael's case: If he learned to acknowledge how terrifying it was to grow up with an abusive, alcoholic father who would rage at him, and allowed himself to feel the hurt, fear, and sadness, he wouldn't need to push away, or push down, those painful feelings when they arise. Nor would he respond by raging at others. Michael could then see his negative behavior patterns for what they are—defense mechanisms that worked to protect him when he was growing up—and learn to recognize that the feelings underneath his urge to rage are what are important.

Then, for the first time, Michael would be more able to express his authentic self and learn that as an adult, it's not only safe to express the feelings in his heart, but doing so might actually help him get his needs met and feel closer and more connected to the important people in his life. It's essential to first feel secure before it is possible to feel safe enough to express our true feelings.

The Original Sin Was the Original Life Lesson

The original cover-up began with Adam and Eve in the Garden of Eden. In the Biblical story, God asked Adam: "Did you eat from the tree from which I commanded you not to eat?" Instead of speaking the truth, Adam became fearful and defensive and blamed his actions on Eve: "The woman that you gave to be with me, she gave me what I ate from the tree." Did Eve do any better? She blamed her mistake on the snake. Did they get what they wanted? No. They were expelled from the garden, cursed with pain.

My interpretation of the Garden of Eden story is that God, who created Adam and Eve, was fully cognizant of their humanity, including their potential to make mistakes. The purpose of their mistake was to provide an opportunity for learning, change, and growth. When confronted with their behavior, Adam and Eve were given the chance to learn an important life lesson and to evolve. Instead, their insistence on covering up their vulnerability by lying and blaming each other caused them—and all their descendants—devastating grief and suffering. The eating of the fruit of the Tree of Knowledge is often referred to as humanity's "original sin." But perhaps creating the cover-up of their fear and vulnerability, rather than learning their life lesson and evolving, is the original sin from Genesis.

Sadly, learning to create the cover-up has become our legacy. Rather than hide from feeling exposed, we need to learn our life lessons and risk expressing to each other our true feelings, thoughts, and needs. That is the "original lesson" that Adam and Eve were supposed to learn. It is a lesson each of us will be given the opportunity to learn over and over again in our lifetime. The cover-up, while expedient in the short term, can only lead to long-term pain and suffering. Think how much healthier Cain and Abel would have been if Adam and Eve had just stopped covering over their vulnerability by blaming. Talk about a dysfunctional family!

It's YOUR fault!
No, it's YOUR fault!

The following tool for transformation will help us identify and separate from our cover-ups, and get to know, value, protect, and share our core sensitivities.

Voice Dialogue:
A Powerful Tool for Transforming the Cover-up

The most effective modality for transformation I have found, one I use both personally and professionally in my practice as a psychologist, is called "Voice Dialogue, Relationship, and the Psychology of Selves." This innovative approach was developed in the 1980s by Drs. Hal and Sidra

Stone, who are licensed clinical psychologists, master therapists, teachers, and inspired consciousness facilitators. Hal and Sidra's psycho-spiritual approach to consciousness is an experiential modality compatible with many theoretical orientations, has its roots in Jungian and Gestalt psychology, and offers a model of consciousness that is both powerful and innovative.

Voice Dialogue is a transformative method for entering into direct communication with a person's inner family of selves—what Hal and Sidra call subpersonalities. Each self has a different energy and way of looking at the world, as well as its own impulses, desires, and methods of protecting the vulnerable Inner Child. Each self also has rules of behavior, feelings, perceptions, reactions, and a history all its own. The terms *subpersonality*, *self*, and *primary self* are used interchangeably throughout this book.

Voice Dialogue allows us to separate from these primary selves in our lives and develop the ability to choose more conscious behaviors. By hearing the needs of the Inner Child, we can learn to express them and make choices that enable our child to feel protected, nurtured, and loved. This enhances our appreciation of ourselves and strengthens our ability to grow, create, and feel more powerful and loving. The goal of Voice Dialogue work is to develop an Aware Ego process that can function apart from what is called the "primary self system," with which we have been identified all along.

As we become more conscious of our inner experience and the different subpersonalities that normally run our life, our operating ego becomes more aware and transforms into an Aware Ego. As such, it is able to separate from the system of dysfunctional ideas, attitudes, and feelings that control our way of being in the world. For the first time, we are able to make real and healthy choices about our behavior, rather than acting out of habits that no longer serve us. Hal and Sidra describe this process in an article entitled "Discovering Our Selves," which is reprinted in Appendix A. "Voice Dialogue is about separating from the many selves that make up the human psyche and creating this Aware Ego ... We feel that the Aware Ego is an evolutionary step forward ... It enables us to follow — safely — our unique paths."

Michael, whose story opened this chapter, needed to develop an Aware Ego that would become conscious of his urge to rage. From an Aware Ego perspective, he could then separate from his "Rager" subpersonality and instead choose to share the vulnerable feelings underneath that subpersonality, which he learned early in life were not safe to share. As an adult, Michael's Aware Ego would help to guide him into the loving, healthy relationships he yearned for but never experienced, growing up with a raging father.

To hear the voice of our core sensitivity, also called the vulnerable Inner Child, and to know what is in our hearts, we need to quiet the many other voices, or subpersonalities, within us that are clamoring to be heard. We do this by first becoming aware of the voices that keep the mind racing, ruminating, and focused outward. Then we begin to separate from them, by realizing that they are just extraneous voices; they do not speak the truth. These voices are simply reading the script they were trained and conditioned to read. They were created to defend against any attacks on our vulnerability; however, as adults these very defense mechanisms, or primary selves, are what set us up for pain and failure.

Our Primary Selves: The Major Players in the Cover-up

Our primary selves are responsible for our survival in what can often feel like a chaotic world. For that reason alone they need to be respected and embraced. They protected our hearts and cared for our vulnerable Inner Child and, in many instances, have allowed us to survive into adulthood. A list of many of the different subpersonalities appears in Appendix B. Let's explore some of the more "vocal" subpersonalities, which are common in many people's experiences.

The Rulemaker

The first self that develops is the Rulemaker. Its job is to figure out, early in life, what the rules are in our particular family and/or environment. To play by the rules, other primary selves, or Heavyweights, develop to support whatever the Rulemaker has figured out is needed to ensure the survival of the little child.

The Heavyweights

Five strong subpersonalities, the Inner Critic, the Judge, the Perfectionist, the Pusher, and the Pleaser, often travel together and are called the Heavyweights. Once we identify the energies of the different subpersonalities, we can uncover our cover-ups and see more clearly what purpose they serve in our lives. We can embrace them for how they have been trying to protect us, and then explore what the authentic self is experiencing under the cover-ups. This develops the Aware Ego process, which is the goal of this approach.

The Heavyweights are most commonly the subpersonalities we need to be aware of and honor for the good job they've done protecting our Inner Child as we were growing up. In order to get past these primary selves who act as guards, we need to first communicate with them, so they know we're on their side. We all want what is best for our Inner Child. As we come to know ourselves better by learning the lessons from the experiences that created these subpersonalities, we're able to manage them more effectively and create healthier options for how to act in different situations. As our responses become clearer and more in alignment with our authentic self, we're able to heal the places in our hearts that have been wounded by these life experiences.

It's amazing how well this system works, because once we learn our life lessons, the dynamics that caused the need for the cover-ups often change, and miraculously, we find we no longer have to deal with those irritating issues or difficult dynamics in our lives.

Behavioral change begins just by honoring and embracing the many selves that make up our personality. Then we can separate from these habitual patterns and make healthier choices that are more relevant to our current situation.

The Inner Critic and the Judge

The heaviest of the Heavyweights is the Inner Critic. The job of this subpersonality is to keep us safe by criticizing us before others do. The Critic comes out when we're feeling anxious—it tries to get us to change our behavior, so we don't get hurt or abandoned. It says things like, "You're never going to amount to anything" or "You're too fat, stupid, ugly," or it looks like the following:

You're an Idiot!   *You'll Never get it right!*   *Did you HAVE to say that?*

The Inner Critic is speaking when you hear the constant inner "shoulds" or the more critical and shame-producing "you shouldn't haves." There's even a New Age Inner Critic that says, "You should meditate more" or "The treadmill is great, but don't forget about doing Hatha Yoga." You see, the Inner Critic reads all the same books you do, but don't let it fool you. It may sound more conscious, but it's still critical.

Hal and Sidra like to say that underlying every Critic is a walking anxiety attack. The Critic is afraid we're going to fail and we won't be loved and accepted. It starts out in life protecting our vulnerability; however, it gets carried away and winds up working above and beyond the call of duty. Often, the Inner Critic assimilates the negative messages we got from our parents and other authority figures when we were young, and then perpetuates these destructive messages without bothering to examine their validity when we're adults.

The Inner Critic is the cause of low self-esteem, self-doubt, guilt, shame, fear of failure, and depression. For most of us, we live life unaware of our Critic. It's been such a constant companion since childhood that we think, "this is me." What a boon to our personal growth to recognize this critical voice as merely one part of us—not all of us—and not a judgment of truth "from Above"! Then we can deal with the underlying fears and make clear, self-loving choices from the perspective of an Aware Ego.

Here is a process you can use to reality-check the input from the Critic when it's pointing out a possible mistake: Access the underlying anxiety that's fueling the Critic, and learn the lessons that our mistakes are here to teach us. At the beginning of a Critic attack, become aware of the Critic's energy, separate from it, kiss the Critic on the forehead, and say, "Don't worry, I've got it under control. We're not perfect, but that's OK. We're not supposed to be."

I've devoted so much space to the Inner Critic because it normally takes up so much inner space! Hal and Sidra wrote an entire book devoted to this subpersonality, *Embracing Your Inner Critic.* You can take the Inner Critic Self-Test in Appendix D to assess how strong this subpersonality is in your life.

While the Critic focuses on criticizing us, the Judge criticizes others to get them to change their behavior when that behavior makes us anxious. If we grew up in a chaotic household that made us feel out of control and scared, we will judge our partner if they have a hard time being organized, are messy, and have problems with being on time—because again, it makes us feel more out of control. Whatever we hear the Inner Critic saying to us, the outer Judge is saying the same thing about others. The Judge tends to judge more harshly those qualities in others that we've disowned in ourselves.

> *Joyce is becoming aware of how extremely judgmental she is of Henrietta when Henrietta's hair is a mess, or she's wearing some outfit that "looks ridiculous." Joyce is dealing with how it is so important for her to be in control and perfect, for fear that she will feel like a misfit and different, which is how she achingly felt growing up. Her family moved so many times, and each time she felt like she didn't fit in. It was traumatic for Joyce, so she disowned the part of her that would make her feel out of control or different. She learned to make sure she knew how to act "perfectly" and be in total control in any situation, so she feels like she fits in.*

The Perfectionist

The Perfectionist subpersonality, which was strong in Joyce, is common in our culture. It sets standards we learn as we grow up to bring us attention and love. These standards are often unrealistic and can never fully be met, since no one is perfect. The Perfectionist was set up to protect the Inner Child from being criticized, unloved, and abandoned. It often succeeds in getting the child attention, affirmation, and acknowledgment. The Perfectionist makes sure whatever we do is good enough to gain approval from others. However, if the Perfectionist continues to be strong in adulthood, given the futility and the impossibility of perfection, it often brings with it physical illness, frustration, and depression.

> *I am working with a client who's building a new home. With a very strong Perfectionist subpersonality, trying to make all the millions of decisions that go into building a house "perfectly" is a nightmare! She's developed fibromyalgia, lost too much weight, is in a constant state of panic, and is seriously depressed. This is a difficult situation, as this client never learned how to separate from her Perfectionist.*
>
> *As this client honors her Perfectionist and understands why she developed this subpersonality—it helped her get affirmed rather than criticized in her childhood—she realizes she no longer needs to worry about being criticized by her mother because she died twenty years ago. Then she can*

separate from her Perfectionist and recognize certain decisions only need to be "good enough – GE," an expression she learned in therapy to repeat whenever the Perfectionist would show up. The process of separating from a subpersonality can take up to two years, so in service to this client's physical and mental health, my client is learning it's OK to make a deal with the Perfectionist that she focuses on a few of the rooms that the Perfectionist can make perfect, and my client can hang out and relax in the rest of the house, which won't have to be quite so "perfect." This allows the decision-making for building the house to be less stressful, as each decision doesn't have to be so perfect. Her experience of the process becomes more enjoyable, and her physical being becomes healthier.

The Pusher

The Pusher's job is to gain approval for what we accomplish. It keeps us learning, striving, and achieving. The Pusher is the one that makes up our to-do lists, tries to get all the jobs done, and never lets us rest, as there is always more to do. Do you wake up in the morning thinking about all the things you have to get done today? That's your Pusher. The Pusher can also prevent us from having the time to quiet the mind and to connect with and experience our Inner Child, as well as the higher energies of our soul-wisdom, which are explored in Stage Two: Soul-Wisdom Therapy. As Hal and Sidra put it so beautifully in their first book, *Embracing Our Selves,* "To recognize soul, one has to stop long enough to discover that there is one."

The Pleaser

Another subpersonality is the Pleaser, who develops to protect the Inner Child by making sure everyone is happy and life is harmonious. If you're at a dinner party with friends, would you not voice your opinion if you think it would be upsetting or different than how your friends feel because it might lead to confrontation, disharmony or loss of friends? That's your Pleaser. This subpersonality takes care of everyone else's Inner Child to the detriment of its own, which is a part of the cover-up. By focusing on everyone else, the Pleaser keeps us from focusing on our own needs.

The Overachiever

The Overachiever subpersonality develops as a way of being affirmed, loved, and acknowledged. Overachievers are great at doing and feeling what they think they should, but are less able to connect with their true needs and desires. The Overachiever, as a primary self, protects us from the fear of not being loved or of abandonment.

Linda came into the therapy session complaining of bouts of depression, which she had experienced most of her life. Her motivation for coming to therapy was to overcome her depression. She described this experience as feeling no energy to achieve. At these times she felt like throwing everything in the closet or sweeping everything under the rug, not being responsible for anything. She called this aspect of herself the "Secret Slob." When asked to describe how she normally experiences herself, she said, "Very responsible, accomplishment-oriented, checkbook balanced to the penny." She called this way of being the "Overachiever," and said she had been that way all her life.

When she explored what benefits the Secret Slob gave her, she realized that only when she felt depressed did she allow herself to take a rest from the drive for achievement and the pressures of responsibility. In fact, she felt as if the Secret Slob gave her a vacation from the pressures of her life. Using the Voice Dialogue approach, we talked to the Overachiever, who described her belief that she always had to be a high achiever. Then we talked to the Secret Slob. Linda realized the Secret Slob deserved an award, because it offered her the opportunity to take a rest in the only way possible, given the Overachiever's belief system.

In the weeks since that session, Linda has been allowing herself to stop and nourish herself without having to do it "secretly." Her bouts of depression have been rare and very short-lived. Linda started viewing the Secret Slob as a friend. Whenever the Secret Slob was around, Linda began to recognize that she needed to take a rest from the Overachiever, and she did. A month after the session, Linda stated that both aspects of herself had become much more balanced, she was much happier, and she felt she had learned an important life lesson.

Eckhart Tolle wisely sums up the process of uncovering our cover-ups in *The Power of Now:*

> Until there is surrender, unconscious role-playing constitutes a large part of human interaction. In surrender, you no longer need ego defenses and false masks. You become very simple, very real. "That's dangerous," says the ego. "You'll get hurt. You'll become vulnerable." What the ego doesn't know, of course, is that only through the letting go of resistance, through becoming "vulnerable," can you discover your true and essential invulnerability. (p. 216)

The Guest House

This being human is a guest house
Every morning a new arrival.

A joy, a depression, a meanness,
some momentary awareness comes
as an unexpected visitor.

Welcome and entertain them all!
Even if they're a crowd of sorrows,
who violently sweep your house
empty of its furniture,
Still, treat each guest honorably.

He may be clearing you out for some
new delight.
The dark thought, the shame, the malice,
meet them all at the door laughing,
and invite them in.

Be grateful for whoever comes,
because each has been sent
as a guide from beyond.

—*Rumi: The Book of Love: Poems of Ecstasy and Longing (p. 179)*

Illustration credit: Rick Garcia

A Client's Experience with Uncovering the Cover-up

I spent my early years as the smallest member of a volatile household and learned in the cradle to have no needs of my own. Not asking for anything meant not drawing dangerous attention to myself. Expressing no needs kept me safe. After my parents' divorce, when I was ten, I supplemented that defense mechanism with a compelling need to serve all those around me—my sad mother, older sisters, adolescent boyfriends—anyone I determined was in need. I arrived, therefore, at adulthood without any sense of who I was. I carried an inner emptiness so vast that without someone else—or something else—to fill me, I feared I would cease to exist at all.

So the woman I was entered marriage intuitively in touch with other people's emotions and ready to serve with an almost knee-jerk intensity. I was empathetic and quick to help. Beneath that I was lonely, angry, sad, and afraid.

My husband, who was raised in a military household, was also taught to have no needs of his own, but found his cover-up in achievement. Being successful ensured his survival; if he never failed, he never lost, he never hurt. The covering up of his vulnerability as a boy brought great rewards, but it led him to enter adulthood a super-achiever … completely out of touch with his emotions. He had covered his vulnerability so successfully that he appeared not to have any. That made him safe to me, and safety was paramount.

The price of safety, however, is frequently numbness. The cover-ups that ensured our early survival had brought together two people who could not feel or expose their vulnerabilities. As a result, we found it difficult to feel any deep connection to each other. It's hard to find a hidden heart and even harder to expose it. Without that exposure, love is an intellectual agreement. Hearts that don't touch can't ignite.

Not long ago I found a black-and-white photograph of my husband at the age of sixteen. He had just said good-bye to the girl he loved, knowing he would never see her again. His father had been transferred to a new job overseas. In the photo, the face of this young man was so full of grief and longing that his pain was palpable. I saw in that photo the boy who still lived within the man I had married—the boy whose uncovered heart could break; who suffered loss and fear, just as I did. In the sudden pressure behind my eyes and the catch in my breath, I felt the passion and depth with which I could love the man that boy had become. I put the photo down, hoping he had not seen how moved I felt. My first instinct was to hide my own vulnerability, even as I responded to his.

It wasn't until years later when I began therapy that I realized that my husband's cover-up of his vulnerability with strength, and my needing to serve others without expressing my own needs, had conspired to sabotage our marriage. I made a commitment to take the risk to express my own needs. Deciding to drop my cover-up is an ongoing process. We peer around the mask and let the other person in, but it takes an enormous desire to change and strength of will. Dropping the cover-up is an expression of faith. It's a decision you have to make in the moment, again and again.

The subpersonalities this client developed when she was young were the Pleaser and the Caretaker, who are often "kissing cousins," meaning they generally appear together. The husband, by contrast, developed a strong Achiever when he was young to protect his vulnerability.

In Practice:
Getting to Know Your Cover-ups

Our cover-ups are the subpersonalities that run our lives and are the ones we most identify with who we are. Try the following exercise. You might want to write out your answers here or in a journal. Journaling helps you develop awareness. By recording what you are thinking and feeling, you free your mind to release the previous thought, knowing that what's important has been written down. This also allows the mind to focus on the next thought or feeling. Journaling facilitates a clearer experience by enabling you to peel off layer after layer of thoughts and feelings until you get to your deeper awareness. Now ask yourself the following questions:

1. *What is your particular way of protecting your Inner Child? Some examples include: By controlling situations, by pleasing others, or by getting angry.*

_____

_____

_____

_____

_____

_____

2. *Describe this primary self. What is its perspective on your life? How would you describe it as a personality (its feelings, its body posture, its general way of thinking)?*

_____

_____

_____

_____

_____

Many people either withdraw to protect themselves or get angry, pushing other people away. As you think about your defense mechanisms, do this in the spirit of self-exploration, not self-condemnation. These protective mechanisms served many of you well as you were growing up; for others, these mechanisms may have created deep wounds, yet as a young child, you knew no other way. Even though they may no longer be effective, you're still using them, because that is what you know. So be gentle and kind with yourself, as this way of reacting has been part of you for many years. Begin to be conscious of these behaviors. Behavioral change happens just by becoming more aware. You don't change by being criticized or by being critical of yourself. What we get from criticism is only lower self-esteem. Awareness, which leads to behavioral change, is the beginning of transformation.

3. *Ask this subpersonality the following questions: What is its job?*

_____

_____

_____

4. *Who trained this primary self to do its job?*

_____

_____

_____

5. *When is it most likely to come out?*

_____

_____

_____

6. *When did it first come into your life?*

_____

_____

_____

7. *How did it protect you when you were younger?*

_____

_____

_____

8. *Give this self a name (for example, Pleaser, Rager, Controller, Wall). Become aware of and write about the energy of this subpersonality.*

_____

_____

_____

9. *Consider how you currently use this same primary self in different relationships or situations.*

_____

_____

_____

_____

_____

10. *Does this subpersonality still work well to protect you today, or do you wind up getting hurt, feeling criticized, or being abandoned when this self comes out in your life?*

_____

_____

_____

_____

Value this subpersonality for the job it did to help you survive when you were younger. We develop these defense mechanisms to protect our Inner Child when we're young. For some, these subpersonalities may have helped us get acknowledgment and praise, or, at least not get criticized or punished, whenever we exhibited these behaviors. For others who were brought up with harsh criticism, the rebellious or oppositional behaviors that developed helped us survive by fighting back.

The power struggles that were put in play by criticism, or aggressive or authoritative parenting, also leave scars, because the subpersonalities that developed in response don't get us affirmed and protected; they lead to punishment and more criticism. However, while rebelliousness is a normal reaction to criticism, the results leave in their wake destructive dynamics.

Even if we develop defense mechanisms that lead to being acknowledged and praised as we're growing up, these same defense mechanisms often inflict the very pain they were set up to avoid once we reach adulthood. Therefore, it's important to learn to embrace, separate from, and transform our defense mechanisms into a more honest expression of who we are and what we are feeling.

11. Which other subpersonalities do you identify with most closely?

You can go back and do this same exercise with these and other protective mechanisms. Allow each self to be heard. Try to appreciate your mind's attempt to create an inner resiliency when you needed these mechanisms for protection. Now, however, you have the opportunity to reassess how your selves are working for you, and to identify all the healthy ways to express, value, and take care of your authentic self.

Questions for Getting to Know a Subpersonality

After listening to what is going on for a client, I'll ask to talk to a subpersonality we've been discussing. Then I'll have them move to a different seat and take a moment to connect to the energy of that subpersonality. I then have a conversation with this subpersonality using some of the questions above in the "In Practice" exercise and the questions below. You can do this for yourself to better understand a subpersonality that has been operating in your life.

Ask the following questions:

> *Tell me about yourself:*
>
> *What happened in her/his life that made you come in?*
>
> *What would her/his life be like if you weren't in the picture?*
>
> *How are you feeling about the job you are doing?*
>
> *If waking time was 100 percent, how much of the time are you out in his/her life?*
>
> *If you were running the show, what would you like to see happen?*
>
> *What do you say to her/him, so s/he knows you are there?*
>
> *Is there anything else you want to share with me?*
>
> *Can we give you a name?*
>
> *Thanks for talking with me.*

2

Transforming Soul Holes into Whole Souls

Real transformation begins when you embrace your problems as agents for growth.

——Michael A. Singer, *The Untethered Soul*

Soul Holes

Children must get their needs met at various developmental stages in order to develop a strong ego and healthy self-esteem. If you come from a dysfunctional family (one in which there is alcoholism; a hostile divorce; sexual, emotional, or physical abuse; parents who are critical, controlling, or raging), your developmental needs may not have been met when you were a child; as a result, you may have grown up with what I call a " hole in the soul."

Many parents are wounded themselves. Therefore, they're not able to truly nurture their children. If children aren't loved enough, they tend to feel that it must be their fault. They believe there must be something wrong with them, which causes a wounded sense of self. If the pain is too great, they try numbing out by succumbing to addictions like alcohol, sex, overeating, and shopping. Or they try getting their own needs met at the expense of others. People who have an injured sense of self can become alcoholics, rageaholics, shopaholics, sex addicts, drug addicts, food addicts, or narcissists.

Like Michael, whose story was recounted in Chapter 1, many people who grew up in a family where there was alcoholism or harsh criticism never learned a healthy way to express their feelings because it was unsafe to be open. Especially for men in our society, who are conditioned and taught not to be vulnerable, these feelings are often expressed in dysfunctional ways—vicious criticism, controlling behavior, and anger—in order to regain a sense of control. Unfortunately, this behavior just makes their lives spiral further out of control. Women, on the other hand, often direct aggressive tendencies inward. Of course I'm speaking in generalities here; the roles may be reversed. For instance, some women learn to protect themselves by directing anger at others. However, I've observed that, more often than not, women turn their anger inward on themselves and develop a strong Inner Critic. They often have difficulty expressing their feelings and therefore swallow them. Unable to have a voice or stand up for themselves, they wind up depressed, feeling victimized, hurt, and resentful. Unexpressed hurt or fear turns into anger. Depression is often described as anger turned inward. This is tragically demonstrated by the National Institute of Mental Health statistics, which find that nearly twice as many women as men are affected by a depressive disorder each year.

Filling the Soul Hole: It's an Inside Job!

When we don't truly love and appreciate ourselves, we may look to others to fill the role of nurturing parent to make us feel lovable and worthwhile. Many people have the illusion that if they can just find Mr. or Ms. Right, they'll be healed. This misconception is described well by John Bradshaw, author of *Homecoming*. He explains that if you aren't whole yourself—let's say you're "half"—and you find someone else who isn't whole, instead of you both becoming whole, the reality is that 1/2 x 1/2 = 1/4.

It's important to realize that we don't heal by getting love from outside if we aren't able to love ourselves. Even if, as adults, we were to find a seemingly nurturing parental figure, it wouldn't totally heal the wounds of the past. Once we become adults, healing those wounds is mostly an inside job. It helps to have a stable, loving relationship, but a wounded sense of self doesn't heal by having someone just love us enough. We have to do the inner work to heal the injured core self, the source of the "hole in the soul." That inner work focuses on learning to love ourselves, which can be facilitated by using the tools taught in this book.

Shawn's father left when Shawn was two years old. As an adult, he grew up feeling shame that he didn't have a father and guilt that he must be unlovable—otherwise, his father wouldn't have left him. He had a hole in the soul, which he tried unsuccessfully to fill with one romantic relationship after another. The relationships would inevitably end with his shutting down and pushing the other person away. In therapy, I did a guided imagery exercise with him, bringing him back to the scenes in his life where he first felt closed down. In one of these scenes, he was four years old and clearly remembered yelling to his mother, "I don't need anybody." By age four, he had already developed a tough-guy subpersonality.

Using the Voice Dialogue method, we talked to Shawn's little Tough Guy, who told us how angry he was that his father left and how different he felt from his friends. I asked Shawn to visualize being with this little guy and to imagine nurturing him. As he gained little Shawn's trust, he was able to put his arm around him and let him know he was there for him.

Shawn had a transformative experience as he poured love into his younger self; his heart was being filled with love. He realized why all his relationships had failed. He hadn't felt as if he deserved to be loved, because he felt unlovable. He learned that searching for love on the outside was futile unless he could feel and receive it on the inside. As big Shawn nurtured his Inner Child, little Shawn felt lovable, trusting, and worthy. For the first time he experienced what it felt like to actually open his heart to receive love. His "hole in the soul" was getting filled by loving himself, rather than by all his attempts to get love from the outside.

Instead of believing in the fallacy that relationships can make us feel whole, it is important to realize what Shawn experienced. Soul holes get filled and healed by allowing the experience of our vulnerable feelings, and by having a healthy, nurturing relationship with this core sensitivity. To heal our "hole in the soul" and feel ourselves as whole, we need to recognize, honor, separate from, and transform these protective mechanisms into a more honest experience of our hearts and a more balanced expression of our growing self-awareness.

"The Road Less Traveled"

When we recognize and embrace the experience of our subpersonalities, we can begin to feel safe enough to hear the underlying truth of our core sensitivity. Listening to our different selves opens our hearts and tunes us into a clearer awareness of our needs. This awareness facilitates an expression of those needs so they may be fulfilled, increasing our sense of empowerment, self-awareness, and self-esteem exponentially.

So, if recognizing and honoring the experience of our selves, and as a result, living more from a self-loving foundation reaps such amazing rewards, why don't more people choose this path? Perhaps it is because our culture is generally outer-directed. Fashion and financial magazines dictate the need to have more material things in order to feel good about ourselves. Our self-esteem is intricately tied to what we do and what we have.

Ram Dass, my first spiritual teacher and the author of the 1971 bestseller *Be Here Now,* and many other books on higher consciousness, has said, "We are a society of 'human-doings,' not human beings." There is no exit off the superhighway with its never-ending "if onlys," as the billboards flash more $$$ in neon lights.

To take the road less traveled means having the wisdom, awareness, and courage to go against this heavy flow of traffic—to go inward. I am not advocating an inner focus to the exclusion of the outer, but a better, healthier balance between the two. The road less traveled is an inner road that takes us past the materialistic focus to an awareness of the emotional, psychological, and spiritual realms of existence. It allows us to get off the superhighway in order to take time to value and support our insights and experiences. We need to take time to share these inner explorations with our family and our community as they pave the way for safe bonding and intimacy.

The paradigm shift that we desperately need is to transform ourselves and, by extension, our society, by moving from a state of "soul holes" to "whole souls." Such a change reveals itself in how we treat ourselves and others. With healthy self-esteem born out of self-awareness, how we care for ourselves, others, and the planet can be impacted in a positive way.

Being conscious and working with our primary selves requires mindful awareness. Being mindful means being awake to the range of outer and inner experiences in the different levels of existence—the physical, emotional, mental, and spiritual realms. Mindful awareness is the process of getting to know ourselves and expanding our consciousness to become aware of what we are experiencing on the inside—our physical sensations, our feelings, our thoughts, our intuitions, and our needs. Our inner experience is a very powerful force in our lives. Whether we are conscious of it or not determines whether this force is a friend or a foe. It can move us in healthy directions and become our most trusted guide on the journey of life. Or, if we are not aware of it, our inner experience can create physical problems, psychological blocks, and emotional lows, like depression, anxiety, and rage. I, myself, have experienced the difference between being bothered by a seemingly inexpressible emotion and learning to express that emotion effectively. Places in my body that felt like knots suddenly became untied, and relationships that had tension relaxed. To live consciously, we need to get to know ourselves and communicate our awareness in clear and reverent ways.

Our Disowned Selves: Part 1

Drs. Hal and Sidra Stone describe a law of the psyche: "We attract to us that which we disown or never learned." In this chapter, I want to introduce you to the concept of disowned energies because they play a huge role in creating our soul holes. In Chapter 6, "The Higher Purpose of Relationships," we will delve more deeply into the effects of disowned energies on relationships.

If we never saw a certain type of behavior growing up or we saw it and were hurt by it, we develop a protective mechanism of pushing that behavior out of our lives and into the unconscious shadows. As Carl Jung said, "What remains unconscious becomes our destiny." To become whole, we need to integrate into ourselves what is in the shadows—our disowned energies. Relationships are often the best way for us to see what we've disowned. The Universe presents each of us with exactly what we need to learn, in the form of the relationships that we attract into our lives, so that we can move from feeling hole-y, to living wholly, and being holy.

> *Two clients, Terry and Hannah, brought in pictures of their nightstands. We laughed, seeing these very clear visual images of their disowned energies. They were able to laugh now because these pictures were a few years old, and they had actually worked through and learned a great deal about the disowned energy that was in their shadows. The picture on the right shows the nightstand of Terry, the Perfectionist in the couple, who would criticize and get angry at the messiness of Hannah, whose nightstand is shown on the left. Then Hannah, the Messy One, would*

29

rebel against Terry's judgments of her, and get even messier. They were off and running, as most relationships are when we are dealing with claiming disowned energies.

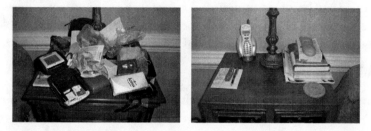

Both Terry and Hannah had similar soul holes that manifested in opposite ways. Having been criticized as children and rarely having their needs met, each of them had low self-esteem. Terry dealt with that by being perfect, because if Terry was perfect, there was less criticism. Hannah grew up with ADHD and was never taught the tools to help her structure her life and become more organized; yet she was constantly criticized for her lack of organization, which made her feel bad about herself.

Today Terry, the Perfectionist, is less perfect and is actually able to let things go, embracing a healthy amount of messiness, which was some of the shadow material for Terry. Not having to be so perfect has given Terry amazing feelings of liberation. Today, the nightstand of Hannah, The Messy One, looks neater. She has embraced her Organized One, is enjoying being able to find things, and is actually feeling good about herself, having learned to incorporate a certain aspect of Terry's organizational ability into her life. Each of them has learned something from the other, and in the process they have each begun to heal their "soul hole" and become more whole.

For Hannah and Terry, the relationship was their teacher. Both had to move from the extreme ends of the polarity of orderliness and messiness toward the center, where they created a more balanced, healthier experience in their own lives.

After the work of claiming our disowned energies has taken place in a relationship, we are able to move into the next stage of relationship, where there is a greater level of acceptance of self and other. When we have worked on claiming some of the disowned energy that our partner carries, and our partner has claimed some of his or her disowned energy, it is easier to be more compassionate and accept our disowned energy in the other person, because it is not as extreme. So, not only is there a healing of our own soul hole, but in the process of claiming our disowned energies, our relationships can become sweeter, deeper, and more balanced as well.

Angie didn't always communicate well. Growing up in a family where she rarely saw anger or individual needs expressed, it was difficult for her to deal with people when they were angry. She also felt uncomfortable expressing her own anger and needs. Angie grew up with a mother who rarely got angry and never expressed her needs. Her mom always took better care of everyone else's needs than her own, and she did it happily. She actually took such good care of Angie's needs that Angie didn't really have any. So the message she got from her mother—not explicitly, but implicitly—was that, as a woman, you don't get angry or express your needs. Therefore, Angie never developed the ability to know or express hers.

It's no surprise that, as an adult, Angie developed a relationship with Michael, the man I described at the beginning of the first chapter. It was a classic case of how we learn our biggest life lessons from our most difficult experiences. Michael expressed anger whenever he felt anxious or exposed; because his needs weren't met when he was younger, it was all about getting his needs met as an adult. Angie, who never learned about her own needs or the expression of anger, had to learn to deal with Michael's anger and find ways of experiencing and communicating her own needs and anger in healthy ways. Michael was Angie's disowned self, and she was his.

The relationship with Michael made Angie find her voice; it taught her how to stand up for herself in ways that would strengthen her sense of self. She felt they needed therapy to work through their individual and couple issues. Yet after a few sessions, Michael decided he didn't need therapy any longer and that he could do the work himself. Angie didn't want to end the relationship with Michael, because she knew that his defenses came from feeling hurt and abandoned in his childhood. However, unless he was willing to work on these issues in therapy, she knew she would be dealing with his focus on himself and anger for the rest of her life. Angie recognized that if she stayed in the relationship, she would be taking care of his vulnerability at the expense of her own.

Once Angie realized this, she ended the relationship. She continued to do inner work both on her own and in therapy. She spent a year keeping a journal of her needs to exercise the muscle that hadn't developed growing

> *up. During this process, there were numerous times when she got to practice expressing her anger and underlying hurt in healthy ways. In time, she came to understand that Michael was one of her best teachers for learning some of the essential life lessons and developing the soul-wisdom that has helped her communicate more fully and navigate more consciously in her life.*

Charlie Whitfield, MD, the author of *Healing the Child Within*, points out that the patterns we develop as children lodge in the unconscious, and therefore we can't always do this work ourselves; we need a trained therapist to guide us. Given that 95 percent of the population come from dysfunctional homes, according to statistics cited by Dr. Whitfield, it is common to feel sad, angry, and victimized by parents who have criticized us, disappointed us, or haven't been there for us. The therapeutic process, where we learn that it is possible to re-parent ourselves, is empowering.

Realizing that we can change the debilitating dynamics that have been obstacles in our lives, so that our upbringing is no longer a prison sentence, can liberate us and allow us to heal the wounds and shame from an unhealthy, unhappy upbringing. You've heard the phrase, "It's never too late to have a happy childhood." It's also never too late to create a happier adulthood for ourselves. We no longer have to hold onto the pain and bitterness that is often directed at our parents, nor do we have to direct the underlying anger and shame at ourselves. By detaching from, learning from, and healing the wounds of the past, we can forgive ourselves, and in the process forgive our parents as well. What a blessing to give, and a powerful gift to receive. Re-parenting ourselves can create an adulthood that is happy, healthy, and loving, which is precisely what we missed during childhood. We can be the parent we always wished we had.

By seeing difficult dynamics with parents or others as life lessons that we need to learn, and by recognizing how such difficult dynamics often reflect our disowned selves, we can actually move into a space of feeling grateful for these "teachers" in our lives. As Rabbi Henry Glazer wisely states in his book, *I Thank Therefore I Am*, "Gratefulness sows the seeds of generosity and compassion, tangible translations into action of thoughts and feelings intimately tied to an awareness of the 'giftedness' of human existence." (p. 51)

A Client Moves from a Hole in the Soul to a Whole Soul

Carla has just graduated from therapy. She shares her story and expresses the joy she feels in her life today:

> *As a single mother on welfare going to school, all I could do was focus on the future and look forward to the time when I could support my two children without feeling as if the rug would be pulled out from under me at any minute. Ten years later, even though I was happily remarried, and had accomplished the goals I had set for myself, I still felt as if my world was on the verge of imploding. I was caught in a cycle of desire, envy, and despair, and I was feeling anxious and trapped. I realized that I had been able to change and improve the external circumstances of my life, but inside I was still ruled by fear and anxiety. While these emotions had helped me push through the hard times, now they were getting in the way of living life. I was making choices that I didn't understand, that didn't make me happy, and that didn't serve my family or me. I knew I had everything a person needs to be happy. Yet I felt stuck and desperate.*

> *Thinking these feelings could be resolved if I found the right career, I sought out therapy to explore the possibilities of finding the "perfect job." Unknowingly, I had begun the greatest journey, one that has forever changed who I am in the world. With the help of my therapist, I learned how my fears and anxieties played a role in protecting me. I got to know some of the primary selves that were running my life—my Worrier, my Victim, and my Inner Critic were my Heavyweights. I began to recognize that the habitual thoughts and behaviors that had served me in the past had become the reasons I felt so nervous and unhappy now.*

> *Gradually, I became conscious of the choices I make automatically, and I began to see the difference between what was true and what was simply part of the myth I had created. As I began to trust that the very truth and peace I sought resided within me, I also recognized how important tools like meditation are for creating inner stillness and space where truth can be nurtured and heard.*

> *As my trust grew stronger, my anxiety and fear diminished. I realized that the destructive emotions I had been feeling for so long were not necessarily who I am. I got better at recognizing my old ways and realizing that I have a choice about how to be with everything in my life. I chose not to be a victim of circumstances or of my own automatic responses.*

The effect on my life has been transformative. I feel like I started with a hole in my soul, always feeling insecure, and now I feel more whole, more sure of myself. For instance, take my relationship with my mother. She is very critical; in the past, her comments would devastate me. Today, because I've developed a stronger sense of self and can communicate more clearly with her, I feel compassion, love, and understanding for and from her. The ultimate proof of how transformative this process has been is that I now enjoy time with my mother. I feel generosity toward her, instead of anger, and I no longer come away from an encounter with her filled with self-doubt. I realize that one of her primary selves, her Judge, was a disowned energy for me, one that would trigger my vulnerabilities. Then I would get angry at her and feel self-loathing, and those feelings would make me doubt and worry about every decision I had to make. I learned to see her Judge and integrate a healthy expression of the Judge, which we called my Discerner. This recognition helps me make choices that I can feel good about and that make me more self-confident.

I began my journey with no hope, unaware of the worlds of possibilities that are everywhere. I continue my journey, after finishing a course of therapy, equipped with tools and knowledge that help me navigate life's path. I am happy to be here, sailing through storms and sunny weather, guided by trust not fear, joy not hopelessness. I know that the greatest gift I could ever give myself or the ones I love is to live this knowledge and share it with everyone I meet. Today, I have a full practice as a health professional, and I am thrilled to be of service and help other people heal. I feel so grateful.

In Practice:
Transforming Soul Holes into Whole Souls

Take a moment and close your eyes. Take a few deep breaths and allow yourself to relax. Notice any tension that you're feeling in your body. Breathe into this place, allowing your breath to open, soften, and relax this area of your body. Then take another deep breath, and as you exhale imagine this breath carrying any tensions out of your body, through your fingertips and your toes.

1. *Think back to any interactions or situations you might have had recently with family members, friends, or at work that are unfinished for you or were disturbing, unsettling, or unclear.*

   _____

   _____

   _____

2. *What happened that disturbed you? What selves in you are you aware of that reacted to these situations?*

   _____

   _____

   _____

3. *How do you feel when these interactions or situations occur? How have you felt at other times when such a situation occurred with the same people or with other people? Can you identify what selves in you felt these feelings?*

   _____

   _____

   _____

4. *Write about the feelings you experience when these interactions or situations occur. How often do these feelings come up for you?*

_____

_____

_____

5. *How would you describe the person (or persons) involved in this situation?*

_____

_____

_____

6. *Does this person remind you of anyone else in your life, or could he or she be exactly the opposite of one of your parents?*

_____

_____

_____

7. *Does this person express him or herself in ways that are foreign or uncomfortable to you? If so, how?*

_____

_____

_____

8. *Do you see in your interaction with or response to this person a recurring experience or pattern, a common thread in the tapestry of your life? If so, describe that experience or pattern.*

_____

_____

_____

3

Our Vulnerability Is Our Strength

The noble heart is one that sheds its armor, opening itself fearlessly to both heartache and delight. It is this process that leads you to full realization of your true strength—the strength that can only come through embracing your vulnerability.

—Pema Chödrön, *The Noble Heart*

To really know ourselves, we need to have a healthy relationship with the part I call our core sensitivity, our Inner Child. It's a wonderful, precious source of truth, wisdom, and guidance, whose home is in our hearts. It's our natural birthright, and it experiences the world as a child does. When this Inner Child feels loved and safe, it's free to express its feelings and needs in healthy ways. Then, as its needs are met, our Inner Child feels valued and embraced, which strengthens our sense of self. Our Inner Child is the true source of our positive self-esteem.

Many of us who come from families with a history of unhealthy parenting grow into adulthood feeling unloved or insecure. If it wasn't safe growing up in our home, then to protect ourselves, it was natural to push these defenseless feelings down and put a lid on them. Whenever we disown a part of ourselves, it is like putting a lid on a pressure cooker—whatever is under the lid expands, eventually exploding. If we "put a lid" on the vulnerable feelings of the Inner Child, trying to feel less exposed, instead of making the feelings go away, this only makes the feelings grow stronger. They expand and create greater pressure and tension. Paradoxically, this leads us to feel overly vulnerable rather than less vulnerable, and, since it isn't safe for us to express these feelings, they often come out in distorted or unhealthy behaviors through dysfunctional defense mechanisms. Our behavior eventually gets us into trouble in the form of being criticized, rejected, and/or abandoned.

When I first talk to clients about the importance of caring for their Inner Child, some make the motion of sticking their fingers down their throat, as if to gag. Many male clients have an innate resistance to calling any part of themselves a vulnerable Inner Child. It makes them feel defensive and defenseless. Men are heavily conditioned by our culture not to be seen as weak. I understand that; therefore, I try to use different language for men, so their resistance doesn't become an obstacle to doing this inner work. I have called on some of my male clients to help me find an expression for this concept that they feel comfortable using. So far, talking about the Inner Child in terms of past patterns and old wounds that affect the heart seems to be useful language.

Once the Inner Child is revealed, some clients resent it and have negative feelings toward this essential part of themselves because they are under the mistaken assumption that their problems of neediness, insecurity, or being overly emotional are caused by their Inner Child. The Child is not the cause of these problems: These problems occurred because the vulnerable Inner Child who was hurt, neglected, or abused had to go into hiding to protect itself. And when we are out of touch with our vulnerability, when the door is closed to that part of ourselves, we live behind the defense mechanisms that are set up to protect us. We live behind a false façade.

> *A practitioner was coaching and doing spiritual direction with a client named Joni. At one point in the process, the client made some references to feeling suicidal. This practitioner felt that she didn't have the appropriate training to continue working with the client.*

> *I began to see Joni, who would periodically make suicidal gestures by taking too much medication. Because of Joni's depression, anxiety, and feelings of not being seen as a child growing up, she would react disproportionately to situations. She would make suicidal gestures after a fight with a friend, when she had a difficult visit with her family, or when she had legitimate needs that she didn't recognize or know how to express.*

In our work together, it became clear that Joni felt neglected and harshly criticized as a child, and had a difficult time feeling heard in her family. Both her parents were highly anxious and she was the middle child, born after the brother she felt was her parents' favorite, and who got a lot of attention. Her suicidal gestures were her ineffective way of getting her needs met, or getting the attention she hadn't received as a child. This strategy was the only way she knew to express intense feelings of hurt, fear, or disappointment.

Joni has made significant strides in healing the wounds from a difficult childhood in which she desperately sought the approval of her parents. When she didn't get it, she would escalate her attention-getting behaviors. This prompted her family to criticize her even more and call her a drama queen. She became the "problem child" and the scapegoat in the family. As Joni learned to connect with her disowned vulnerability and the nurturing adult part of her began to develop a positive relationship with her Inner Child, she finally began to feel safe. She has done a great job of taking care of herself, by expressing her needs in healthy ways. If she wants an extra session in a week, or more time for a session, she is able to ask to have her needs met in more direct ways.

In this journey that we've been traveling together, Joni has come a long way. There haven't been any suicidal gestures for a few years. She has learned to "check in" with her Inner Child (see "In Practice" at the end of this chapter), trust her feelings, and then follow through with whatever she needs to do to take care of her Inner Child in healthy ways.

Joni is feeling clearer emotionally and stronger psychologically than ever before. Her Inner Child is getting her needs met more often, and Joni has been successfully able to separate from some of her other primary selves that were obstacles in her life. Her Inner Critic and her Rebellious Daughter used to cause a lot of static, keeping her mind churning with negative thoughts. Today, more often than not, she's able to quiet her mind and connect with a depth of wisdom that continually amazes me. When she's dealing with a difficult situation with one of her parents, a sibling, or a friend, for example, I'll ask her to "check in." Remarkably, she'll get a quick response characterized by insightful, intuitive wisdom. Her self-esteem is getting stronger as she's identifying with this wise, knowing self, rather than the kid who had to create drama in order to be heard.

It's natural for children to assume that their difficulties in life are their own fault. They don't realize that is the job of the adults in their lives to affirm and love them. Some of us develop strategies or cover-ups to try to get our needs met when life situations create an unsafe environment to be vulnerable, as was Joni's case. These cover-ups can make life even more difficult, forcing the Inner Child into hiding. Taking the Inner Child out of hiding is essential to expressing our needs in healthy ways and getting our needs met. How do we go about recognizing, embracing, and valuing our Inner Child?

Getting to Know Our Inner Child and Our Inner Nurturing Parent

For the gaggers in the group, or for those who are uncomfortable with their inner emotional world and who are more concrete thinkers, this section may be a stretch. However, it really is important, so I invite you to keep an open mind. Healing ourselves by healing our relationship with our Inner Child can make a profound difference in our lives.

In a sense, we work to 're-parent' our child. As with real children, it takes time, patience, consistency, and a lot of holding and loving the Inner Child to help him or her trust and feel safe enough to begin to come out and talk to us. For others, the Child might be ready to be with you, but may not be old enough, or may be too traumatized to talk. In this case, just be with the Child as you would be with any preverbal child. Envision holding him or her, cuddling him or her, stroke his/her hair, and, as Dr. Elisabeth Kübler-Ross said, "Marinate the child in love." Even if the Child cannot talk, you may be able to sense what the Child is feeling, so you can be with and comfort your Inner Child.

There are actually a number of Inner Children. There are the magical child, the playful child, the abused child, the abandoned child, and others. I often lead clients on a guided imagery visualization to meet their Inner Children. This exercise is included in Appendix C.

It is equally important for us to get to know our Inner Nurturing Parent. Many of us didn't grow up with role models who were nurturing, so it is sometimes difficult for people to know how to nurture their Inner Child. If our parents weren't caring, supportive people, there may have been other role models in our lives who were. Often there is a natural instinct that comes out with pets or babies. Tapping into the feelings that we have at those times and generalizing those feelings to nurture our Inner Child can be the beginning of an important relationship between our Inner Nurturing Parent and our Inner Child, who needs to feel safe and valued. Our healthy sense of self and development in life depend upon it.

As Joni learned, we can develop the ability to nurture, love, and protect this precious, sensitive being who lives within each of us. To do this, we need to communicate with our Inner Child to find out what s/he is feeling, and what s/he needs. Once the Child feels heard, and therefore valued, healing and growth occur, self-esteem increases, and the Inner Child becomes a wonderful guide on our journey of life. Our Inner Child can be a source of discernment for us, letting us know if people and situations are safe for us, or whether we need to veer away.

Home Is Where the Heart Is

Our hearts are the home of our Inner Child. It's through this doorway that we need to walk, to spend time, to feel comfortable, and to rest in the realization that our vulnerability is the source of our strength, clarity, truth, and love. When we're connected to our feelings and our needs, the door to our heart is open. Being aware of and expressing what we are feeling and needing may not always get our needs met, but it certainly increases the likelihood of doing so. Often just knowing and expressing what's in our hearts and on our minds can strengthen our sense of self and enhance our experience of empowerment. It's this intimacy with ourselves that opens the doorway to a more fully intimate and loving experience with others.

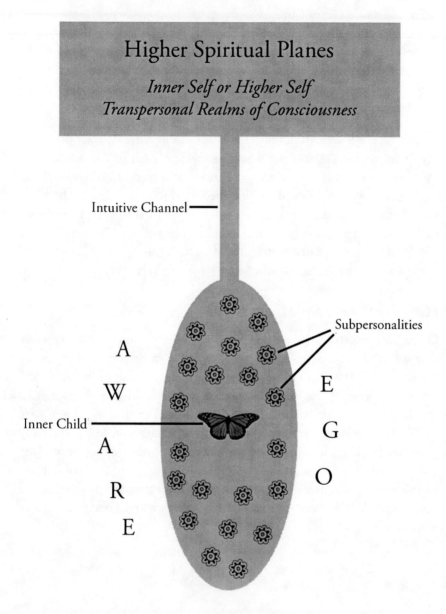

Ego-Personality-self

The illustration on the preceding page helps to clarify this framework. What I call "my egg diagram" was adapted from *Psychosynthesis*, a transpersonal approach to psychology developed by Roberto Assagioli, MD (1888-1974), who was an early student of Freud and Jung. The large egg in the diagram represents the personality, also called the ego or the small "s" self. At the center is the vulnerable Inner Child, surrounded by all the different subpersonalities, which we develop to protect this core self. The subpersonalities are how we identify who we are: Parent, Friend, Rulemaker, Perfectionist, Inner Critic, and so on. We use these labels to describe ourselves. They make up our personality, our body, our feelings, and our mind. This is the realm of personality development where the work of learning our life lessons occurs.

Stage One of *LASTING Transformation*, Life-Lesson Therapy, leads us to develop a strong sense of self by embracing our Inner Child and the subpersonalities or primary selves that we've developed to protect ourselves. Then we learn to separate from these selves we're identified with, and discover and explore the ones we have disowned. By doing so, we develop a strong Aware Ego, through which conscious choices are made in one's life as to which subpersonalities we want to express and when. We become the conductor of our inner orchestra of selves, choosing who plays, what gets played, and when. This is the Aware Ego process.

In the diagram, the Intuitive Channel connects the personality/ego/self to the Higher Spiritual Planes, often called the Inner Self, the Higher Self, or Transpersonal Consciousness. In Stage Two, if we've learned to take care of our Inner Child in healthy ways by listening to our Inner Child's needs and expressing them so they more often get met, the voices of the subpersonalities quiet down.

Once the mind quiets down, we're then able to open the intuitive channel and experience the intuition—that still, small voice within—which is the voice of our Wise Being. This is the subpersonality that's connected to the higher spiritual planes of consciousness, which are home to the soul, the Source, Higher Power, God, Love, or whatever you feel comfortable calling this Force that is greater than we are. These dimensions of soul-wisdom, and how to access our intuition, will be discussed further in Stage Two—Soul-Wisdom Therapy.

We Are All Vulnerable

The "egg diagram" shows our vulnerability residing at the center of our existence. Realizing that others are also vulnerable is essential to living life fearlessly and fully. Understanding that everyone has an Inner Child who's also afraid of not being loved, and of being rejected and abandoned, evens the playing field and allows us to be more conscious, in control, and compassionate in our interactions.

For example, when we encounter a defense mechanism of anger in another person instead of the person's true feelings of hurt or fear, we can choose more effectively how to engage the angry person. Rather than escalating the anger by attacking the other, we can respond with awareness of their hurt or fear, and in so doing, defuse the situation and successfully deal with the problem. Another example is dealing with a critical person's defense mechanism. Rather than taking the criticism personally and getting defensive ourselves, we can be aware that the critical energy is masking anxiety. Even if the other person isn't aware of this, we can respond to their negative energy with awareness, not take it personally, and respond to the anxiety rather than react to the criticism.

Knowledge of the vulnerable Inner Child allows us to be far more powerful than we can imagine. When we realize that in relationships, everyone is vulnerable, and that in fact it is precisely this vulnerability that creates connection and intimacy, we can behave with compassion and kindness, feeling stronger and more secure.

In her audiobook, *The Noble Heart,* the American-born Tibetan Buddhist nun Pema Chödrön describes how vulnerability is our greatest spiritual resource in overcoming life's difficulties. It is in this direction that we need to move, to spend time, to feel comfortable, and to rest in the realization that our vulnerability is the source of our strength. Our vulnerable Inner Child is an essential guide on the journey to health, happiness, and wholeness.

Our Vulnerability Is Our Strength—
The Highly Sensitive Person

The Highly Sensitive Person (HSP) is a good example of how our vulnerability can be a strength. Mary Strueber, a psychotherapist who specializes in working with HSPs, has contributed this section about the Highly Sensitive Person, a term coined by Dr. Elaine Aron, author of the book, *The Highly Sensitive Person: How to Thrive When the World Overwhelms You*. Dr. Aron's research has found that high sensitivity is a normal trait for about one-in-five of us, and is not a sign of a mental disorder. Rather, as Dr. Aron points out, the HSP has a nervous system that is simply hard-wired to notice more subtle environmental influences. This sensitivity causes the HSP to be more easily aroused by influences that others might miss. We all have "arousal comfort zones," and too much arousal can lead to feelings of depression, confusion, anxiety, and low self-esteem.

These influences tend to exist below the radar of most people. Increased awareness of environmental stimulus and subsequent over-arousal can also create negative feelings about oneself, as typical social activities like going to malls, parties, or large family gatherings, or experiencing college dorm life can all spell over-arousal for the HSP.

Because Highly Sensitive People have a capacity for awareness that's more developed than others', this trait can be a major strength when it comes to being aware of our inner world and outer world. Many gifted people are HSPs. Their sensitivity and depth of processing make them naturally adept at being advisors, therapists, artists, educators, musicians, writers, poets, spiritual teachers, religious leaders, energy healers, and body workers from all modalities. Because HSPs are more physically and emotionally empathetic, this trait would actually be valuable for any profession that would benefit from practitioners who are able to quiet their minds and be exquisitely sensitive to the deeper physical, emotional, mental, and/or spiritual worlds.

Unfortunately, most HSPs never identify their sensitivity and generally assume that others have similar experiences but somehow manage them better. They aren't aware that the experiences of their sensing bodies, and of emotional empathy, are highly unusual for the majority of the population.

If a person does have HSP as a trait, it's important to identify it. Recognizing that we may have a highly sensitive personality is the first step toward dealing with it. That step is available by taking the HSP self-test by Elaine Aron. There's a link to it on the InnerSource website: www.innersource-inc.com. HSPs may appear inhibited, but only because they have a stronger "pause to check system" when encountering novel situations and experiences. This could be because they're taking in so much more information and are thus more aware of all the possibilities in a situation. They pause before acting in order to reflect on all that could happen. That's a positive trait! But in a culture that values confident, bold extroverts, HSPs can be easily stigmatized.

When we recognize and identify our experiences as an HSP, we become a better advocate for our needs. This enables us to more deeply understand our career, social, relationship, and environmental needs. With a model for understanding our experience of the world, and with education and support, we can begin to put together a picture of the unique way that our mind, body, and senses experience, absorb, and process incoming information. We can make the most of our heightened awareness.

Optimizing life as an HSP is a tremendous step forward. But it takes effort and courage. However, once we identify our sensory needs, temperament, and learning style, self-criticism can give way to self-acceptance and self-knowledge. We can experience how our highly sensitive nature is not a burden, but rather a gift for living a deeply meaningful life.

Mary's Experience of Vulnerability as a Strength

As a girl, my parents encouraged me to get the most out of life. I was urged to date and go to parties, mixers, camp, dance classes, and, of course, shop—all things my sisters and friends enjoyed. But as much as I tried to be like them, I couldn't. Even going to the movies seemed a chore.

Instead of enjoying myself, I felt oddly tired, confused, and stressed. I felt overwhelmed no matter how hard I tried to enjoy myself. Why was it so easy for others to engage the world and so difficult for me? Why did I lack energy or a sense of belonging when I was with groups of people? Why was selecting a gift so confusing? Why did other peoples' moods impact me so strongly?

What was wrong with me?

My self-doubts were unwittingly supported by peers who called me a party pooper, a stick in the mud, or too sensitive. Well-meaning adults labeled me shy, anxious, depressed, or lacking in confidence.

Discovering that I was a "Highly Sensitive Person" was liberating. Suddenly life fell into place. I learned that high sensitivity is not a disorder, but rather an innate difference found in 15 to 20 percent of people. One of the main differences is that our brains process more sensory information. Because of this heightened sensory awareness we are naturally more sensitive to pain, caffeine, medications, temperature, light, sound, hunger and even other people's moods and mind states. But we are also more reflective, learn more gradually but thoroughly, and tend to be unusually conscientious and deeply moved by beauty.

Having a way to understand and work with my experience as an HSP was a great relief. At the same time, I felt grief for all the years I'd spent being identified by labels that didn't fit. On the road to getting to know my true nature, it was extremely important that I found support for digesting the meaning that all this had for me: To know not only that I wasn't crazy, but that my exquisite sensitivity was a real gift—a strength I'd never appreciated because I'd spent so much of my life feeling weird and different.

Discovering that I am a Highly Sensitive Person has made it possible for me to create a life that is meaningful and enjoyable. Since this discovery I have had the great pleasure of working with other HSPs individually and in groups. I find that HSPs are unusually creative and productive workers, attentive and thoughtful partners, and intellectually gifted individuals.

—Mary Strueber, LCPC, Assistant Director of InnerSource

In Practice:
The "Checking-In" Process

This is an exercise for "checking in" with your Inner Child. Whether you're an HSP or not, listening to your Child tunes you in to a clearer awareness of your deeper needs and allows your Inner Child to feel valued and loved, which increases your self-esteem.

Take a moment and close your eyes. Take a few deep breaths and allow yourself to relax. Notice any tension that you are feeling in your body. Breathe into this place, allowing your breath to open, soften, and relax this area of your body. Then take another deep breath, and as you exhale imagine this breath carrying any tensions out of your body, through your fingertips and your toes.

1. *Think of a situation when your Inner Child experienced feelings you weren't clear about. It may be a situation when someone said something or did something, or you might be aware of an interaction that feels unfinished and as a result you feel an imbalance inside of you. If you're in touch with a current experience that you are dealing with, it may be easier for you to "check in." It will be helpful for you to write about this situation in your journal or below. Who was involved in the interaction, and what happened?*

_____

_____

_____

_____

_____

_____

_____

2. *After you finish journaling, take a moment and close your eyes. Imagine your Inner Child in your heart. Ask this Child what it is feeling. Now focus on your heart and become aware of any sensations or feelings you might be holding that are connected to this experience. See what feeling actually describes the sensations or emotions that you experience when you allow yourself to "check in" with your Inner Child. To do this process, actually try pairing the feeling in your heart with the feelings in the list below and see which feeling describes what your Inner Child may be experiencing. Write about this experience below. You can select from the following list of feelings or feel free to add others to this list.*

Hurt	Resentful	Hopeless	Happy
Scared	Angry	Envious/ Jealous	Excited
Needy	Frustrated	Detached	Loving
Anxious	Depressed	Restless	Grateful
Vulnerable	Embarrassed	Lonely	Hopeful
Ashamed	Concerned	Isolated	Peaceful
Unhappy	Rejected	Mischievous	Awed

_____

_____

_____

_____

3. *Once you're aware of what you're feeling, ask your Inner Child what happened that caused the feeling. If the feeling is hurt, did someone say something that hurt your feelings? Are you anxious because you need to talk to a coworker and you're afraid he or she will be angry? Write down the source of the feeling.*

_____

_____

_____

_____

_____

_____

_____

4. *From your Inner Nurturing Parent's perspective, write what you might do to take care of the situation that is causing the feelings your Inner Child is having. Follow through with whatever you are aware of, so that your Inner Child will feel valued, loved, and protected.*

_____

_____

_____

_____

_____

_____

_____

4

Vulnerability Is the Key to Intimacy

Heaven favors the daring.
—The Talmud

If we can't be vulnerable, we can't be intimate. It's as simple as that. I personally think men have it the hardest when it comes to vulnerability. Living on planet Earth up through the twenty-first century, men have basically been robbed of their sensitivity. To cry, to acknowledge fear, needs, or vulnerability, is viewed as "wimpy" by our society. Males who were raised in critical families tend to be put down for any display of vulnerability, and are often made to feel like sissies. The message boys learn from society at large and from their parents who may be alcoholic, critical, controlling, or wounded, is that it's not okay to feel exposed, anxious, or out of control.

What a travesty to the soul and an impediment to building healthy relationships with ourselves and others. To relearn being vulnerable, we need to remove the "macho" consciousness as an ideal to aspire to. Instead, men need to learn to be strong enough to cry, to express their needs, and to honor and acknowledge their feelings. We need to stop sending the message that big boys don't cry.

My father, Dan Rosen, who passed away as I was writing this book, is a great example of a strong and sensitive man. He was a blessing in my life and in so many lives. He was a successful man by society's standards, and yet he was also able to be sensitive and cry. One of my favorite pictures was taken at a joyous occasion when we were dancing cheek to cheek. Tears of joy were streaming down his face.

When I look at the picture, I feel love and admiration for him, appreciating how far he had gone along the road less traveled in our society. He was a man who was truly strong, because he was able to remain connected with his feelings and was not afraid of expressing what was in his heart.

If It Isn't Safe To Be Vulnerable, Then It's Not Possible To Be Intimate

For both men and women, safety is a prerequisite for intimacy. Safety necessitates being in situations where there is respect, support, and a sense of feeling honored and seen for who we are. Men and women need to be able to express what is in their hearts in healthy ways. While men may be considered too soft if they express vulnerability, women also have a difficult path to travel with this business of being intimate and vulnerable. Women may be seen as too aggressive, or demanding and controlling when they express their feelings—especially hurt and anger—and the needs that stem from those feelings. Historically, women have been the more receptive, nurturing gender—focusing on meeting their partners' and families' needs more often than their own. But if a woman can take care of herself by speaking her truth and communicating her feelings honestly and clearly, she can experience a sense of safety that is self-generated, which can lead to trust and intimacy. I am talking in generalities here. In my practice as a psychologist, I have also seen these roles reversed.

Both genders need to learn how to communicate assertively, not aggressively. To do this, men and women need to know what they are feeling. If they can't be open, or can't express their feelings and needs because of societal conditioning or earlier upbringing, they encounter a block to healthy relationships. This block interferes with true intimacy, preventing two people from sharing their innermost thoughts and feelings. Unfortunately, this often results in a no-win situation. No wonder there is a 60 percent divorce rate in our culture, according to James M. Robbins in "The Costs of Rising Divorce Rates Across the US."

If it isn't safe to be vulnerable, then it isn't possible to be intimate, which is why it's so rare to find relationships that are truly happy and healthy.

"For Successful Marriage, Do What She Says"

This was the headline in a 2001 *Los Angeles Times* article reporting some interesting research on what makes relationships work. University of Washington psychologist John Gottman and his colleagues studied 130 newlywed couples for six years. Their study was designed to identify factors that contribute to a successful marriage so they might be brought into play in therapy. The study, which was reported in *Journal of Marriage and Family,* found that marriages that did work well all had one thing in common—whenever possible, the husband was willing to give in to the wife. Indeed, those husbands who adopted an autocratic style and failed to listen to their wives' needs, greeting them with stonewalling, contempt, and belligerence, were doomed from the beginning. But the study didn't let wives completely off the hook. A woman who couched her requests in a gentle, soothing, even humorous manner when approaching her husband was more likely to have a happy marriage than one who framed her needs and requests more belligerently.

Gottman explains how changing the attitudes of men "is a very powerful lever" in changing the course of a marriage. While this study may seem to belittle the role of the husband, by having him simply "yes" his wife, it underscores the importance of expressing needs and feelings, as well as creating a safe environment for true intimacy by responding to expressions of vulnerability. This study also implies that men who feel safe in their marriages and more secure in themselves aren't afraid of sharing power with their spouses or being more receptive to their needs at appropriate times.

Sometimes it helps to experiment with "trying on" more positive behaviors as a rehearsal for true and lasting change in attitudes and behaviors. As one of my clients put it, "You've got to learn the moves before you can do the dance." The client who showed me Gottman's study, for example, is a physician. After reading the article, he tried "yes-ing" his wife in a tongue-in-cheek manner. But then he told me that the results were so positive that he grew to understand the deeper significance of what it meant to be a friend to his wife by supporting her perspectives and needs, rather than putting up resistance from a fear of being controlled.

He, in turn, has been more willing to share his more sensitive emotions and needs and is feeling heard and responded to more often. They both agree that they're experiencing some very positive, even revolutionary shifts in what had been destructive, stagnant patterns. They're enjoying a delightful playfulness and a growing trust in their relationship—not to mention an increase in their lovemaking!

As women are able to express their feelings and needs, and thus feel safe and supported, this engenders a greater openness to sexuality and intimacy. As the study found, women who express their needs in less critical or hostile ways are learning to take care of themselves. In this way, women can experience a feeling of safety that is self-generated. If a positive response to the need isn't forthcoming, sometimes it doesn't even matter. Just expressing the need may make a woman feel empowered, strengthening her self-esteem and sense of safety. When she takes the risk of expressing her needs, this allows her to feel emotionally safe enough to trust herself and share her feelings more fully, which is the key to intimacy.

The Ratchet Effect

Many relationships fail because of what I call the Ratchet Effect. A ratchet is a tool that can open really wide—or it can totally close. At the beginning of relationships, the ratchet starts to slowly open. Once we feel safe, we start sharing our thoughts and feelings. A uniting occurs, along with feelings of connection and safety. The ratchet then opens wider. Egos merge. The ratchet is wide open. However, the first time we feel hurt or rejected, the ratchet may close down a notch.

How we navigate this experience is essential to the feelings of trust and safety in the relationship. Unless we deal with the hurt or rejection in a wise way, the ratchet may eventually close completely. Every time something happens that causes a feeling of separation or fear, we ratchet down our willingness to be open and vulnerable even more. Oftentimes, we have a tendency to withdraw, withhold, and isolate ourselves; or, we get critical, angry, and push the other person away.

The Ratchet Effect is what we do to protect our hearts; we close down to the other, leaving no openness to connect. Relationships are about being in relation to someone else—that means feeling and being connected, sharing and allowing the other person into our inner experience. When the going gets tough, and a disconnection occurs (for whatever reason), our instincts are to withdraw and build walls to protect our heart and ensure our safety. Yet these are precisely the times when we need to speak our truth. Even though this is probably the most difficult time to share our feelings, it's exactly the time when it is most essential in order to have a healthy, loving relationship that works. Clearly, couples could benefit from training in how to create functional relationships. Most of us have neither seen nor been taught healthy ways of interacting.

The story of a client I'll call Tess is a beautiful example of how the act of honoring and learning to speak the truth of the Inner Child leads to healthy relationships that work. When the Inner Child takes its rightful place in our lives, healing from abuse, neglect, and abandonment can occur.

Tess grew up with a very rejecting father. As a youngster, she would continually try to gain his approval and attention, but felt constantly criticized by him. She developed a subpersonality she called "the Wall," which protected her from feeling his abusive comments. The Wall allowed her to pretend not to care about getting her father's love, since that wish was futile. She became very rebellious and rejected her father before he could reject her. This worked for Tess to some extent, and probably helped her survive a painful childhood. The Wall protected her Inner Child from getting devastated in this dysfunctional family.

However, as an adult, her Wall subpersonality kept her softer, loving side hidden, so she was never able to get the love she needed. Whenever she entered a relationship, the Wall would go up. If a man got too close, she would find an excuse to push him away before he could reject her. She would withdraw if she felt hurt, rather than share her true feelings. Her partner would feel shut out, not understanding why she'd withdrawn her love, making it difficult for him to respond to her real needs.

Thus she never felt the intimacy she needed in order to feel safe and loved. In effect, she rejected the men in her life just as her father had rejected her. The very Wall set up to protect her from feeling hurt and abandoned wound up perpetuating Tess's feelings of being alone and unloved.

In therapy, Tess has worked on getting to know the Wall, the subpersonality that would withdraw from and reject every man in her life before he could abandon her. She has learned to embrace the Wall for the important job it did protecting her from her critical and rejecting father. She's also learned to recognize the behavior when it shows up and to make the conscious choice to separate from this primary self. After six months of therapy, she was finally able to begin a sustained relationship with Jim. After years of this behavior pattern sabotaging relationship after relationship, she was able to break through the Wall and communicate in emotionally open ways with the new man in her life.

She nurtured her Inner Child by sharing her true feelings. When her Aware Ego became strong enough to recognize that the Wall was about to go up, she'd "check in" and realize she was scared that Jim would reject her, or that he didn't love her, and shared her fears with him. He then had the chance to care for and reassure her that he loved her and wasn't going anywhere. Little Tess felt safe and protected by Adult Tess, and loved by Jim. The more she broke through the Wall, the more empowered she felt, and her self-esteem grew stronger. This allowed her to take more risks. As Tess and Jim grew closer, Tess experienced an intimacy that she'd never felt before.

A few months later during a therapy session, she announced that they'd broken up. In listening to her, I could feel the Wall talking. Jim had gotten to a point in the relationship where his fears of commitment had surfaced. Tess heard his defenses and took them personally (it's hard not to). This triggered her fears of rejection and abandonment so strongly that her old defenses took control. Without realizing it, the Wall made the choice to end the relationship before Tess got rejected.

Tess was vehement that Jim wasn't the man she wanted to spend her life with. Yet, as we talked, she realized who was making this choice. Tess separated from the Wall. She did the "Checking-in" process to talk to Little Tess, who was terrified of getting hurt but also devastated at having lost this wonderful love. Through this experience, she recognized what Little Tess needed from Adult Tess and what her truth was—she needed to share how she had reacted out of her childhood fears of getting hurt and abandoned. She wanted to support Jim's fears, try not to take them personally, and express her needs and boundaries so that Little Tess could feel safe.

Tess left the session feeling much clearer about the whole situation, and much stronger. Truth is more solid than any wall.

The end of the story … Tess is now happily married.

The Truthsayer

As we develop intimacy with our own Inner Child and realize that everyone has one, it allows us to risk speaking our truth and open to a deeper, richer experience with others. As we replace walls with windows, letting others in, and open doors that allow others inside our hearts, we create a healthier paradigm for ourselves and others. This paradigm shift encourages the transformation of defense mechanisms that cover our vulnerability and supports the healthy expression of our authentic feelings.

We need to be willing to take the risk to know and share our needs and joys with people in our important relationships. Once we have a clear sense of what we are feeling, the next step is to communicate that feeling as honestly as possible from what I call the Truthsayer. This is the self within us that can stand in front of our vulnerable Inner Child and protect her or him by verbalizing what we're feeling and needing from a place of truth, strength, and clarity.

As Tess experienced, sharing the authentic feelings of our Inner Child no matter what the other's response allows us to become stronger, more empowered, and free. The liberation and sense of confidence that come when we speak our truth allow us to gain access to both our vulnerability and our strength. It takes an exquisite balance of listening to the wisdom of our heart, which is where the vulnerable Inner Child resides, and knowing how to hold firm, clear boundaries for what our Inner Child needs to be heard and valued.

The art of conscious communication comes down to this: Being able to hold our vulnerable Inner Child gently in one hand, and our Nurturing Parent securely in the other, and expressing them both through our Truthsayer.

The Truthsayer stands in front of and speaks for the Inner Child. When s/he feels safe and protected, this is the key to intimacy—one that can deepen and strengthen the foundation and the bonds of all our relationships. This is truly the art of conscious communication.

The Truthsayer uses the Formula for Conscious Communication (see below) to convey feelings of the heart and other truths from a place of strength and empowerment. The Formula for Conscious Communication can facilitate this process by converting protective mechanisms into healthy expressions of our growing self-awareness. When this is done in a way that creates safety, clarity, and intimacy, the formula enables us to express whatever we feel in constructive ways, so that difficult situations get resolved and relationships improve.

The Formula for Conscious Communication

1. Support the other person by beginning your communication with an expression of appreciation for and/or understanding of how the other person feels.

For example, you can begin by saying:

"I can understand that _____"
or "I can appreciate _____"

This step creates safety for the person with whom you are communicating. It allows him/her to feel that you understand his/her experience.

2. Express how you feel about the situation using "I" messages as opposed to "you" messages.

Express your feelings from the Truthsayer who protects your vulnerability.

3. Share what you want and need with the other person.

Whether or not the other person is able to respond to your wants and needs almost doesn't matter. Just the ability to stand up for yourself can increase your self-esteem and create a sense of empowerment in life.

The following is an example of the Formula for Conscious Communication:

Jane came home from work tired and is critical of Russ when he gets home because he didn't call to say he would be late.

Jane yells: *"Where were you, and why didn't you call me? I'm sick and tired of having dinner alone and worrying about where you are!"*

Rather than get defensive and retaliate, Russ decides to use the Formula:

Russ*: "Jane, I can appreciate that you've been working hard and that you're tired, but I feel angry and criticized when you talk to me that way. When you're upset about my being late, I need you to tell me what you're feeling, rather than yell at me for what I did wrong."*

Jane: *"I understand that sometimes you have to stay late at work, and I got upset and yelled, which hurt your feelings. Yet when you're late and don't call, I feel abandoned and unimportant. I need you to call me when you're going to be late."*

Russ: *"I had important paperwork to do at the office, and I should have called. Next time I will. Perhaps I can bring work home from the office and do it after we've had dinner."*

You can see in this example the three-step formula:

1. Support the other's vulnerability.

Russ: *I can appreciate that you've been working hard and that you're tired…*

Jane: *I understand that sometimes you have to stay late at work…*

2. Express your feelings using "I" messages.

Russ: *I feel angry and criticized when you talk to me that way.*

Jane: *When you're late and don't call, I feel abandoned and unimportant.*

Hint: When communicating your feelings, if you say *I felt that,* you've just expressed a thought, not a feeling. Here's an example: "When you didn't call me, *I felt that* your work was more important than I was." Compare this with the example from the Formula: "When you're late and don't call, *I feel* abandoned and unimportant."

When Jane communicates her feelings, it encourages the conversation to move in the direction that allows her needs to be met by Russ.

This is a subtle distinction, but the "*I felt that*" phrasing can take the conversation in a direction that isn't as useful in directly addressing Jane's feelings. Russ's work is important to him, and he might get defensive in response to that phrasing, as opposed to addressing Jane's feelings and needs.

Hint: If the feeling is followed by *because you,* then you've just used a "you" message couched in an "I" message. *Example:* I feel frustrated *because you're* always yelling at me.

While this sounds like an expression of feelings, it is actually a direct attack on the other person. It slams the door on the conversation. It makes the other person feel defensive, rather than receptive to hearing your feelings.

3. Ask for what you need.

Russ: *I need you to tell me what you're feeling, rather than yell at me for what I did wrong.*

Jane: *I need you to call me when you are going to be late.*

In the example above, Russ and Jane communicated using this three-step formula: (1) They supported each other's vulnerability, (2) they stated their feelings using "I" messages, and (3) they asked for what they needed. You can, too!

Russ and Jane connected with, and communicated from, the strength and protection of the Truthsayer. Communicating this way clarifies our feelings and creates a sense of self-confidence and a trust in the other. It allows people to get their needs met and connect. Resolution occurs, so couples experience more emotional security and greater intimacy.

A Client's Experience of Vulnerability
as the Key to Intimacy

Despite being a well-respected professional, community, and family member, who's strong, capable, confident, and caring, I was prone to emotional collapses and sudden, overpowering bouts of worthlessness. The fact that I was intelligent and perceptive made matters worse, because it seemed as if I should "know better" and be more together.

My interactions were centered on my unconscious need to please others and use their approval and acceptance to feel lovable and good about myself. I was skillful at caring for others, perceiving their needs, and devising ways to meet them, which helped them feel good about themselves. What was largely missing from the equation was an awareness of the parts of myself that were causing me to feel worthless and prompting my need to please others—these were the primary selves that held the key to my own healing and happiness.

The Voice Dialogue process has been a wonderful tool for me, and my therapist's skillful, insightful, loving, and genuinely benevolent guidance has been an amazing gift in my life. Reconnecting to the disowned aspects of myself took great courage on my part and required an experienced guide to safely contain and positively frame the energies of the emerging selves. While the theoretical background satisfies the needs of my mind, the healing happens through new experiences in the emotional and spiritual realms.

I learned to listen within and to invite the frightening energies into my conscious awareness in small doses. The gold in the shadow was the very currency I needed to heal myself. As I learned to have affirming relationships with those parts of myself, my therapist guided me to integrate the information through an Aware Ego, a state of consciousness that can hear the voices of all the selves and separate truth from illusion. By modeling an Aware Ego and showing me how it functions, my therapist helped me birth one of my own. She demonstrated how it could serve both as my inner guide and as the interface between Self and other.

At first, when I used the Formula for Conscious Communication, I did a perfect "textbook" job on the surface. The words were great, but there were dissonant undertones of hidden agendas and Critic energy. I learned to listen for the anxious voice behind my Inner Critic. Through hearing and addressing my own needs, rather than beating myself up with inner criticism or distancing or punishing others in response to my inner judgments of them, I was able to become energetically congruent with my spoken words. I learned to balance the Pleaser personality that had been so other-directed that it drained me and left me feeling frightened, unsafe, worthless, and resentful. I am becoming skilled at finding the voices at the roots of my inner conflicts as they arise, and I am feeling more comfortable and confident that I can safely negotiate those turbulent waters, even enjoying them as an exciting adventure in self-discovery and awareness! The more I listen to and support my own feelings and needs, the less anxious and critical I am, and the more I am able to be present for others in a balanced, clear, and genuine way. As I learn to create honest, appreciative, and respectful relationships with my own once-feared and now-beloved fragmented selves, I find myself less often caught in the distressing reactive patterns that used to overwhelm me, and I experience appreciation and peace more often with myself and with others—and this feels so good!

Walking this path hasn't been easy. It's taken me from feeling crazy at times, to sobbing at feeling so alone and empty, to feeling grateful and blessed that I am who I am, connected to my Inner Self. Inevitably and consistently, as I take the risks to share my vulnerability with others and speak from my Truthsayer, a bridge appears, which leads directly and deeply to their heart and soul, and back to mine. It is a path of love, clarity, joy, and empowerment.

In Practice:

Using the Formula for Conscious Communication

1. *Think about a current situation in your life in which communication feels incomplete. Describe the situation as you experience it.*

_____

_____

_____

_____

2. *Take a moment to quiet your mind, use your breath to relax, and release any tensions you may be holding in your body. What does your Inner Child feel about what has happened? Allow any awareness to come into your consciousness about the situation and write down what you receive.*

_____

_____

_____

_____

3. *Who are your primary selves in this situation? What do they have to say about what is occurring?*

_____

_____

_____

_____

4. How do you imagine the other person's Inner Child is feeling? Try to journal about this situation so that you can elicit your ability to be compassionate and appreciate the other person's experience from an Aware Ego perspective, rather than being identified with a particular subpersonality.

    _____

    _____

    _____

    _____

    _____

5. From an Aware Ego perspective, what needs to be expressed from either your Inner Child and/or other subpersonalities? Using the Formula for Conscious Communication, how could you complete the communication with this person, supporting his or her vulnerability, making an "I" statement about your feelings, and expressing your needs?

    _____

    _____

    _____

    _____

    _____

5

For Men, Mainly

It's hard to know whether to laugh or to cry at the human predicament. Here we are with so much wisdom and tenderness, and—without even knowing it—we cover it over to protect ourselves.
—Pema Chödrön, *The Places That Scare You*

The process of honoring and allowing the expression of our hearts is difficult for both men and women. However, since societal and familial conditioning gives men messages like "big boys don't cry" and "if you're sensitive, you're a wimp," men face the biggest hurdles in overcoming the conditioning that creates the cover-up of vulnerability. For these reasons I felt it was important to devote an entire chapter to men. If you're a man reading this, then you are at least curious about—or have actually signed on for—the journey. Congratulations! You have the strength, the vision, and the courage to explore the road less traveled.

Obviously, I'm not talking to all men. Some of you already know how to delve into the world of feelings and can communicate from this inner realm in healthy, effective ways that create connection and intimacy. This chapter is for those who haven't yet undertaken this inward journey. Hopefully, through books like this, and more men doing their inner work, then encouraging their sons, brothers, nephews, friends, and fathers to do their own inner work, we can change society, one man at a time. Women also have their work to do. But due to gender-specific expectations, in terms of transforming the cover-up of our hearts, men generally have more to overcome.

The Times, They Are a Changin'

The rules of what it means to be a man have been changing since the sixties. As women have begun to work outside the home, many no longer need men for protection and security. They want partners—someone with whom they can share physically, emotionally, mentally, and spiritually. Not all women care about sharing on every level. But among the couples who have come to me for counseling, most women aren't interested in being physically intimate unless they feel emotionally connected. Conversely, most men need to first be physically intimate in order to feel close emotionally. Sometimes, when joking around with clients, I say this difference in the sexes is the second mistake God made—the first being mosquitoes. Given the problems this difference causes in relationships, one might wonder whether God has a weird sense of humor, or if there's some inherent purpose in this dynamic other than men and women just making each other crazy.

My version of the Garden of Eden story, as described in Chapter 1, hints at a possible explanation for this difficult dance between men and women. If Adam or Eve had been able to be truthful with each other, and had acknowledged making a mistake when they ate from the Tree of Knowledge, rather than covering over their vulnerability by defensively blaming each other, we would have inherited a very different model for relationships—one that uses conscious communication. If Adam had acknowledged his vulnerability instead of blaming Eve, and if Eve had acknowledged her vulnerability rather than blaming the snake, perhaps the story would have turned out differently. There's one thing we know for sure: It was hard for both Adam and Eve to take responsibility for their feelings of vulnerability, and it remains difficult for many men and women today.

For a man who's never learned to acknowledge his feelings and to know what's in his heart, a relationship with a woman who needs him to be emotionally open will no doubt cause him a great deal of anxiety. Even if a man is able to access his feelings, he was probably taught to put a lid on them because expressing feelings was not considered "manly." Those repressed feelings can, in turn, manifest as anxiety. So both evading and repressing feelings can cause a lot of anxiety for men. And voilà, there you have it—a recipe for a no-win situation for both men and women.

Addressing anxiety within a relationship is critical, since it's probably one of the biggest culprits in the 60 percent divorce rate in the United States today.

We Attract to Us That Which We Disown

The concept of attracting what we disown is addressed in greater detail in the next chapter; however, this dynamic affects all our relationships, so it's important to address it in this chapter as well.

When we disown a particular set of emotions or behaviors because they hurt us as a child, or we've never experienced them, we attract those emotions in the form of relationships that will help us move in the direction of balance. Strong, controlling, and domineering men tend to marry women who need to learn to have a voice and express their needs; men who can't deal with anger generally marry angry women; men who feel unsuccessful and fearful of taking risks are often married to strong, accomplished, risk-taking women. The work of coming into balance is the work of relationships. It's often the only way we learn the lessons we need in order to grow. You will see this dynamic play out in the different types of men and women described below. (See also Appendix E: Primary and Disowned Selves.)

Different Types of Men/Different Expressions of Anxiety

Many men I work with in my practice are dealing with anxiety. Some, having never developed a strong sense of self, don't feel successful in their careers. Low self-esteem prevents them from achieving their full potential. They're anxious and fearful of taking risks as a result of being brought up by critical parents. While they can rage when they feel vulnerable or out of control, these men have a tendency to more often suppress their aggressive tendencies. They're often married to very strong women who are very successful in their careers.

Other male clients are softer, gentler types who shy away from confrontation. They either grew up with very confrontational and overly emotional parents, or, conversely, they just didn't see a lot of emotions, like anger, expressed as they were growing up. Thus when it comes to the realm of emotions, they have a tendency to withdraw or become invisible for fear that their emotions will get out of control. Although these men find it difficult to express vulnerability, they feel equally uncomfortable expressing strong emotions of any kind, including anger or rage. Such men are often married to women who express a lot of anger.

Some clients have grown up in dysfunctional homes with domineering, controlling, and critical parents. This scenario often leads to problems with anxiety as well—not only because their needs weren't met when they were younger, but, to add insult to injury, no matter what they did, it was never good enough. Because it wasn't safe in their families to be emotionally exposed, as adults, any time these men feel vulnerable, they also feel anxious. Sometimes they're also dealing with anxiety caused by a genetically inherited biochemical imbalance. Sadly, the anxiety these men experience because of impaired parenting is compounded by the inherited biochemistry. Anxiety that goes unexpressed often turns into irritability, anger, and rage. The greater their vulnerability, the stronger their anxiety, and the more intense their expressions of anger will be, resulting in even more critical, controlling, and domineering behavior.

This strong, aggressive approach can make them very successful in their careers; however, it often doesn't work in their personal lives. If these men have a tendency to get angry when they're feeling vulnerable and/or their needs aren't met and they rage when they feel out of control, their marriages often wind up falling into that 60 percent divorce statistic.

NCCDPD

NCCDPD is an extreme manifestation of the category of men described in the previous section. Think of Michael, whose story began this book. His needs weren't met growing up, so he compensated by making his relationships as an adult all about getting *his* needs met. This is the definition of narcissism.

I have coined a term—NCCDPD—to "endearingly" describe people like Michael who have a **N**arcissistic, **C**ritical, **C**ontrolling, and **D**omineering **P**ersonality **D**isorder. NCCDPDs often grow up in families where there is a lot of anxiety, criticism, and often trauma. As a consequence of the emotionally disconnected experiences when they were younger, their needs didn't get met; so, as adults, these men and women become focused on getting their needs met—often at the expense of others.

Feeling out of control in their dysfunctional families creates the defense mechanism of always needing to be in control as adults. They develop a subpersonality that's so impenetrable, it's difficult for them to enter into a therapeutic relationship. These men and women simply can't see themselves as being at fault, and even if they do come into therapy, they rarely stay, as they are unable to take responsibility for their behavior.

Tragically, unless something devastating happens to them, they're unlikely to engage in a process of becoming more conscious, self-loving, and caring of others. One fantasy I have is to put all the NCCDPDs on an island together. Over time, as they bump up against each other in their attempts at domination and control, their hard edges will get worn down, and hopefully, they'll become more peaceful and less defended.

Now   *Ten Years Later*

Such men are often married to women who are strong Nurturers and Pleasers, who need to find their own voices, express their needs, and stand up for themselves. Of course, these roles can also be reversed, with the woman being critical, controlling, and domineering, and the man more conciliatory.

If Anxiety Is a Problem, You May Have a Biochemical Imbalance

As I mentioned at the beginning of this chapter, anxiety often stems from suppressing feelings of hurt, fear, insecurity, or sadness. Anxiety may also be caused by genetics; that is, it may be inherited from the maternal and/or paternal sides of the family. I used to recommend herbal or homeopathic remedies for emotional or psychological problems, but I would rarely recommend psychotropic medication. I have grown to have a respect for the appropriate use of herbal and/or psychotropic medication, depending on the situation and the person, when a biochemical imbalance is causing anxiety. In this case, it's extremely helpful to have physiological medicinal support—whether holistic or pharmaceutical—as a way to bring one's system into balance. In my many years of practice, I've seen too many instances in which individuals and couples who resist medication go through crisis after crisis and unnecessary stress, all because they feel ashamed or apprehensive about having to take any kind of medication.

Diabetics, for instance, know they must take insulin to survive. The same is true with a biochemical imbalance that creates anxiety, depression, manic depression (also known as bipolar disorder), obsessive-compulsive disorder, post-traumatic stress disorder, or any other psychological disorder. Disorders like these are not your fault: You're doing nothing wrong, so there's no need to feel ashamed about addressing it. This kind of disorder is genetic—you inherited it. True, it would be better to inherit money, which you would gladly accept and invest for your future, but if you inherit a biochemical imbalance, accept it and do what you need to do to make an investment in your future happiness.

Taking medication can help you function at your optimal level and allow your relationships to thrive without the unnecessary strife and stress that a biochemical imbalance can create. Sadly, I've seen too many tragedies involving people who refused to take medication when it was needed. Don't become another statistic simply because you're afraid that taking medication means you're the problem—it might be the smartest choice you'll ever make.

A useful tool for self-evaluation is *Rating Your Inner Critic Self-Test* in Appendix D. If, after taking the test, you believe that you may be dealing with a big or huge Inner Critic, then given that underlying every Inner Critic is anxiety, it is likely that you are also dealing with a significant amount of anxiety as well. If the level of anxiety is more debilitating than what is considered a normal amount, or is significantly getting in the way of daily functioning and activities, it's important to consult a family physician or, preferably, a holistic physician or psychiatrist. Ask your health care professional to test you for a biochemical imbalance. Discuss the use of supplements such as

B-vitamin complex; fish oil; vitamin D; and Inositol, which is similar to a B vitamin. Also helpful for anxiety are 5-HTP, L-tryptophan, L-tyrosine, and SAMe, which are amino acid-based; or herbal remedies like Rescue Remedy. You can also ask about psychotropic medications such as SSRIs (selective serotinergic reuptake inhibitors) for anxiety or one of the psychostimulants for ADHD. Explore the benefits—as well as the possible negative side effects of taking any medication—with your health care professional.

If you and your medical professional decide that herbal remedies or psychotropic medications may be an effective choice, try it for an agreed-upon time period. Then evaluate the results objectively. You might even ask people in your life whom you trust if they notice a difference in your overall demeanor. Try to be honest with yourself, and avoid covering up your anxiety with risky behaviors that only perpetuate this dangerous cycle. Other reactionary behaviors may include road rage or using sexuality, drugs, or other addictions to numb out feelings of anxiety. You might find yourself being critical and domineering as a way of controlling others in your environment. In its extreme form, addiction can be a way to self-medicate your anxiety with your "drug" of choice. Alcoholics, rageaholics, sexaholics, shopaholics, foodaholics—all are numbing out their anxiety. While addicts need to work on their addictions, eliminating anxiety would make this process much easier and more enduring.

Getting to Know Your Inner Emotional World

Men—here's the bottom line for this chapter: In order to be happier and feel loved and emotionally secure in your relationships, take time to become familiar with your inner world and communicate your feelings in effective ways. If you discover that anger, critical energy, or lack of self-esteem is controlling your life, learn to recognize the underlying feelings of anxiety. Remember, this anxiety stems from having to suppress feelings of vulnerability labeled as "weak" or "unmanly"—yet putting a lid on them creates even more anxiety. Deal with it head on! Rather than getting angry, critical, or withdrawn, find a better way to deal with this anxiety, as those behaviors are obscuring the anxiety.

First, learn how to identify the anxiety underlying the more aggressive emotions. Then you can reach underneath to your core needs and vulnerable feelings and learn to express them in healthy ways.

Many people find it difficult to become aware of their feelings. They spend so much time thinking that they aren't even conscious of the emotions that are truly driving them. Training ourselves to be more aware of our inner emotional world is like training to excel at a sport. For example, we use our bodily sensations to cue us as to the right timing to throw a basketball toward the hoop, or to hit a golf ball so it heads for the green. It's not much different when it comes to getting to know our inner emotional world.

One way is to get to know what physical sensations arise when emotions are percolating just beneath the surface. What are our particular bodily cues? Does our chest or jaw get tight? Does our heart race? Do we feel we have a lump in our throat? We need to get to know ourselves well enough to recognize that when our stomach gets upset, we understand it might be a sign that there's something going on in our inner emotional world that we're having a hard time stomaching.

Once we connect our bodily cues to an emotion we may be feeling, these cues will act as early warning signs that something is going on inside us. This awareness helps to make it possible for us to figure out what's going on in our inner emotional world, and then consciously talk about what we're feeling in a constructive, healthy way.

A Step-by-Step Guide for Identifying and Dealing with Anxiety

Now I am going to walk you through the steps, using a client as an example:

John's wife asked him to get into therapy to become more comfortable with his feelings. They have a lot of love for each other; however, she gets frustrated that she doesn't have a partner with whom she can share emotionally. When she isn't feeling connected to John because he's not emotionally available, they have major fights, disagreements, and breakdowns in communication that can go on for weeks. These fights also create a lot of frustration for John. His wife withdraws from him, which is very difficult for him. So, he's willing to work in therapy on what he can do to change his side of this negative pattern.

Step 1: The first step is to get to know the particular defense mechanism you use to cover over your vulnerable feelings. Refer back to the practice exercise in Chapter 1 and work through the steps.

John's defense mechanism of choice is to keep so busy that he doesn't have time to feel. His Workaholic is one of his primary selves. If vulnerable feelings surface for him, rather than acknowledge them he often becomes irritable and tries to exert control over the external situation. He might wind up yelling at the kids, or not focusing on what his wife is trying to share with him, and instead take phone calls he's constantly receiving from work.

Step 2: The second step is to name the feeling. Often, just naming what you feel can take the discomfort and charge out of the experience. Use the "Checking-in" process described in the practice exercise for Chapter 3 to figure out what you are feeling.

In therapy, we identified a situation in which John could feel himself shutting down and getting irritable with his wife. John "checked in" to name what was going on inside him. He became aware of feeling sad and lonely, especially when he was about to leave town on business. So instead of sharing what he was really feeling, he'd keep a stiff upper lip and withdraw. He was afraid if he shared his sadness and loneliness, his wife would have a hard time dealing with her own feelings of abandonment.

When I asked his wife about this, she acknowledged that his fears were justified. She said it used to be impossible for him to leave on business. They'd both go through a terrible time, so they came to believe that things were better when they didn't discuss how they were feeling. They sidestepped the emotional difficulty by avoiding talking about his leaving, but that defense robbed them of the opportunity to deeply connect and get support from each other at a more honest and satisfying level.

Step 3: Explore the feeling. Is it familiar? Do you remember feeling this way growing up? What triggered it then? Does the present experience feel stronger, as it re-creates the same feeling that you had in the past? Often, when you feel as if your reaction is much stronger than what the current circumstances seem to warrant, it's because the current situation mirrors an earlier, similar one that was traumatic.

It's important to get to know—and trust—your inner experience before you can share it. You have to become intimate with yourself before you can become intimate with others. This step may take some practice to master, but just as you did when you learned to drive a car, just keep doing it until it becomes second nature.

To drive a car there are many different areas to focus on and important steps to remember to do at the same time; yet as adults, driving is second nature to most of us. You don't have to think it through—it seems to come naturally. It's the same when it comes to mastering the realm of the emotions, even though it may seem like a monumental task at the outset. Mastering your emotions will increase your self-esteem, and also create positive relationships that thrive on conscious communication and respect.

John is working on step 3, learning to get to know and trust his inner experience. Together, we're exploring his reaction to being away from his wife. His mother gave birth to four children in four years. Clearly, his emotional needs couldn't have been adequately met. His separation anxiety now is so intense that when he parts from his wife, he gets sick to his stomach. This is what happened when he was younger and his parents left him. These feelings of abandonment are triggered every time John and his wife have to leave each other.

As John recognizes the feelings stemming from his separation anxiety and names them as a re-creation of his past, he'll be able to regulate these feelings and calm his anxiety. Then he won't have to use his defense mechanism of energetically pulling away from his wife before they separate to avoid feeling the pain of separation.

His wife could feel this happening even before John was conscious of his withdrawal, and she'd feel abandoned. Then she closed down to protect herself, which then exacerbated his separation anxiety. It became a vicious cycle, which was devastating for both of them.

Step 4: Share your feelings with a significant other (or someone you trust). Use the Formula for Conscious Communication described in Chapter 4.

John and his wife can deal with their feelings in supportive ways by sharing them with each other. They can experiment with the process of moving from a warm, connected personal space that's nurturing when they're together, to a cooler, more self-contained, impersonal energy when John has to leave town. Knowing how to move into this kind of "impersonal energy" is an important tool in consciousness work and in relationships. Hal and Sidra Stone describe the process of moving into the impersonal as a way of creating healthy boundaries.

By consciously approaching their time apart and finding ways to be self-nurturing, John and his wife will still be able to feel their connection, while at the same time feeling a sense of being more self-contained. They'll no longer have to stifle their feelings of abandonment, sadness, or loss because they'll be able to share their feelings and experience the intimacy engendered by those feelings, then make a choice to consciously move into a more self-contained space. Such periods of separation can then become a time for strengthening their relationship with each other. When they're back together and more focused on their relationship, they can return to that self-nurtured state. This will make their relationship stronger and more intimate.

If more people could open to this process of recognizing anxiety and embark on this journey of consciousness, their lives would change for the better. Relationships would improve, and society's 60 percent divorce rate would surely be dramatically reduced.

Because many women now have their own careers, they no longer need to stay married for financial reasons. As they discover that their needs for emotional connection and safety aren't being met, these women are making the choice to leave their marriages. As Celine Dion sings in "Real Emotion," "Women want a man who can do real emotion, I need real emotion / Feel, gotta feel it inside." Those who are willing to go against society's conditioning and take the risk to feel and express their emotions will be richly rewarded. They will be loved, adored, and appreciated for meeting their partner on the emotional plane. This connection is what many women need in order to feel safe enough to open up to greater physical intimacy. Both genders will feel a stronger bond, which will create a deep sense of security. Men will once again feel like the kings and masters of their castles and their lives! The greatest winners of all will be the children, who will grow up in a loving, intact, functional family.

My hope is that men will read this chapter with open minds and choose to take this inner journey. Imagine the different kind of role modeling they'll be exhibiting for their brothers, sons, and nephews. They'll be able to teach the next generation of men to be more conscious of their inner world and more successful in their relationships. Eventually, we can all live in a society where the inner journey will no longer be the road less traveled.

An Experience of Transformation— from a Man's Perspective

As an attorney with an extensive family practice, I often referred my clients to therapists or other mental health specialists. It took going through a divorce and being depressed before I realized that I needed to seek help myself. I didn't know what I was feeling. I'd repressed my feelings for so long, I didn't even know I had any! When asked what I was feeling, I responded with what I was thinking. This led to problems in relationships. My needs weren't being met because I was unable to express what they really were. These suppressed needs manifested themselves in various levels of impatience, frustration, or anger. At one point I realized that if I kept doing what I was doing, I'd keep getting what I was getting. This made me continually depressed, compromising my happiness in many ways—especially in my relationships.

I was fortunate to recognize that it takes a stronger, healthier person to know when to seek guidance and support from a professional. After working with a therapist in whom I had a lot of trust and confidence, I began to change behaviors that were sabotaging me. Using Voice Dialogue and other modalities, I quickly realized, for example, how much influence the Inner Critic had in my life. Often, I'd literally feel the Critic sitting on my shoulder, talking in my ear. The Critic still surfaces, is quick to question my judgment, and makes me feel guilty about what I'm feeling or doing. But, I'm getting better at recognizing when the Critic is there, and I'm able to reduce the effect this primary self has in my life. This significantly lowers the level and frequency of anxiety and depression, and enables me to stay in touch with my feelings.

I made a commitment to myself to risk sharing what I am feeling. Whenever I do this, it reinforces the positive benefits of taking such risks. I'm becoming more trusting of myself and others. My self-esteem is stronger, I actually wind up getting my needs met more often, and my relationships are much better and more fulfilling.

In Practice:
Learning to Recognize Anxiety

Your goal is to begin to recognize the feelings of anxiety that come from having to suppress feelings of vulnerability. Develop the ability to delve underneath the anxiety to the deeper, sensitive feelings in your heart and then express them. Anxiety is just one emotion, although it acts as a powerful force for many people. If you're experiencing an emotion other than anxiety, and would like to learn to recognize what it is, substitute that emotion for anxiety in this exercise. To further illustrate these principles, I've included a client's story in italics.

1. *Become aware of any physical and behavioral cues that let you know anxiety is present. Sometimes it's hard to tune into physical cues and the presence of certain behaviors that you use to push down the anxiety. It may be helpful to name them, so when you experience physical cues, they'll alert you to the underlying anxiety.*

    When Larry feels anxious, for example, his chest gets tight and his heart races. These are his physical cues. After participating in couples therapy with his fiancée, he learned to identify additional emotional and behavioral cues, such as anger and his righteous indignation. Through hard work and a commitment to taking responsibility for his own actions, he learned to acknowledge that he has a tendency to become critical and blame his fiancée and her children whenever things in his own life go wrong.

    Larry learned this from his father, and it's become his major defense mechanism. When he feels vulnerable, he gets anxious and winds up attacking others as a way to protect himself.

What are your physical and/or behavioral cues that let you know anxiety is present?

_____

_____

_____

_____

_____

_____

2. *Next, name the feeling underlying the anxiety. Ask your vulnerable Inner Child what s/he is feeling and check in. If you need help connecting with the feeling, refer to the menu of feelings in the In Practice exercise in Chapter 3 called, "The 'Checking-in' Process."*

The menu of different feelings includes hurt, scared, resentful, angry, unhappy, happy, embarrassed, grateful, and needy. Focus on these feelings and check in to see what feeling actually describes the sensation or emotion that you experience underneath the anxiety.

_____

_____

_____

_____

_____

_____

When Larry checked in, he realized he was feeling scared about whether his fiancée was the right partner for him. Because she had been holding back sharing emotionally and sexually, he was afraid that he wasn't going to get his needs met in this relationship.

3. *Further explore the feeling to see if it's familiar. Have you experienced it before in your growing-up years or adult life? Is it a pattern in the tapestry of your life? Why do you repeatedly experience this feeling? Taking this step necessitates that you examine your life, become aware of your actions and behaviors, and take responsibility for what's working and what's not and for what's healthy and what's destructive.*

_____

_____

_____

_____

_____

As Larry began to explore feeling scared that he wasn't going to get his needs met, he remembered that he'd spent most of his childhood feeling sad, fearful, and lonely; his needs for warmth and affection were rarely met. He also realized that he'd had the same experience with his ex-wife, who eventually shut down any feelings of warmth and intimacy. It was happening again with his fiancée. Larry had to look at this recurring pattern and the part he was playing in it. We explored this in couple's counseling. His fiancée shared that she loved Larry, but that every time he would rage and tell her they were breaking up, she withdrew further and further from him to protect herself emotionally.

She was also aware of how those actions triggered Larry's rage and was working on that in her own individual therapy. Given the trauma she experienced growing up, it was hard for her to share on a personal level, which is what Larry needed to feel secure and safe in the relationship. So, they both had their personal growth work cut out for them.

4. *The next step is to share your feelings with your significant other, or with whomever you need to communicate your feeling to, in order to resolve the situation. This comes after you've gotten to know, and learned to trust, your inner experience.*

   Larry took all he'd learned about himself and used "The Formula for Conscious Communication." He was able to share his deeper feelings of vulnerability underlying the anxiety, the anger, the blaming, and the raging with his fiancée. He said, "I can appreciate how hard it is for you when I get angry with you or the kids. I realize that I do that when I'm feeling scared that our relationship won't work. I spent so much of my childhood feeling lonely and unloved, that when I feel you pulling away emotionally and physically, I get terrified I'm going to spend the rest of my life that way. I guess I just need to share my fears with you, because I know how the raging pushes you away."

Larry felt loved, appreciated, and very secure after showing up emotionally and sharing his vulnerability with his fiancée. Learn to communicate your inner world of feelings consciously, and you will, too!

6

The Higher Purpose of Relationships

One of the greatest—and most rewarding—challenges for each and every one of us is learning how to communicate vulnerability in relationship while at the same time remaining in touch with the parts of us that carry our strength.

—Hal Stone, PhD, and Sidra Stone, PhD, *Partnering*

Have you ever wondered why there is such a strong emphasis on relationships in our culture? From day one we are engaged in relationships. Even when we are alone, our thoughts often have to do with relationships. It may be thoughts about relationships with a significant other, with a family member, at our jobs, with friends, with children, or even relationships with our pets. Relationships can result in our feeling on top of the world, or feeling hopeless and alone. But the bottom line is that relationships enable us to grow and are a path to self-awareness. It is through relationships that we often learn the most about ourselves. Relationships are the crucible in which, if the vessel is strong enough, hearts and souls are polished into diamonds. If the vessel can't hold the pressure of this alchemical conversion, then the coal turns into dust. How do we strengthen the crucible? How do we use the gift of relationship to learn life lessons and develop soul-wisdom?

By creating conscious relationships, we open ourselves to the understanding that those who are in the crucible with us are there to teach us, and vice versa. From this perspective, we work on ourselves and our relationships with the vision that we are not victims. On the contrary, we have actually attracted these people into our lives because we each have something to learn from the other. The people and the situations we attract give us the opportunity to learn the lessons that allow us to grow.

Many of us have noticed that there are certain patterns in our relationships that continually recur no matter how many times we end one relationship and begin another, whether with spouses, friends, coworkers, or others. We tend to repeat old patterns from the past, drawing people to us who help us play out these dysfunctional patterns, until we begin to question and do the inner work to change these patterns. The secret is this: We do it over and over again until we do it right! The cast of characters may change, but the basic script remains the same. We repeat the pattern until we learn the lesson that the relationship is trying to teach us. It's as if something in us knows what we need for our hearts to open and we keep bringing these situations to us. As we gain awareness, we can identify the problematic patterns, dialogue with the inner selves that take the lead in participating in these dysfunctional situations, and begin the work of separating from these subpersonalities. Once we achieve the wisdom that comes from knowing our primary self or what I call being able to "name that tune" and then learn the lessons that this life experience is here to teach us, the recurring pattern of suffering and disappointment often disappears.

> *Babs ended a relationship with Tom because he was too critical and controlling. The next relationship that ended was with Sam, because he was too narcissistic and self-involved. Then Babs thought she'd changed the pattern when she met Carl, who was more giving, but too insecure and unhappy with his life. The external dynamics with each of these men were different. However, there was a recurring theme: Babs became involved with men who were narcissistic, critical, and controlling, like Tom and Sam. Or she got into relationships with men like Carl, who were insecure, had no backbone, and had a strong Pleaser subpersonality. Underneath all these different expressions was an insecure, wounded little boy. Tom developed the Inner Critic to protect his wounded child; Sam's defense mechanism was to become self-absorbed and make sure his own needs got met; Carl thought that by adopting the Pleaser subpersonality as his primary way of relating to the world, people would like him, so he wouldn't be abandoned. Each of these situations kicked Bab's Pleaser and Nurturing Mother into overdrive.*

As we have seen in earlier chapters, all the defense mechanisms in the world never heal our wounds. Instead, these outmoded patterns just make us feel more wounded because they can never compensate for the love and security we wanted and needed growing up. The little boy inside each of these adult men was wounded and became insecure because he grew up in a home where one or both parents were alcoholics, overly critical, demanding, and controlling; or, for different reasons, unable to give him the unconditional love he needed to grow up with a healthy sense of self. Sometimes, the circumstances might have been beyond the parents' control because they might have been dealing with illness, or death, or poverty. Often, the parents had been abused themselves, either emotionally or physically, and therefore also had a wounded Inner Child making them incapable of healthy parenting. If parents never do the inner work to heal their own wounds, these unhealthy defense mechanisms are passed down from generation to generation.

> *Babs, on the other hand, grew up with a mother who was very loving and had a very strong Nurturing Mother subpersonality. Her mother rarely expressed her own needs and never complained. So Babs didn't learn to communicate hers, either, and subconsciously felt that expressing needs was tantamount to complaining. Babs's psyche attracted narcissistic men, whose focus on their own needs forced her to express her own. In other words, she had to learn "healthy narcissism." This was the lesson that the relationships she had attracted into her crucible had to teach her—learning to become aware of and communicate her needs.*

Stages of Changing the Dysfunctional Patterns

As we begin to understand the patterns that contribute to the self-defeating dynamics in our relationships, we have a choice to change the way we relate to others. Once we understand what lessons we need to learn to heal the wounds and reshape the patterns from the past, then we can change the script. The first stage in this change is described by Clarissa Pinkola Estes in her book, *Women Who Run with the Wolves*. According to Estes, we develop the maturity to know when to veer. This means that when we see the pattern repeating itself, we can make a conscious choice to move away from it. Babs, in the example above, has become adept at recognizing when she meets a man who has the characteristics that match the mold of narcissistic, critical, and controlling, and she consciously chooses to veer away; that is, to avoid such men. She has also learned to recognize men who are absorbed in protecting their wounded Inner Child in other ways, as Carl did by over-identifying with the Pleaser. She no longer gets involved in relationships with these kinds of men. However, even as Babs becomes more conscious of attracting such men, they continue to appear in her life, as she hasn't yet finished the second stage of actually learning her lessons.

The second stage goes beyond merely recognizing and veering away from the situation that is similar to ones we have been hurt by or that have been difficult in the past. The next step in changing the dysfunctional patterns is to disidentify from the selves we have developed to protect our vulnerability, because they no longer serve us. For Babs, that entails changing her defense mechanisms of the Pleaser and the Nurturing Mother that cover over her feelings and needs—subpersonalities that she learned from her own mother. They will be replaced by Babs's awareness and healthy expression of her own needs and wants. As she learns to speak her truth, she will feel more empowered and successful in getting the love she wants.

Babs has decided not to get involved in relationships while she is working on unlearning what she experienced in her upbringing. She is practicing experiencing, embracing, and expressing her needs and vulnerabilities when they arise. Babs is learning to speak her truth and stand up for herself when her needs aren't being met. When Babs is able to claim her disowned energy, feel and express her anxieties, and then communicate her needs, she will no longer attract unhealthy narcissistic relationships to be her teachers. When she reaches this stage of awareness, a transformation will occur in her life.

Women like Babs feel uncomfortable asking for what they want. Dr. John Gray offers a great explanation for this in his book, *Men Are From Mars, Women Are From Venus*. He says,

> Venutions are telepathic. They never needed to
> ask on Venus. Men are Martians and don't read
> minds. The only way women are going to get their
> needs met is if they ask. They need to know they
> have a right to ask and it doesn't mean that the
> person doesn't love them. It just means that they
> are not from Venus. (p. 298)

A friend of mine once said, "Men and women are two different species. They just happen to be sexually compatible." I know John Gray agrees with him, and sometimes I do, too. To learn to love another "species," you need to know both your own heart and the heart of your loved one. It's also important to know what the boundaries are that make each of you feel safe, valued, and cherished. Loving with this level of awareness can open up both your hearts so the vulnerable Inner Child can heal.

Our Disowned Selves: Part 2

In Chapter 2, under "Our Disowned Selves: Part 1," I mentioned a law of the psyche, described by Drs. Hal and Sidra Stone, founders of Voice Dialogue: The law says we attract to us that which we have disowned or never learned. It is important to be aware of our disowned selves and learn to incorporate their expression as a representation of our authentic self. A disowned self is created by either our experiencing, seeing, or observing a behavior in our role models (most often, our parents) that we were hurt by, frightened by, or didn't like. A disowned self can also be created when we were criticized for exhibiting certain behaviors. Sometimes, as in Babs's case, a disowned energy is a way of behaving that we never learned. Whatever causes a disowned self to emerge, the result is the same: A set of thoughts, feelings, and behaviors are deemed totally unacceptable and are therefore repressed, but not destroyed. They remain alive in our unconscious. Often, we only see our disowned selves in relationships, in our dreams, or in our meditations. We attract these disowned selves in the form of our friends, partners, bosses, children, and even our pets.

Voice Dialogue is designed to facilitate an Aware Ego process through which we become aware of a primary self with whom we have identified, embrace the opposite energy of the disowned self, and then make a conscious choice that is in our highest interest. By examining our own personality, we can begin to see the dynamics of primary selves and disowned selves that underlie our relationships and how they function as teachers. Primary and disowned selves travel in pairs and are often extreme and opposite expressions of the same character trait or behavior (see Appendix E).

For example, if one of our primary selves is the Pleaser, chances are we will attract a person who is hostile or selfish. Each of these is an extreme manifestation of balancing our own needs and the other person's needs in relationship. If we have developed an Aware Ego process, then we can recognize that we have disowned the energy of the Selfish Self. Perhaps the fear is that by being selfish we would alienate friends and family, and we would be rejected and abandoned by those we love. Another example is the Pusher and the Beach Bum, also known as the Lazy Self. The Pusher, as a primary self, fears that no matter how much is accomplished, it is never enough. The Pusher might emerge out of a fear that being lazy would cause our life to collapse, because we would never accomplish enough. The Beach Bum, on the other hand, is content to enjoy the moment, with no concern about goals and accomplishments. As illustrated, it just might behoove the Pusher to take on a little of the disowned energy of the Beach Bum and vice versa.

The point of being aware of our disowned energy in our relationships isn't to become like the other person. Having attracted that person into our life—and this is probably a recurring pattern—means that we need to claim a small amount of our disowned energy in order to be in better balance. Hal and Sidra talk about needing to incorporate only a homeopathic dose, or 2 percent, of the energy that the other person exhibits. Once we've realized that the person we've attracted into our life is manifesting the same behavior that we've disowned, we can then understand how this behavior is actually a part of ourselves that we need to get to know in order to become whole. We'll no longer feel either victimized or righteously judgmental.

Feeling victimized usually means that we are identifying totally with our vulnerability and have disowned an important aspect of our being. Feeling righteously judgmental, on the other hand, means that we identify with the power side and have disconnected from our vulnerability. Either way, this person in our life is an important teacher. By observing the other person's energy, which we have disowned, we can experiment with how we want to incorporate that disowned energy into our life. For the first time, we have a choice about how to respond. We can communicate with the other person from a place of clarity, with an awareness of the inner dynamics that set up the disowning of the energy. Conscious communication means being able to express our vulnerability, feelings, needs, and fears, as well as our awareness, strength, and power.

Bonding Patterns

All relationships have what Voice Dialogue calls bonding patterns, which are re-creations in the present relationship of psychological/emotional interactions that we experienced in our childhood. A bonding pattern occurs when an internalized Parent of one person relates to the Inner Child of the other person.

> *Let's return to Jane and Russ, the couple I introduced in Chapter 4. Their relationship illustrates how couples express the disowned energy of each other. I have been seeing Jane in therapy. She can be hostile, critical, and definitely outspoken about her needs. Her husband, Russ, hates confrontation and bends over backwards to please Jane and everyone else. Each of them carries a missing piece of the other.*
>
> *Jane and Russ have been in a strong bonding pattern of Critical Mother and Conciliatory Son since they got married nine years ago. They haven't made love since their honeymoon night. Mother-son bonding patterns don't do well in bed! Jane talks about Russ in a critical, yet motherly way. She needs him to develop his power side and stand up for himself in order for her to respect him. Russ is resentful of how Jane treats him, although he realizes that he lets people walk all over him, which is also creating problems for him at work.*
>
> *Jane and Russ both need to learn about the disowned part of themselves that the other spouse holds. Russ needs to separate from his Pleaser and Conciliatory Son and connect to his power side by learning to stand up for himself and deal with confrontation more effectively. Jane needs to separate from her critical, controlling self and access her softer, more vulnerable side. Since Jane's own mother, her most important role model, was very critical, Jane grew up feeling unlovable and filled with shame. Although Jane appears strong and powerful, she actually feels weak and*

has low self-esteem. She learned to develop the Inner Critic and the Judge as a way to protect her vulnerability. Her Inner Critic criticizes Jane, and her Judge criticizes others. Both of these subpersonalities serve to deflect criticism of Jane from others. Because this defense mechanism tends to alienate people, she never feels successful in her relationships, which increases her feelings of low self-worth and shame. As Jane has learned to connect with her feelings of vulnerability and communicate effectively with others without being hostile or critical, her relationships with her employees and friends have begun to improve. She feels this progress, which increases her self-esteem, and she is beginning to feel less self-critical and more empowered.

It is often less threatening to try new behaviors with people who are safer, like coworkers or acquaintances, since they may not pose as much of an emotional risk. Once you feel more comfortable with the new behaviors, you can begin to use them with family members. As Jane develops better communication skills and feels more successful in her dealings with her employees and friends, her self-esteem will increase. Then it will be less threatening for her to express her vulnerability with Russ and with her family.

As we learned in Chapter 5 and from Babs's experience, the same bonding pattern of aggressive, Critical Parent and the Pleaser/Conciliatory Child can be played out in reverse, with the man being the one who is more aggressive, critical, and controlling. Yet whoever is in the position of the aggressor needs to learn how, as an adult, to share the authentic feelings underlying the anger or rage. Conversely, whoever is the Pleaser/ Conciliatory Child needs to become more assertive. The important thing is that each of us needs to understand the dysfunctional patterns we have developed to protect our hearts. No matter what primary selves are complicating our lives, we can learn to express our feelings in constructive ways. This can only happen after we do the inner work to develop a healthy relationship with our Inner Child so we know what our Child needs. The experience of expressing these vulnerable feelings often allows the Child to be heard, get his or her needs met, and feel empowered. This inner process helps us to learn a new pattern of communicating in healthy ways, allowing us to feel safe being vulnerable. In conscious relationships, where both partners can express their truth, each one learns from the other. As we each claim our disowned energy, we move naturally from the extreme positions of our opposing primary selves toward a healthy expression of behavior and a more balanced, truer expression of who we are, as individuals and as a couple.

Energetic Linkage

One of the most subtle and exquisite aspects of Voice Dialogue is the depth of focus on the energetics of relationship. Hal and Sidra Stone use the term *energetic linkage* to refer to a source of connection or to the vitality of a relationship. This relationship happens in a myriad of ways: Each subpersonality carries its own source or power, and the awareness of how each self is experienced is important. We relate to each of our subpersonalities in different ways, and we connect in innumerable ways to the people, animals, places, and things that enter our world. This could include how we respond to our family members, our work, our pets, our computer, our television set, our money, or our connection to food, alcohol, exercise, or even our "to do" lists.

Hal and Sidra describe on their website in "The Basic Elements of Voice Dialogue, Relationship and the Psychology of Selves" just how important it is for professionals to learn about energetic linkage. "Experienced facilitators are able to work at deeper and deeper levels as they become more at home with the energetic realities that are in us and that determine so much of what happens in our lives and in our relationships."

The energetics of Voice Dialogue is what elevates it to an art form! Being aware of this powerful flow in relationships makes all the difference in the world. People can unhook from negative bonding patterns, which are devastating to relationships, become aware of the internal dynamics, and make a conscious choice to link in vital ways that support the deepening of intimacy in a relationship and the growth of the individuals who are in the couple.

When we see our relationships as purposeful—as essential to our process of growth and development—we can understand that there may be a method to the madness. To heal our wounded self-esteem, we need to develop a relationship with our Inner Child by valuing, honoring, and nurturing this precious part of ourselves. We each need to love and nurture ourselves in order to be able to have loving relationships with others or, as the Beatles taught, "And in the end, the love you take is equal to the love you make." Then, with greater self-awareness and an awareness of the other, we can cultivate loving relationships that can be an important step in promoting a healthier family, community, and society.

Hal and Sidra illuminate the focus of this chapter, "The Higher Purpose of Relationships," in their book, *Partnering: A New Kind of Relationship*.

> When we link energetically with choice and awareness, a soul connection is made. We begin to develop a new kind of sensing in which the visible and invisible worlds become as one. It is in the silence of this linkage that we are able to open the basket of the Star Maiden [which contains the magic of who we are and what we hold most precious in life] and find the riches that lie within it. (p. 115)

Clients' Experience with the Higher Purpose of Relationships

To improve myself and my chances of inviting love into my life, I invested in numerous personal growth seminars over a twenty-year period. I thought I had learned a great deal about myself, as well as what to look for in a future mate, and I practiced good communication skills that are imperative for a healthy relationship. I had even made a lengthy list of all the pertinent qualities I wanted in a partner. I was clear about what I was seeking—I did not want another failed relationship. My ex-husband had been quite a controlling man, and I had resisted confrontation. Through the seminars, I became more confident in myself, enjoyed the freedom of "walking to the beat of my own drummer," and became comfortable with confrontation.

So when I got to know "Seth," who met 90 percent of the criteria on my list, and with whom I was easily able to discuss many important issues, I felt very comfortable agreeing to marry him. But once we were married, it suddenly became difficult for me to discuss a problem or an issue. No matter how I framed it, Seth would deny that anything had happened.

He would tell me that I was wrong to bring it up, saying that it wasn't an issue. I found myself losing respect for him. My attempts to discuss any personal issues with Seth evoked for him the need to avoid my personal problems. Over time, my confrontational "fangs" grew longer as I would attempt again and again to "reframe" the issue; each time Seth became more adamant that I was overreacting. Eventually, his insistence that it was my fault and that I was the "bad guy" took on a life of its own—the original issue got lost in the shuffle. Only once did he express anger. I became his cheerleader, saying, "Tell me more. What else?" He was so shocked that he did not know how to react.

Often I would blow up, becoming more and more like a Critical Mother. The pattern that evolved was this: The day after my "explosions," he would become the "Conciliatory Son," acting like a child attempting to get back in Mommy's good graces. This behavior was a big turnoff for me, each time deepening my loss of respect for him. There was nothing healthy about this dance we were doing. I felt I could not trust Seth, which resulted in my distancing myself from him. I had even considered leaving after dozens of these experiences. I did not like myself when I was around him and did not like the person I was becoming. I had viewed myself as an innately positive person, and I was experiencing far too many negative thoughts.

Thankfully, I was guided to reach out to a therapist for personal therapy and after a few sessions, she invited my husband to come into the office. What we have learned about ourselves is amazing. The wounded child within each of us was preventing us from cultivating the healthy relationship we each longed for.

When I was seven, my father was transferred from our home in Virginia (where we had an extended family and a broad base of friends) to upstate New York. We moved into a smaller, more modest home during a January snowstorm. My father traveled during the week and my one-year-old brother was always sick. My mother had left her beautiful home and family support system for a cold climate where she knew no one. These were rough times for all of us.

From my first day in second grade at a new school, the children started taunting me about my stupid clothes and how dumb I must be. It was a very lonely time for both my mother and me. Though I knew my mother loved me unconditionally, I now realize that she did not have the emotional energy to wisely and patiently listen to my feelings about my painful rejections. There was no one to talk to, no one to hear me. Those lonely years from second through fourth grades indelibly affected my life. I developed a strong "Pusher" to cover over my wounded, lonely, rejected seven-year-old. I learned to push to be heard, and I became skilled at detaching from incidents that would threaten my security.

Because I had such a hard time being heard early in life, what were minor irritations to others became major transgressions in my view. These would trigger "explosions" when the same scenario occurred repeatedly. For example: My husband loved orange juice. Early on, I explained that I could not drink it because the acid upset my stomach. He continued to ask me to try it because it would be good for me. His offering me orange juice was like a broken record, which played over and over again. I finally "blew my top" because he refused to hear me. I would ask for salt and he would say, "Do you want pepper, too?" I snapped, "If I wanted pepper, I would have asked for it." I was begging, please just listen to me. I was becoming the "Critical Mother" nag, and I did not like her.

Through therapy we learned that because Seth had such a domineering, critical mother, he had developed a "Pleaser" personality, so that he would get his mother's approval, rather than her criticism. He was so attuned to his mother's criticism that he ducked or denied anything that even "smelled like it." Being a Pleaser became so deeply ingrained that it made it hard for him to hear my requests, whether large or small; he was so focused on doing what his Pleaser thought would make me happy, so that I would like him and not criticize him, that he missed what I was actually saying to him.

A light bulb went on for both of us when we realized that Seth was viewing me as his mother and I was seeing him as rejecting me, reflecting each of our major childhood wounds. I worked individually on getting to know my Critical Mother, which emerges because of the trauma my seven-year-old went through. An awareness started to develop where I would see my Critical Mother start to creep in, and I would catch myself and realize that I didn't want to repeat that pattern. Instead, I learned how to share my vulnerability with Seth when I didn't feel heard, which now allows him to be there for me because he doesn't have "to duck." With the new tools I've been given by my therapist, I'm able to "check in" and really hear my seven-year-old, who no longer feels lonely and rejected because I am more available to be there for her. I feel better than I have in forty-five years. Seth has also worked individually on separating from his Pleaser and is able to speak his truth more clearly and directly, which is allowing him to feel stronger and better about himself. I also respect him and trust him more because I know he is being honest with me, rather than allowing his Pleaser or Conciliatory Son to cover over his true feelings. Now that we can see each other's wounded children, we are more compassionate, understanding, and accepting of each other. The work we have done on ourselves and the relationship has dissolved the dance we had been doing for years! We have come to realize that being in this relationship has precipitated a depth of healing for each of us individually that would not have occurred had we not been married—one of the unexpected gifts of this relationship. Thankfully, we are now closer than we ever dreamed possible.

In Practice:
Getting to Know Your Primary and Disowned Selves

1. *Think about one of the relationships in your life, other than an intimate relationship, in which you are having a difficult time (e.g., with a coworker, a boss, or a sibling). This can be a relationship with someone you may resent, reject, despise, or judge harshly. This person may be carrying your disowned energy. The thought of this person creates a sense of self-righteousness and maybe even indignation. You can also discover your disowned energy by focusing on people you greatly esteem, maybe even put on a pedestal. For example, do you admire any particular movie stars, or political or historical figures? Do you know people whom you admire so much that you feel inadequate when you compare yourself to them? Choose a person who elicits in you either strong positive or strong negative feelings.*

   Write his or her name here: _____

2. *Now list the qualities that describe this person under Disowned Selves, and the opposite qualities that describe you under Primary Selves. For example, if you listed "hostile" or "selfish" under Disowned Selves, how would you describe yourself in relation to that quality—nice, caring, giving?*

Primary Selves	**Disowned Selves**
....	....
_____	_____
....	....
_____	_____
....	....
_____	_____

3. *What are the qualities listed under Disowned Selves that might be useful to you in some situations? As you contemplate this possibility, consider how the quality would change your personality if it were expressed at a 2 percent homeopathic dose that would be more balanced for you.*

_____

_____

_____

_____

_____

_____

4. *Describe how different your life would be if you were to separate from your primary selves and claim some of your disowned energies.*

_____

_____

_____

_____

_____

_____

5. *Write down any new awareness that may have come to you as a result of doing this exercise.*

_____

_____

_____

_____

_____

_____

7

How Behavioral Change and Transformation Happen

In the end, it is important to remember that we cannot become what we need to be by remaining what we are.

—Max De Pree, *Leadership Is an Art*

The Process of Behavioral Change

Slowly, with great perseverance, behavioral change and transformation can begin to occur through expanded awareness. Let's look at behavioral change first. Once we begin to acknowledge our behavior, the primary self we want to change, and become familiar with the situations that precipitate this behavior, we're on the road to anticipating and ultimately changing the behavior. Viewing the behavior as a defense mechanism that no longer serves us creates the motivation to embark on this journey of conscious behavioral change.

> *Georgia was traumatized at age two when she witnessed her grandmother's death in an accident with a bus. Her father left the family when Georgia was very young and her mother, Anna, was emotionally absent throughout Georgia's life. Understandably, Georgia developed a strong defense structure with an underlying belief that she didn't matter; otherwise, her father wouldn't have left, her grandmother wouldn't have died, and her mother would have been more emotionally available to her. Anna had low self-esteem and was narcissistic, so she couldn't pass a strong sense of self on to Georgia or give her emotional support; she was too focused on herself and her own needs. Anna was also an extreme extrovert and, as*

the center of attention, left Georgia feeling as if she were always standing in her mother's shadow. As a mother, Anna wasn't capable of meeting Georgia's emotional needs in a way that would have made Georgia feel that she mattered and was important. As an adult, whenever Georgia had to decide whether or not to go to a social event or a meeting, she would invariably wind up not going because she believed that it didn't matter whether she showed up or not. She didn't let people get close to her, she didn't risk reaching out to people for fear of being abandoned or rejected, and when she was with people who were extroverted and getting all the attention, she would react with an edge of anger. These situations would trigger the same dynamic that she experienced with her mother, and she would wind up feeling rejected.

When Georgia came to see me, she felt extremely lonely and isolated, and had little in the way of a social support system. She enjoyed her work, had a meaningful career, and was good at what she did. However, she felt isolated and lonely when she wasn't working. Georgia has become aware of how her defense mechanisms have led to her feelings of loneliness. Because of the traumatic events of her childhood, making behavioral changes has been difficult for her. First, she learned to express her feelings and needs in healthy, effective ways. She was amazed that this strengthened her relationships, rather than creating rejection. Then she worked on her mind, which had set up the subpersonality of her Inner Critic, telling her that she didn't matter. Georgia named the subpersonality that would avoid going to events the Isolator. Georgia became aware of her Isolator and her Inner Critic who would repeatedly say to her, "It doesn't matter if you go to that party, no one will care." Her Inner Critic and her Isolator would inevitably come up with very good reasons why she shouldn't go out to parties, meetings, lunches, dinners, or any event that she was invited to attend.

To begin to work on changing these destructive behavioral patterns, we made a deal that for one month she would say yes to any invitation, whenever it was possible, no matter what her Isolator told her to do. In a gradual process, we worked with her traumatized selves, since her defense mechanisms had clearly formed in response to early traumas. For instance, we talked to the self that felt abandoned by all the key people in her life, and that made her feel as if she didn't matter. The protective mechanisms of criticizing herself so that others won't, and isolating herself so that she doesn't feel abandoned, have made it difficult for her to change the behaviors that she would like to transform. Georgia is a very interesting and intelligent woman who has much to offer others. Yet her negative beliefs about herself have kept her from having the life she wants. The more she is able to hear and separate from the voices that carry her negative self-referencing beliefs, the more she is able to make new and positive choices that take her in a healthier direction.

The Process of Transformation

Transformation is more than behavioral change. When we only change our behaviors without addressing the deeper layers of our unconscious, there is a possibility of a reversal, a return to an earlier pattern of behavior—a relapse, so to speak. When lasting transformation occurs, by contrast, there is an internalized shift. We have moved to a new and deeper experience of being, closer to our essence or true nature. We have grown larger and freer as a result of our experience of life. It is no longer possible to regress to a smaller, more limited sense of self. It is like the butterfly trying to return to the chrysalis—it simply can't happen.

One of my colleagues, Jay, has a wonderful metaphor for this process of transformation. The chambered nautilus shell is created when the little sea urchin outgrows the chamber it has lived in and burrows a hole through the chamber wall. As it comes through to begin building its next home, bigger than the last, the first thing it does is seal off the hole it just came through. That wise little sea urchin knows there is no going back.

This process of transformational change is an awe-inspiring endeavor that can take several years to complete. While behavioral change can begin to happen immediately, it takes more time for the kind of full transformation that results in the permanent cessation of self-defeating behaviors, when we can look back at a behavior and say, "Amazing, I don't do that anymore." According to Hal and Sidra, this journey, from the initial moment of awareness of a subpersonality, to behavioral change, and then to complete transformation, can take up to two years. Shifts can begin immediately as we become aware of a behavior we want to change—but the Aware Ego process that leads us up the mountain to transformation may take longer. Indeed, depending on the complexity of the defense structure we needed to survive, it can take up to two years, if we really focus on the process of transforming a particular behavior. As we navigate the twists and turns up this steep path, the tools that were acquired during the process of life-lesson therapy (Chapters 1–7) will help us stay the "consciousness course," as will the qualities of patience and compassion. Attaining lasting transformation is truly an adventure that makes life full, exciting, and at times confusing and difficult—but that is always in service of our growth.

Letting Go of the Past Creates Change in the Present

In moving toward change and transformation, we need to acknowledge and accept our past, so that we can focus on the present. As Jay puts it, "It's difficult to change behavior; it's impossible to change history." For this reason, if our past includes loss, we must do the work of grieving. The process of holding on to past hurts, and blaming others or ourselves for our difficulties, keeps us stuck in the past. To break out of this impasse, we need to allow ourselves to feel the feelings from the past so that we can heal, learn the lessons from our life experiences, and develop the wisdom that these experiences were in our life to teach us. Even in the present, it's important to continue to work to let go of the patterns we developed as a result of our history, and to take responsibility for the choices we've made. Then we can use these life lessons and the soul-wisdom we've earned to make conscious choices in the present. Behavioral change and transformation can only happen in the present.

Mussar: A Spiritual Wisdom Tradition

This process of transformation I've outlined is not just a twenty-first century concept, but can be found in various spiritual traditions. Mussar in Judaism, for instance, draws on a body of ancient ethical teachings that have evolved over the past thousand years by great Jewish thinkers and spiritual seekers. Mussar is not just for Jews; it is universal and applicable to everyone. Mussar guides people to examine their soul-traits and character traits, and maps out a daily practice whose purpose is to build character and create possibilities for transformation. Rabbi Moshe Chaim Luzzatto (1534–1572), whose work had a profound influence on the Mussar movement, describes this purpose in his book, *Da'ath Tevunot* (Discerning Knowledge, or The Knowing Heart): "The one stone on which the entire building rests is the concept that God wants each person to complete himself, body and soul." When I first discovered Mussar, I was very excited and inspired, because Mussar laid out a map that was very similar to the process I use with clients for behavioral change and transformation.

The word *mussar* means "correction" or "instruction." It also means "structured transmission," "to hand over," or "to deliver." Behavioral change and transformation do not happen haphazardly; they occur as a result of working in a structured, conscious way, carefully correcting what does not work. We have to let go of the old stories about our lives that are no longer true, along with dysfunctional behaviors and limiting self-concepts, using our new understanding of the Aware Ego. Mussar is a way of life that shines light on the causes of suffering and instructs us in how to correct our way of navigating through life, so that we experience the journey as more meaningful and authentic. The focus of Mussar is to help us become more whole and complete by refining our character traits, called *middot* in Hebrew. Alan Morinis, author of *Everyday Holiness*, defines the singular form of *middot, middah*, as "measure." He says,

> We can find in this root [*middah*] a Mussar insight. Each of us is endowed at birth with every one of the full range of the human traits, and what sets one person apart from another is not whether we have certain traits while someone else has different ones, but rather the degree or *measure*, of the traits that live in each of our souls. Through introspection and self-examination you can identify the traits that are hindrances in your life, either because you have too much or too little of them. Awareness of your inner imbalances pinpoints the work you can do to transform those challenging inner qualities. (p. 19)

To change behavior and transform our subpersonalities or character traits, specific steps must be taken in order for us to move forward on the journey. The teachings of Mussar are reflected in the following two steps for behavioral change and transformation.

Steps for the Behavioral Change and Transformational Journey

Through the "In Practice" exercises at the end of each chapter, you have been identifying selves, or subpersonalities you have developed to protect your vulnerable Inner Child, many of which are no longer working for you. You can pick one of these subpersonalities to focus on as I lead you through the following process of behavioral change and transformation.

Step 1: Awareness—In order to complete ourselves, body and soul, we need to differentiate between those primary selves or subpersonalities that are working in our lives and those that hinder us. We need to become attuned to our inner world and the thoughts and feelings that underlie our behaviors. The sooner we develop this awareness, the sooner we will have a choice to change the behavior to one that is more aligned with what we truly want in life. Using a Voice Dialogue perspective, we can name the subpersonalities that we have utilized to protect our vulnerability, and develop an awareness of how these subpersonalities are playing out in our lives.

> *For example, Georgia, whose story we described toward the beginning of this chapter, needed to become sensitive to the Inner Critic that made her feel as if she didn't matter, as well as her Isolator who didn't want her to take risks for fear of being rejected. Georgia became aware of these two subpersonalities who would repeatedly say to her, "It doesn't matter if you go to that party, no one will care if you go." The feelings underlying the Isolator are feelings of insecurity. By talking with this insecure self, Georgia can separate out from this identity and strengthen the Aware Ego. This way a more conscious awareness will emerge whenever the energy of that subpersonality comes up in her life. By getting to know the Isolator, understanding where it comes from, and identifying what happened in her life to create those feelings of insecurity, she can begin to embrace this subpersonality. She can also become aware of the anxiety that underlies her Inner Critic. She can then stop the pattern of being unconsciously ruled by this critical self and understand its needs for protection. The Isolator and the Inner Critic work together to keep Georgia safe by making her feel bad about herself—so that she isolates and then doesn't reach out and risk getting rejected or abandoned.*

Step 2: Behavioral Change—Behavioral change occurs as we become aware of the primary self that is directing us. After focusing on the behavior that we wish to change, we gradually become more aware; at first this awareness occurs *after* our actions, perhaps three hours or three days later. Gradually, however, the awareness occurs closer and closer to the moment when the behavior happens. At a certain point in our journey of behavioral change, awareness will awaken in us right before the behavior is about to take place. In that moment, we will be able, for the first time, to separate from that primary self before it expresses itself. This is the critical moment when behavioral change is possible and we can make a decision to act in a different manner.

What is at work in this process I've just described is discernment—one of the most important spiritual attributes. Through discernment we can decide to choose a different response to a specific situation, using self-restraint to eliminate the behaviors that were at one time destructive, or that no longer work. Voice Dialogue is a powerful tool for developing the ability to be conscious of the behaviors that we want to change.

By naming the self and identifying the voice that would isolate her from reaching out to connect with others, for instance, Georgia could "name that tune," and not believe what the Isolator was saying to her. She could actually hear the voice of her Isolator; within a few seconds she could make a choice to separate from its seductive message, instead of acting on the voice saying "you don't matter." As her discernment sharpened, Georgia's behavior changed; she began to attend events and to even have a good time. In those moments of awareness, she was able to change a self-defeating behavior into a healthy one that enhanced her life.

Step 3: Transformation—We can decide to act in ways that are in greater alignment with a healthy, wise, and responsible Aware Ego. An Aware Ego allows for healthier choices, which has the potential to more fully nourish our essential Self. Mussar teaches us to strive toward the positive and strengthen the opposite trait of the one with which we are struggling. It is important to identify the positive quality, which will serve as an antidote to the self-destructive subpersonality we are exhibiting. In Voice Dialogue, subpersonalities often come in pairs, existing on the same continuum as, but often on the opposite side from, the subpersonality that is the disowned self.

The parts of Georgia that were afraid of taking risks, that carried her low self-esteem, and that isolated her from others were clearly primary selves that had created extreme feelings of loneliness in Georgia's life. Throughout her life, her Isolator was triggered every time she came in contact with an extrovert. But as she became aware of how she attracted this extroverted energy that she disowned, it became possible for her to recognize how extroverts exemplified the opposite energy that she needed to integrate into her life. She learned that if she could take in just a little of this opposite energy (based on the 2 percent rule: that is, taking in just 2 percent of the Extrovert's energy that her mother exuded), then she would be able to transform the subpersonality she named the Isolator.

A Comprehensive Model for Shifting Consciousness

My doctoral dissertation, titled "The Transformation of the Mind into Wisdom: An Understanding and Practical Applications," was an exploration of Patanjali's Yoga Sutras. Patanjali, who lived three or four centuries before Christ, recommended a series of guidelines to reverse the negative tendencies of the mind. A Hindu yoga master, Patanjali presents a comprehensive model for shifting consciousness through gradually learning to observe and control thoughts, bodily functions, and social relationships in an objective manner. Sutra 33, for example, describes the process of focusing on the opposite. I. K. Taimni *(The Science of Yoga)* translates this sutra as follows: "When the mind is disturbed by improper thoughts, constant pondering over the opposites is the remedy." By choosing to withdraw energy from negative thoughts and emotions, for example, and replacing them with thoughts and emotions of a higher, more positive quality, the mind becomes calmer and the individual gains greater balance and control in living.

In her book, *The Language of Love*, Susan Polis Schutz describes this process:

> All that we are is the result of what we think. How then can a man escape being filled with hatred, if his mind is constantly repeating he misused me, he hit me, he defeated me, he robbed me? Hatred can never put an end to hatred. Hate is conquered only by love. (p. 19)

A process I often use to effect behavioral change and transformation combines Voice Dialogue, Patanjali's Yoga Sutras, and a Mussar practice, which focuses on identifying negative soul-traits and their opposite or positive soul-trait. As Alan Morinis suggests in *Everyday Holiness,* a good way to begin is to identify our "personal spiritual curriculum" by creating a list of those traits that interfere with our feeling fulfilled in life. Let's use the example of developing a Liar subpersonality as a way to lessen anxiety-provoking situations by protecting the part of ourselves that feels fearful or insecure. Along with working with this subpersonality and identifying its feelings and needs, we could then use the Aware Ego process to begin separating from this subpersonality. The next step in the process of behavioral change and transformation is accessing and strengthening its opposite—the Truthsayer. In another example, a tendency to be fearful could be transformed by strengthening the subpersonality of the Courageous One.

The process that leads to transformation also involves understanding what is motivating the negative behavior of a particular self. It is important to identify the underlying feelings of vulnerability that have contributed to the formation of that self. The tendency to lie may be coming from feelings of insecurity, of feeling like we're not good enough and therefore we need to inflate the truth. In *Everyday Holiness,* Morinis explains, "To be completely freed of the negative soul-trait requires that this causal trait be reprogrammed, not with ideas but with the sorts of direct experiences that can wire new patterns of thought and feeling from deep within" (p. 259). This is why the Voice Dialogue method is so powerful—it leads to a deeper sensory experience of the thoughts and feelings that are operating under and driving the subpersonality. Once this is experienced directly, a behavioral change that leads to a transformation can occur on a conscious level, and this process informs and thereby strengthens the Aware Ego.

> *Let's turn to Georgia again. Underneath Georgia's Isolator were feelings of insecurity and lack of self-love, which stemmed from a self-involved mother, Anna, who was not very nurturing. Anna's extreme Extrovert covered over her lack of self-confidence, and therefore she wasn't able to pass on a strong sense of self to Georgia. After first speaking to the Isolator, using the Voice Dialogue Method, we also spoke to Georgia's Inner Critic, who contributed to Georgia's insecurity and lack of self-love. By helping Georgia connect to her Inner Nurturing Mother, the opposite and positive subpersonality, she could begin to re-parent herself and feel more secure and self-loving. Another opposite and positive trait of the Inner Critic could be wisdom. For Georgia, the Wise One or Inner Teacher was the subpersonality who could see things from a higher perspective and thus help her become less self-critical.*

The behavioral change and transformation experiment, outlined in the "In Practice" section at the end of this chapter, offers a daily practice that you can do in your own life to focus on your "spiritual curriculum"—the behaviors that you want to consciously change and ultimately transform.

A Client's Experience of Behavioral Change and Transformation

What happened to me in therapy has changed my life forever. How do I put into words a process that saved my life, without losing objectivity and reducing the words to pure gratitude? What happened to me is so powerful and close to my heart that it is difficult to talk or write about it. But write about it I must: It would be a disservice not to let people know that the process works and can change your life.

While thinking about my life, especially the part that involved sailing, I realized that what happened to me was nothing short of a sea change, a total transformation. I had been a sailor for most of my adult life, and so putting it in this perspective made a lot of sense to me.

I was brought up in a Catholic orphanage and learned early on that the way to survive was to become invisible. I learned never to be the focus of a person in authority; in my case, that meant the nuns or the civilian prefect. Discipline was maintained by corporal punishment and meted out without regard for innocence or guilt, but rather proximity. Being invisible allowed me to escape the severe corporal punishment and in later life repress my feelings of shame, guilt, and unworthiness brought on by being abandoned after my mother died.

For the next five decades after leaving the orphanage, I ricocheted through life, leaving emotional scars on everyone foolish enough to enter my private life. I failed miserably in three marriages and never made a friend. But I was successful in my professional life. I realized that I had no social skills and therefore had to rely on being more knowledgeable and better prepared than any of my peers. This brought me a grudging respect and a certain measure of financial success, and allowed me to remain anonymous as a person. I rejected every attempt at intimacy, expressions of love or friendship, and was passionate in protecting my shame, guilt, and unworthiness. Through all these years, I hated my father for abandoning me, and rejected my religion for the harsh treatment I received during my childhood. I relied totally on myself and rejected anyone who got too "close" to my emotional self. I made it into retirement alone, miserable but intact—or so I thought.

While preparing my sailboat for a trip to the Caribbean, where I would get hired to captain the boat for people, and start a new phase of my life, I had an accident that resulted in the loss of one of my legs. Overnight, I became a disabled person with all the ramifications and connotations associated with a physical disability. As a person who was emotionally invisible, this was something that I could not deal with. My invisibility disappeared overnight. I was "reduced" to a wheelchair and for the first time in my life, I was totally visible. I had been "outed" in a most significant way. I had no defense for this most obvious of conditions. In my "cold gray light of dawn moment," I seriously considered ending it all. I believe it was the incredible care, both physical and emotional, that I received during my three months in the rehabilitation hospital that finally swayed me to reject this option and that gave me the strength to make the phone call that would transform my life. A therapist whom I knew by acquaintance and reputation agreed to take me on in spite of the mountains of baggage that I dragged into the therapy room.

I have now been in weekly therapy for almost five years. I am still disabled, but my emotional self, my soul, my heart, and my understanding of who I am have all been changed forever. I am now able to live without the fear of being found unworthy. The intense anxiety of being found out, which interfered with my getting close to anyone, no longer plagues me. The shame of my existence has been replaced with a worthiness I never knew existed. I have replaced cynicism with awareness and caring about other people. The guilt, which isolated me from intimacy, no longer holds me prisoner. The father I hated is now remembered with sorrow, understanding, and sadness at not having had the chance to know or love him. I have accepted my disability.

How did all this happen? No, it is not a fairy tale! It happened because I was blessed with a skilled and caring therapist. A therapist who accepted me as I was, and who applied her skill to my situation using all the processes at her disposal to bring the "Inner Child" I had been protecting out into the open, finally allowing me to understand the how and why of my wanting to be "Invisible." She is the first person I have ever trusted, and through this trust she has gently peeled away all the layers of my defense mechanisms. She has led me down the path of awareness and worthiness, helped me find my spiritual self, enabled me to know that I mattered and was a good person. These are not simple matters. They were at the heart of my unexamined life. I am now able, for the first time in my life, to accept love and intimacy and return them in kind. There is a new intensity to my life, a life now worth living, as I share my life with and care about other people. I am now able to trust and take the risk of allowing someone to get close to me. It is now an examined life. I am by no means perfect. I still have pangs of fear at exposing myself, but in spite of this, I now move forward and take the risk, and that makes all the difference. I have undergone a "lasting transformation." Psychotherapy works, and I will be eternally grateful to my therapist for transforming my life.

In Practice:
Behavioral Change and Transformation Experiment

1. *Take out your journal. There are aspects of your personality that you have developed to protect yourself, parts of you that are no longer working. You have explored these subpersonalities in other chapters. Make a list of the ones you want to change and transform.*

Subpersonalities I would like to change:

a. _____

b. _____

c. _____

d. _____

Some say it takes twenty-eight days to change a habit. In Judaism, forty days is frequently connected to purification and transformation. I find that reinforcing a change for forty days gives people time to experience a feeling of deeper behavioral change.

For the next forty days, choose one soul-trait or subpersonality to focus on. Sometimes it is easier to identify a subpersonality, and sometimes it is easier to identify a soul-trait.

Example of a soul-trait: Punctuality (being on time)

Example of a subpersonality: The Inner Critic

Soul-trait or subpersonality to focus on:

_____

Beginning date: _____

Forty days from now: _____

2. *Create a daily reminder, a short and pithy phrase that accurately captures the essence of the positive quality or opposite energy of the subpersonality you want to cultivate. Try out different phrases until you find one that feels right to you and that helps you feel stronger and clearer on the path to change the behavior on your list. Write it out on a card that you can place in a spot where you will see it every morning—on your bathroom mirror, on your car dashboard, by your morning coffeepot, or on your screensaver. By focusing on your morning phrase, you create an intention to change whatever behavior or personality trait you are working on transforming.*

_____

_____

_____

Sample phrases:

For the soul-trait of punctuality: Time is of the essence.

For the subpersonality of the Inner Critic: I am enough.

3. *Create an exercise that will allow you to focus on what needs to happen for you to change whatever behavior you are working on transforming.*

_____

_____

_____

Examples:

For punctuality: Each morning, I will think of what time I need to be at my first appointment and work backwards to figure out what time I need to start getting ready.

For the Inner Critic: I will name the voice of the Inner Critic that is saying no one cares if I show up or not, and separate from that negative energy. I will choose to hear the voice of my Inner Nurturing Parent, telling me that I am a caring, interested, and interesting person, and that I can choose to enjoy myself when I go out.

4. *At bedtime, you can write below, or take out your journal and identify events during the day that show the presence of the specific quality you are cultivating. You can record any incidents, thoughts, or experiences that relate to the quality you are cultivating in your daily life. Record in your journal, each night, how well you did in accomplishing the exercise you assigned yourself. It's important to get into the habit of writing each night. Even if you are too tired to write anything significant, writing down that you are too tired to write will perpetuate and strengthen the focus on writing each night. Writing in your journal is very important because it helps develop awareness, which is the key element in effecting behavioral change, so eventually, down the road, there will be a transformation.*

_____

_____

_____

_____

_____

Examples:

Punctuality: I did really well in getting to my morning meeting on time. I realized when I was doing the exercise of calculating how much time I needed to get ready and prepare for the meeting, that I needed two hours and I was right. Good work!

The Inner Critic: I actually enjoyed going to the party at Barbara's house tonight. I could hear my Inner Critic starting that endless loop when I was walking up to the door, and I just chose not to take it in. Instead, I found some people that I knew and started talking with them, which kept me involved at the party. People seemed to enjoy talking with me and I liked meeting some of the new people that I didn't know. Whew, that was a whole lot better than my Critic said it would be!

5. *Find a book relating directly to the subpersonality you are focusing on during these forty days. Read a section from that book each day. If you can carve out time to study with a partner, this will enrich your experience of reading the material. Studying with a partner can be a powerful experience that can take you deeper into the process of learning.*

_____

_____

Examples:

Punctuality: *Take Time for Your Life* by Cheryl Richardson

The Inner Critic: *Embracing Your Inner Critic: Turning Self-Criticism into a Creative Asset* by Hal Stone, PhD, and Sidra Stone, PhD

Stage Two:
Soul-Wisdom Therapy

Laini Nemett, *Meditations,* 2008. Oil on linen, 16×13 in.

8

Grow a Conscious Self—Know Your Inner Self

Happiness does not depend so much on circumstances as on one's Inner Self.
—Lady Randolph Churchill, playwright and mother
of British Prime Minister Winston Churchill

In Stage One we focused on personality development by changing behaviors that no longer serve us. These behaviors were established to protect our vulnerability, as represented by our Inner Child. We can integrate a stronger ego, or sense of self, by valuing and communicating with this Child aspect of ourselves. This allows for a growing sense of self-acceptance and love for ourselves and others. In Stage Two, however, we shift the focus to our soul development. Our soul is our pure essence; it is the center of consciousness, and it is immortal. Our soul existed before we were born, and it will continue to exist after we die. Some spiritual teachings hold that prior to birth our soul picks the situation into which we are born in this lifetime in order for us to learn, so that our soul will grow. From this perspective, that is the purpose of creation and of having a human birth—our life is about being in a classroom with a "soul" curriculum where we will learn the wisdom that will help grow the soul. As Gary Zukav describes in his book, *Soul to Soul: Communications from the Heart,*

> Everything in the Universe moves toward ever-increasing awareness and freedom. Every personality in the Earth School has lessons to learn and gifts to give that have not yet been given. Every soul, also, participates in the continual

> movement toward fuller and fuller expression of
> wisdom and compassion. (p. 218)

We can tell when we are dealing with soul experiences because these experiences often form a thread that runs through the tapestry of our lives. These soul lessons generally have a great impact on our life.

A Transpersonal Approach to Transformation

My psychotherapeutic philosophy comes from my experience exploring spiritual planes of consciousness for over thirty years. These deeper realms of consciousness are home to the soul and to that inner source of wisdom within each of us, the Inner Self, which is the authentic center of our Being. The Inner Self is the center of the realm of the soul, just as the ego is the center of the realm of the personality. We rarely learn about the Inner Self as we are growing up. Very little in our society supports us in the quest to discover, nurture, and strengthen our connection to this sacred place.

Traditional psychotherapy conditions us to believe that we are merely our personality, our ego, or our small "s" self—nothing more. The work of traditional therapy is to strengthen and actualize the ego. It is important to develop a strong ego and sense of self, because we can't transcend something that we don't have. Transpersonal psychology builds on the strengths of a healthy ego, yet looks beyond the ego to connect us to the Divine in a profound way. By Divine I mean any force, higher power, or source of love or inspiration that touches us at the core of our being. The ultimate goal of transpersonal psychotherapy is to transcend the ego and experience these higher spiritual planes of consciousness, also called the Inner Self, the Higher Self, or the Transpersonal Realm. Unless we become aware of a spiritual perspective, we never learn that we are more than our ego. We can actually grow to identify with the capital "S" Self, which is our true Soul essence, and the inner source of wisdom within each of us. It is this process of integrating and transcending the small self to experience the Inner Self that makes up the transpersonal psychotherapeutic journey.

As a transpersonal psychologist, I have witnessed how transformational it is for clients to experience the Inner Self. It changes everything. Transpersonal psychotherapy affirms people wherever they are on the consciousness continuum and supports their continued evolution to live their lives consciously. We can also integrate the wisdom of the Inner

Self so that it permeates and speaks through the small self. It is through the alignment of the personality with our spirituality that we develop a sense of wholeness, undergo lasting transformation, and learn to see life's experiences as lessons to be learned and soul-wisdom to be integrated.

The search for soul-wisdom is beautifully expressed in a story from India. In this parable, all the gods got together. There were a lot of them, because in India they have more gods than we have flavors of ice cream. The gods were sitting around talking and were very concerned. They knew that there was a great power in the Universe, yet they were afraid that unless human beings were very developed and were conscious of the importance of this power being used for good, it would fall into the wrong hands. So they thought and thought about where to put this powerful force. One god said, "Why don't we put it at the very top of the highest mountain so it will take great effort to reach it?" Another god said, "No, in the future, humans will know how to build big birds and they will be able to fly to the top of the highest mountain." Another god said, "I've got it! Let's put it down at the bottom of the deepest ocean." Someone else said, "No, in the future they will also learn to build big fish that will take them to the depths of the ocean." Finally, after much discussion another god said, "The one place that most people will never think to look will be within. Only the very dedicated and wise ones, who will be willing to go in a different direction than the masses and travel long distances on an inner journey, will be able to discover this precious power."

So that is what they did. They placed this power of love, strength, joy, and wisdom at the very center of each human being, just waiting to be discovered. Once we discover it and learn to trust the guidance from this Inner Source, it becomes a friend, a true guide, and a constant companion on our journey to the realization that who we truly are is the Inner Self.

Realizing the Inner Self: The Goal of Meditation

As explored in Chapter 7, the Hindu Yoga master Patanjali presented a comprehensive method for realizing the Self. This method can lead to an understanding of the larger reality where one is motivated more by the goal of "Self-becoming," rather than the material goals of becoming wealthy, famous, or professionally successful. Patanjali's theory is not only a noteworthy theoretical framework, but also a novel concept for the West.

A holistic therapeutic approach, it accomplishes the primary goal of Western psychology, which is the formation of a healthy, harmonious personality and ego structure, along with the Eastern psychological perspective of transcending the personality, thus enabling the mind to focus on the higher spiritual planes of consciousness. The state of our mind determines the state of our life experience. Therefore, when the mind is focused on the Inner Self, it leads us to the most sublime and constant experience of joy, wisdom, love, and peace.

Knowledge of the Inner Self is important, but knowledge can take us only so far. We need to have an actual *experience* of the Inner Self. Swami Muktananda, my spiritual teacher for many years, described the experience of the Inner Self in his book called *Meditate*:

> Only in meditation can we see the Inner Self directly. That which lives in the heart cannot be found in books. Since that being is our innermost consciousness, it is necessary for us to turn within to have a direct experience of it...As we see it more and more, we become transformed. (p. 18)

By expanding our awareness to include experiences of the Inner Self, we remove the limitations, negativities, and blocks to incredible inner beauty, joy, and wisdom. Freed from these blocks, we can fully perceive ourselves and the world as it truly is. However, as long as we identify with the personality, which is made up of the body, the feelings, and the mind, our experience of life is limited. The goals that some people pursue, such as money and power, don't bring lasting happiness, as those things that we depend upon for external gain are transient and eventually die or deteriorate. Thus the true goal of life is to shift away from our identification with our personality toward developing the soul-wisdom to realize and identify with the Inner Self. The experience of the Inner Self does not change; it persists in the face of external challenges.

Stages in the Realization of the Inner Self

There are many stages along the way to realizing the Self. These stages may be thought of as progressing from an outer to an inner focus, or from a grosser to a more subtle Self-consciousness. This journey of becoming aware and uniting with the Self may also be thought of as taking place along a spiral, a metaphor I use with my clients. Sometimes, it seems to them that they are not progressing—that they are just going around and around in circles. When I reframe their process using the model of a spiral, they quickly comprehend that what seems like endless circles are actually slow, steady movements upward along the turns of the spiral.

At the outset of the transformational journey we tend to believe that we are simply the personality and the ego. Here our self-perceptions are on the order of: "I am a good person"; "I am sad"; "I am smart"; or "I am not enough." As we gradually begin to know ourselves and understand our personality, we arrive at the stage of self-acceptance. The tools I have presented in the first seven chapters can facilitate this process of self-acceptance as we journey around the spiral.

At the higher end of this spiral we reach the true goal of life. From the transpersonal psychological perspective, this goal is the realization of our true nature, the Self. This stage goes beyond self-acceptance to an experience of Being. Here the experience is one of "I am," without any labels or judgments. The experience of "I am" is the experience of the Self. This means living in a state of pure awareness that I am a manifestation of Unity, which connects me to all of life; I am able to transcend my identification with my personality and experience the Self that dwells within. E. Norman Pearson describes this goal of Self-realization in *Space, Time and Self*:

> The Ultimate Consciousness within each one of us is the True Self. It is, and will forever remain the Self. To find our way successfully through the many difficulties and illusions of life, we should always be aware of this one fundamental fact. To quote the words of an ancient scripture: "I am that Self; That Self Am I." (p. 167)

Only a few truly enlightened human beings experience permanent and ongoing identification with the Inner Self. The rest of us mere mortals may experience fleeting moments of true connection with the Inner Self. Though brief, these moments can change our lives forever, catapulting us higher along the spiral on our journey toward Self-realization.

Preparing to Meet the Inner Self

In order to experience the Inner Self residing within each of us, we need to learn to relax our bodies, quiet our minds, and turn our attention 180 degrees from our normal focus—out there—to an inner focus. The many demands of everyday life put us in the habit of directing the majority of our thinking and behavior outward. Even if we do take the time to relax, we are bombarded by all the thoughts of the unending "to-do" lists, or the "You shouldn't have done that" critical messages, or the future fears I call the "awfulizing" thoughts of the "what ifs" or the "if onlys." Clearly, we can benefit by learning strategies for quieting and controlling the mind.

The most thorough research, experimentation, and development of techniques to transcend the intellect and access the higher mind come from the "Easts"—India, China, Tibet, and the Middle East, including Israel and Saudi Arabia. Among the spiritual traditions that teach meditation and other tools for quieting the mind are Hinduism, Kashmir Shaivism, Tibetan Buddhism, Zen Buddhism, Sufism from the Islamic tradition, and Kabbalah, a Jewish spiritual tradition. Meditation and transcendence are actually inherent in the Judeo-Christian tradition, however these teachings are not widely taught or known about; therefore, over the past four decades, Westerners have increasingly turned toward the East to study with teachers from the Hindu, Buddhist, and Sufi traditions. During this time, Western science has increasingly begun to embrace the disciplined quieting and transcending of the mind that Eastern psychology has explored for three thousand years. Practitioners of the modern disciplines of Western psychology and medical science are just beginning to realize how much the West has to learn from the East in terms of understanding the nature of the mind.

This historic confluence between the East and West played a pivotal role in shaping my own life and work. In 1982, I helped to coordinate the Seventh International Transpersonal Psychology Conference, which took place in Bombay, now called Mumbai, India. The conference title was "Western Science Meets Eastern Wisdom." Mother Teresa, Swami Muktananda, and many others from India were the keynote speakers. Scientists, physicists, psychologists, priests, ministers, and rabbis from the West came to learn from those who were the spiritual leaders of the East. Those who attended the conference learned a great deal about the spiritual technologies that have been used for millennia to relax the body and quiet the mind in order to experience the Inner Self. Some of these techniques include meditation, relaxation, breathing exercises, guided imagery, music, and yoga.

These technologies from the East can bring us into the right state of consciousness to connect with the Inner Self. They can open us to other dimensions of our soul's wisdom. By learning to meditate (the focus of Chapter 9), we can quiet the chatter of the world and of our own busy mind. A quiet mind allows the intuition—that balanced and wise "soul" source of guidance—to open (intuition is the focus of Chapter 10). The intuitive channel connects the personality to the higher spiritual planes of consciousness.

As we increasingly access our Inner Self and its wisdom through the spiritual journey, it allows for a sense of faith to grow. This is often experienced as an inner knowing that a higher wisdom directs our lives. When we develop faith (discussed in Chapter 11), we realize that there is nothing to worry about, and that things are happening for a reason. Thus even during times of great stress, faith allows us to be at peace, to stay conscious, to learn the lessons, and to be grateful for the journey. The more we can enjoy the journey and feel awe, rather than fear, the more we can experience and express compassion and love for ourselves and others. This shifts us away from being "self-serving" toward becoming the "Serving Self" (the focus of Chapter 12). As we journey around the spiral, we develop healthy, deeply intimate relationships with Self, the Source, and significant others. As we gain soul-wisdom and learn to adopt and communicate a transpersonal perspective effectively, we can help to transform the society in which we live.

As Hal and Sidra Stone alluded to in the Foreword to this book, the journey of transformation works best for those who have allowed themselves to gradually ripen as they travel higher along the spiral. As they wrote, "They don't need to chase after wisdom any longer; it seems to emerge more and more in the form of 'downloads from the Universe.'" Amazing things happen as we make connecting with the Inner Self a priority in our life.

Just as I finished that last paragraph, I experienced an inspiring example of how having faith in a higher wisdom can direct our lives. I was at my beach house, alone for the weekend to work on this book. It was ten o'clock at night, and the beginning of winter. All the windows were closed, and a fire was blazing in the fireplace. I realized I needed some papers, so I put down my computer and ran upstairs to get them. When I returned two minutes later, a beautiful butterfly was lying in the middle of my computer keyboard. Although it was dead, its colors were vibrant, and it was centered and straight—as if a hand had placed it there for a purpose.

Butterflies have a special significance for me. Every client who graduates from therapy with me gets a butterfly. It may be a butterfly candle, earrings, or a butterfly wind chime. No matter what form it takes, the butterfly gift to my clients symbolizes their emergence from the chrysalis, with wings to freely fly on their own. So when I saw the butterfly on my computer, I was in a state of shock—my mind couldn't believe what it was seeing. Where had the butterfly come from? I'd taken a walk on the beach, but had been in the house for over four hours. It was winter; I hadn't seen any flying butterflies, much less dead butterflies. In almost two years, I'd never seen a butterfly inside the house. How had it suddenly appeared? And what was the significance of its appearance as a lifeless form? I tuned into what was trying to be communicated to me. After some reflection, it seemed to me that the message from a Higher Source had to do with telling me to relax about the writing of this book, and the publishing deadline, which was soon approaching. Then I laughed and had to share the experience, so I would have a witness to the reality of what just happened. It was too late to call most people, and too early to call others living in other time zones. But I knew that my sister, Diane, would understand the amazing significance of what had just happened. And she did! In that moment, I experienced that sense of a higher wisdom directing the process of my writing this book. I felt grateful knowing that the message of the butterfly was to reassure me, and to know and have faith that I, too, am about to come out of the chrysalis.

My Most Powerful Experience of the Inner Self

I studied with Swami Muktananda, an Indian meditation master, from 1974 until Baba, as he was endearingly called, passed on in 1982. I first met Baba in San Diego, where I was living in 1974, and then continued to spend time with him in India, as well as in a number of his ashrams in the United States. He was a powerful role model and an incredible teacher for what it is to be a "true" psychologist. It was under his guidance, while studying with him in India from 1977 to 1978, that I had my first experience of the Inner Self—an experience for which I am eternally grateful. As my teacher, Baba gave me the gift of awakening my spirituality and my connection with the Divine.

I was in a class at Baba's ashram in Ganeshpuri, India, when I went into a deep meditative trance, a state of consciousness that I'd never experienced before. In the middle of the class, I picked up my belongings and walked out into the gardens of the ashram, where I sat and meditated. During this transformative meditation, I experienced an inner fountain overflowing with love, wisdom, joy, and peace. In that moment I could feel how this same fountain that was flowing within me was also the exact inner source that resided within everyone. It was an underground tributary that was a flowing river, and it connected and came to the surface in each living, beating heart. I actually experienced what all the great spiritual masters have taught: That we are all truly one! The inner source that was this overflowing fountain of love, wisdom, joy, and peace was an image of that Inner Self that resides within each of us.

That experience has stayed with me as the foundation for my philosophy in life. Almost fifteen years later, when Ruth Berlin and I opened our Center for Psychotherapy and Healing, we chose the name InnerSource, and an overflowing fountain became the center's logo. InnerSource continues to flow and grow today.

Fountain of Love, Wisdom, Joy & Peace

Our InnerSource

In Practice:
Disidentification and Self-Identification

Patanjali, a great Indian sage, composed a series of aphorisms, or sutras, to explain the purpose of yoga to his contemporaries. According to Patanjali, yoga is designed to turn our attention inward, where the Self resides. Patanjali believed that ignorance is the false sense of identification with the lower vehicles of consciousness, like the personality, rather than with consciousness itself. By constantly practicing disidentification from the planes of consciousness that make up the personality—that is, the physical body, the emotions, and the mind—we are able to break the false sense of identification that creates the drama of life, or suffering. Identifying with the personality is a habitual pattern that is very difficult to overcome; it takes a long time and much practice for us to be able to identify with the Self. By identifying with the true nature, the Self, we can experience life as an enjoyable "play of consciousness." Roberto Assagioli discusses this process in *The Act of Will*.

> We must realize that the mind is in reality an "instrument," an inner tool from which we must disidentify ourselves if we are to make use of it at will. While we are wholly identified with the mind we cannot control it. A certain "psychological distance," a certain detachment from it is needed. (p. 9)

The following disidentification and Self-identification exercise has been adapted from *Psychosynthesis* by Roberto Assagioli. Someone else can read it, or you can tape it yourself and play it back.

1. *Put your body in a comfortable and relaxed position, and slowly take a few deep breaths. Then say the following affirmations silently to yourself, slowly and thoughtfully:*

   I have a body, but I am not my body. My body may find itself in different conditions of health or sickness, it may be rested or tired, but that has nothing to do with my Self, the real "me." I value my body as a precious instrument of experience and action in the outer world, but it is only an instrument. I treat it well; I seek to keep it in good health, yet it is not my Self. I have a body, but I am not my body.

2. *Now close your eyes, recall briefly in your consciousness the general substance of this affirmation and then gradually focus your attention on the central concept:* "I have a body, but I am not my body." *Attempt, as much as you can, to realize this as an experienced fact in your consciousness. Then open your eyes and proceed the same way with the next two exercises.*

> *I have emotions, but I am not my emotions. My emotions are diversified, changing, and sometimes contradictory. They may swing from love to hatred, from calm to anger, from joy to sorrow, and yet my essence—my true nature—does not change. "I" remain. Though a wave of anger may temporarily overwhelm me, I know that it will pass in time; therefore, I am not this anger. Since I can observe and understand my emotions, and then gradually learn to direct, utilize, and integrate them harmoniously, it is clear that they are not my Self. I have emotions, but I am not my emotions.*

> *I have a mind, but I am not my mind. My mind is a valuable tool of discovery and expression, but it is not the essence of my Being. Its contents are constantly changing as it embraces new ideas, knowledge, and experience. Often it refuses to obey me! Therefore, it cannot be me, my Self. It is an organ that connects both the outer and the inner worlds, but it is not my Self. I have a mind, but I am not my mind.*

3. *Next comes the phase of Self-identification. Affirm slowly and thoughtfully:*

After the disidentification of my self from sensations, emotions, and thoughts, I recognize and affirm that I am a center of pure Self-consciousness.

Focus your attention on this central realization: I am a center of pure Self-consciousness. Attempt, as much as you can, to realize this as an experienced fact in your awareness.

4. *When you finish this exercise on disidentification and Self-identification, you may want to write in your journal or write below a description of any experiences that you may have had and want to remember. These experiences come from the following recognitions:*

   I am not my body, I am not my emotions, I am not my mind. I am a center of pure consciousness and Will.

Learning the process of disidentification will help you in separating from the subpersonalities that you are focusing on transforming, as well as accepting those you have disowned. It will also facilitate the process of meditation described in the next chapter, "Communicating with the Source." Source is the term I use to refer to a Higher Power, God, Love, or whatever you feel comfortable calling that which is greater than we are.

9

Communicating with the Source: The Power of Meditation

With innocence and openness we return to the simplicity of direct experience.
When we step out of the current of thoughts, letting go of "how it was and
how it should be," of "how we should be," we enter the eternal present.
—Jack Kornfield, *After the Ecstasy, the Laundry*

In Sanskrit, the word for meditation is *dhyana*. Derived from the root verb *dyai,* "to meditate," it refers to a method of loosening our identification with the mental and physical realms of existence, which opens us to an experience of the spiritual realms of consciousness. In meditation, we learn to develop our Inner Witness, who watches thoughts pass and emotions arise without identifying with these fleeting thoughts and emotions. In this way, our behavior and actions can be chosen consciously, rather than directed by random thoughts and emotions that are creations of the mind. When we're not distracted by continuous, and often frenetic, negative or critical thoughts, our personalities can function in greater alignment with our authentic self. Meditation clears the way for true connection with the Source.

Meditation also creates a state of relaxation by reducing external and internal stimuli. Meditation is a powerful tool for quieting the mind's thoughts and thereby reducing stress. In an article titled "Psychophysiological Therapy Based on the Concepts of Patanjali," published in the *American Journal of Psychotherapy,* N. S. Vahia and colleagues state:

> In a constantly changing environment, recurrent cycles of pain and pleasure are unavoidable. The only way to maintain freedom from anxiety and its consequences under different kinds of life situations is by unlearning being preoccupied with externally oriented pleasure and pain and relearning to channel mental and physical faculties in an optimum fashion according to one's intrinsic capacities. (p. 557)

It is through meditation that we have the experience of our intrinsic capacities.

Meditation is a powerful tool that can be an antidote to anxiety and depression; it is very important for relaxation and healing of many physical disorders. It can help to lower blood pressure, decrease chronic pain, and alleviate headaches. It can also be a complement to medical treatment for cancer, heart disease, and AIDS. Learning to meditate can help with numerous stress-related disorders, including sleep disturbances, digestive problems, seizures, skin disorders, and panic attacks. As you can see, the psychophysiological benefits of meditation are extensive.

Meditation as Medication

Choosing a Meditative Path

There are many different forms of meditation. Most spiritual traditions, both Eastern and Western, have their own specific techniques of meditation designed to facilitate the transformational journey. Each tradition is distinct, and every person's journey is unique. Therefore, I encourage you to do some experimenting with different approaches. As you move deeper into your meditative and spiritual journey, you may find a particular path that feels like "home" to you. Or perhaps it will find you. This journey may unfold over many months or years, or over a lifetime. It has for me.

I spent five years learning Transcendental Meditation, and learning and teaching Arica Meditation (developed by Oscar Ichazo from Chile). While I was teaching Arica in San Diego I met Swami Muktananda, or Baba, and spent the next ten years studying Siddha Yoga intensively. I spent a year in India with Baba on two different trips, returning from my first trip to run a Siddha Yoga meditation center in San Francisco. I eventually became Baba Muktananda's administrative assistant and worked directly with Gurumayi Chidvilasananda, who was Baba's translator at the time, at the international headquarters in upstate New York. I left the center in 1981 and helped coordinate the Seventh International Transpersonal Psychology Conference, which took place in India, with Baba as one of the keynote speakers. Gurumayi became the head of the Siddha Yoga lineage after Baba passed on in 1982.

A year later, I traveled around the South Pacific for six months, exploring the spiritual traditions of the native people in Tahiti, New Zealand, and Bali. I came back to the United States for my nephew Todd's Bar Mitzvah (a rite of passage into adulthood in the Jewish tradition). In a synagogue in New Jersey, much to my surprise, I had a wonderful and powerful spiritual experience. In that moment I realized that I had spent fifteen years studying the spiritual traditions of the "East," both from India and the South Pacific—when what I was seeking, which was a deeper connection to my Inner Self and to God, was right there in the tradition in which I'd been raised.

I came home to Judaism as a spiritual path, remembering what Carl Jung had said: that the clearest path to enlightenment is in the tradition in which you were brought up because the symbolism is in your unconscious. My meditation practice and spiritual path have evolved over many decades, with each step leading to the next in unpredictable, yet related and seemingly guided ways. The Jewish spiritual path I now follow is deeply informed by my experiences with Eastern spirituality, and yet draws from traditional Jewish practices, such as the study of Torah (the Hebrew Bible), observing the Holy Days, keeping kosher (following

Jewish dietary laws, or kashrut*), and keeping the* mitzvot, *which are commonly translated as good deeds but are more accurately understood as religious obligations or commandments. Torah, holy days,* kashrut *and* mitzvot *are the stepping-stones within Judaism that I have been exploring and practicing as my way to experience a spiritually deeper connection with God.*

I also discovered a rich but overlooked meditative tradition in Judaism. One word for meditation in Hebrew is *hitbodedut,* which means self-isolation. Aryeh Kaplan in his book, *Meditation and Kabbalah,* quotes Rabbi Abraham Maimonides (1186–1237), who wrote about internal and external isolation. "External *hitbodedut* is physical isolation, which is desirable when one wishes to meditate. Internal *hitbodedut,* on the other hand, consists of isolating the soul from the perceptive faculty. When the mind is completely hushed in this manner, one becomes able to perceive the spiritual realm."

I have been meditating for forty years, and for me it has been the most powerful tool I've found to develop intuition, connect with the Inner Child, the Inner Self, and the Divine.

As I pointed out earlier, there exist numerous traditions of meditation from all around the world, including Jewish, Christian, Buddhist, Hindu, Taoist, and Islamic. My meditative experiences have focused on Siddha Yoga (a tradition from India) and Jewish spirituality, however, because I want to help people find their right path, whenever possible, I will bring in information and practices from various spiritual disciplines. You can experience other paths up the mountain in order to find one that feels like home to you. Resources for further exploration into other traditions can be found in Appendix G.

So, prepare to become what is called a "seeker" on this spiritual journey, or one who is open to exploring the different paths up the mountain. You are about to engage in the adventure of your life. It is a sacred journey.

How to Meditate

While in the last few decades meditation has been popularized as a tool for stress reduction, healing, and feeling peaceful in a challenging world, the ultimate goal of meditation throughout the centuries has been to experience the Inner Self and our connection with the Divine. (See Chapter 8 for a discussion of the Inner Self.)

The method of meditation explored in this chapter involves four major components: (1) the breath; (2) the posture; (3) the attitude; and (4) the object of meditation.

While meditation is part of most spiritual traditions, and each varies in its practices, one of the basic aspects to meditation across the traditions is the importance of the breath.

The Breath

The first step in meditation is to become aware of our breathing. Mindful breathing balances the emotions, quiets the mind, and relaxes the body. How we breathe is a reflection of our inner state of being. There are two basic types of breathing: chest breathing and belly breathing.

Chest breathing is rapid and shallow. This type of breathing occurs when we are feeling anxious and stressed out, and it results in anxiety and fatigue. It stimulates the sympathetic nervous system, producing a widespread stress response. A vicious cycle ensues in which stress leads to chest breathing and the physiological consequences of this shallow breathing magnify the stress response.

For meditation we use belly breathing, or what is called diaphragmatic breathing. The diaphragm is a large sheet of muscle, like a piece of rubber balloon stretched over the bottom of the lungs. When breathing is natural and relaxed, the diaphragm expands down on the in-breath, pushing the abdomen out. On the out-breath, the diaphragm relaxes back into its original position, pushing air out of the lungs.

To deepen this experience, try putting one hand on the chest and one hand on the belly and feel what moves. On the inhalation, allow the belly to expand or push out, and on the exhalation feel the belly flatten. Now imagine the belly as a balloon, inflating on the inhalation and deflating on the exhalation. Take a moment to notice any feelings that arise. Learning to breathe diaphragmatically, which is a slow, steady, and controlled form of breathing, automatically shifts the body's physiology out of the stress mode into the relaxation mode. The heart rate will slow, blood pressure will decrease, and the level of our sympathetic nervous system arousal will decline, leading to a subjective sense of relaxation and a decrease in anxiety and restlessness.

Our bodies, emotions, thoughts, and spirits are all connected, and together they make up the whole person. In order to meditate, we need to reduce the constant internal stream of thoughts, worries, images, and emotions that we experience in our normal state of consciousness. By becoming aware of our breathing, we can gain a powerful tool for consciously aligning and quieting our body, emotions, thoughts, and spirit.

Miriam Millhauser Castle elucidates this point in her beautifully deep and practical book, *The Breath and Body of Inner Torah:*

> Our true authentic breath that lies underneath the restrictions and holdings we've developed over a lifetime, knows exactly what we need in any given moment. Through this breath we are able to be in touch with all levels of existence, not only with the conscious and unconscious, but also with the wisdom of the soul … The sensitivity of breath to everything that happens inside and outside of us—to our thoughts and feelings, to our interactions with others, to everything we hear, see, touch, and smell—is in service of maintaining balance. Breath helps us mediate all of these internal and external influences so that we can stay in right relationship to them. (p. 48)

The Posture

The posture is the second important aspect of meditation. The posture, the breath, and the mind are all intimately connected. There are different postures in which you can sit for meditation. Hindu Yoga, Buddhist Vipasana (also known as Insight Meditation), and Zen Buddhism all share the following postures.

Sit in a comfortable position, either on a chair, a cushion, or a mat; many Buddhist practitioners prefer a low, specially designed meditation bench called a seiza bench. Posture is very important. Try to keep your back straight. If you are sitting on a chair, keep your feet flat on the floor. Many traditions other than Judeo-Christian approaches to meditation suggest a posture of sitting on the floor. There are four floor-seated postures to choose from. Progressing from the easiest to the most difficult, they are:

1. *Sitting with your back straight against the wall and legs straight out in front. If you would like to sit on the floor in a cross-legged position, sit on a cushion to raise your hips, since that makes it easier to keep your back straight.*

2. *Sitting in a comfortable position, with both legs folded in front of your body, but not crossed over each other. Bring one heel in toward your groin. The other foot may rest on the floor in front of the other foot. In Hindu Yoga meditation, this position is called* sukasana, *the easy pose. In Buddhist meditation this is called the Burmese posture.*

3. *Sitting with your legs folded, the right foot placed on top of the left thigh, with the left foot underneath the right thigh. This position is called the half-lotus pose.*

4. *Sitting with your legs folded, the right foot placed on top of the left thigh, and the left foot over the right leg on top of the right thigh. The soles of each foot are face up on the thigh of the other leg. This position is called the full-lotus pose. This is not an easy posture. But according to Hindu meditation traditions, when mastered it is very purifying for all the nerves in the body.*

Whichever position you choose, the body should be relaxed and comfortable. Hands can be folded, one on top of the other with palms up in the lap with thumbs touching. In Zen meditation, this is called the *cosmic mudra.* Hands can also be placed gently on the knees, palms down or palms up. If the palms are up, the thumb and the index finger should touch. Viewing the body as a generator of energy, these hand positions, or *mudras,* with fingers touching each other or the body, close the circuit, so that energy isn't dissipated.

You can also lie flat on the floor with your arms at your sides and your ankles uncrossed. However, in my experience, lying on the floor guarantees that I will fall asleep, rather than meditate. Some traditions focus on being comfortable and encourage meditators to gradually shift their position to avoid discomfort in the body. However, it is important to do this in moderation, because the more still the body, the quieter the mind. Zen meditation is strict about staying still. *Zazen,* the Zen practice of meditation, is done with the eyes open. In Insight Meditation, meditators keep their eyes partially closed, and in Hindu yogic traditions, eyes are generally kept closed.

With the right understanding and attitude, meditation brings us to the experience Baba describes in his book, *Meditate*:

> As the posture becomes steady, the prana [breath] automatically becomes steady. As the prana becomes steady, the mind becomes steady, one begins to drink the joy that is in the heart. (p. 41)

The Attitude

Sharon Salzberg, cofounder of the Insight Meditation Society and the Barre Center for Buddhist Studies, beautifully describes in her book, *The Kindness Handbook*, the attitude that is essential for meditation:

> Evolving a spiritual practice is not about having and getting; it is about being more compassionate toward ourselves and others. It is not about assuming a new self-image or manufactured persona; it is about being compassionate naturally ... Compassion is like a mirror into which we can always look. It is like a stream that steadily carries us. It is like a cleansing fire that continually transforms us. (p. 27)

At Baba Muktananda's ashram in India there was a sign at the entrance to the meditation area that read: *Leave Your Ego with Your Shoes*. In meditation we don't need to try to become something, or to try to have any particular kind of experience. On the contrary, the aim is to just "be." There is no "right" meditative experience. What happens to each person is right for that person's process. Some people may have visions, see lights, move spontaneously, cry, or laugh. Others may sit quietly and rarely have any of these experiences. One student came out of meditation feeling very disappointed that nothing had happened. He said, "I just felt a lot of calm and peace." That is precisely one of the goals of meditation—but his mind told him that it was not good or dramatic enough, and this idea destroyed his peaceful feeling.

It is important to be aware of any expectations we may have about meditation. Expectations are creations of the mind; they tend to get in the way and block what we would otherwise experience. It is only by quieting the mind's activity that we are able to experience the place beyond the mind, the Inner Self, which is where the still, clear lake of peace and wisdom exists. The waves of the lake—the restless activity of the mind— need to calm down before the beauty and depth of the inner world waiting submerged beneath the lake can be experienced. That world awaits us when there are no waves of thoughts or barriers of expectations to get in the way of experiencing what is truly and constantly there.

The way to quiet expectations or thoughts that arise is to just let them be. Notice these thoughts without getting involved in them or trying to stop them. When a rock is thrown into a lake, it creates waves. If we go into the lake after the rock, the waves get even bigger. We can't stop the waves—it would be useless to try. If we simply watch the flow of the waves, the ripples from the rock will soon subside. In his book, *Meditate,* Baba Muktananda describes the attitude and awareness that is best for the process of meditation:

> Let your mind spin as much as it wants to; do not try to subdue it. Simply witness the different thoughts as they arise and subside ... no matter how many worlds of desires, wishes, and positive and negative thoughts your mind creates, you should realize that they are all a play of consciousness ... If you meditate with this awareness—your mind will become calm very soon, and that will be high meditation. (p. 36)

The Object of Meditation

Meditation is inward concentration. The goal is to quiet the mind, as the uninterrupted flow of attention is turned toward the Inner Self. We move in the direction of our thoughts and images, whether we want to or not. Therefore, it's important to focus on something that will facilitate the connection with the Source, as this is the higher purpose and goal of meditation.

To maintain inner concentration and direct our attention toward an object that elevates our thoughts and images, it is helpful to use a focus of meditation, such as a mantra, which is a sacred phrase; the breath; or a candle. A sacred image can also be used, such as a mandala that consists of concentric geometric figures that direct the viewer to the center, the six-pointed Star of David, the Christian cross, or a Navajo sand painting. In addition, we can focus on a place on our body, like the area behind the space between the eyes, which is called the intuitive center, or the "third eye."

Peaceful scenes within nature can also be used to focus our meditation. Sitting to meditate by the water's edge or in a forest, or listening to the sound of the wind in the trees, can facilitate the experience of a higher state of consciousness. The sense of awe we feel before the miracle of creation in nature allows us to feel the palpable presence of the Divine.

There are many different paths of meditation. Each path offers a different object to meditate on in order to help the mind focus and quiet. Whether we are meditating using a mantra, the breath, phrases, a candle, a mandala, or doing a walking meditation or sitting in nature, we will find that after a short time our mind will begin to wander. This is natural, as it is the nature of the mind to produce thoughts. For example, we might wonder what we will do later on that day after we finish work; then we remember that we are supposed to be meditating, and refocus on whatever we are using as an object of concentration. A moment later, our mind may start thinking about a conversation we had earlier that day; we find ourselves feeling upset about how someone talked to us. Then we realize that we are thinking, and quickly and gently, without being critical of ourselves, we bring our focus back to the object of meditation. Soon we feel a pain in our back; and we shift our position and wonder how much longer it will be until the timer goes off—then we remember again that we're supposed to be meditating, and we return to our focus. Staying in the present, we once again repeat our mantra; it feels so good, until we remember that the day after tomorrow is a loved one's birthday, and we need to remember to buy a present.

And on and on it goes. We will do this over and over again, probably hundreds of times, during every meditation session.

Further directions for developing a meditation practice are given in the "In Practice" exercise at the end of this chapter and in Appendix F.

The Nature of the Mind

I talked at great length about the nature of the mind in Stage One: Life-Lesson Therapy. The more we can learn about the mind, the more choices we have. Meditation is the vehicle for learning how the mind works and for developing the witness who can break away from the strong pull the mind has on us—the pull that makes us believe whatever our mind tells us.

Meditation can be a powerful tool for dealing with depression and anxiety, which in part are created by the mind.

I see a client, Marcus, who is married, with children. He deals with anxiety and depression, which he inherited from his father. He is a dedicated doctor and a very caring, kind, and concerned human being. He is very open to spirituality. Inwardly, he holds himself to standards that would be hard for anyone to meet. If he is dealing with a difficult case and didn't perform up to his standards, his Inner Critic comes out and he spends days under a "Critic attack." I asked him if he would be willing to do a metta meditation, which is a Buddhist concentration practice that cultivates kindness for oneself and others. The phrases that are mentioned in The Beginner's Guide to Insight Meditation *by Arinna Weisman and Jean Smith felt appropriate for Marcus. Between becoming more aware of his Inner Critic and learning to separate from that self, as well as doing the following metta practice, Marcus is learning how to reduce his anxiety and his depression, and to feel better about himself.*

> *May I be kind to myself and all others.*
> *May I love, honor, and respect myself.*
> *May I live without fear.*
> *May I embrace all that is difficult with an inner resiliency.*
> *May I be happy.*
> *May I be healthy.*
> *May I be peaceful.*

Committing to a Path, Finding a Teacher

After exploring different paths, whether for weeks, months, or years, it is good to choose one path and stick with it. This way we can avoid what Baba called "spiritual promiscuity." Otherwise, we can waste a great deal of time circling the base of the mountain, trying different paths, and never committing ourselves to a tried and true path that takes us to the top.

It can be helpful on the spiritual journey to find a teacher: A guide who has traveled the road before us, and who can help direct us along the way. As I said in previous chapters, the mind can be our best friend or our worst enemy, so it is important to have someone we can go to for support and guidance. Sometimes what happens in meditation can be disconcerting. We may reexperience difficult, traumatic memories that cry out to be healed. We may receive messages from our minds that direct us down paths that lead away from learning our life lessons and our soul-wisdom. Oftentimes, we can greatly benefit from having someone as a spiritual guide, so we can ask questions and get a reality check.

Meditating in a Group

If we find an approach that feels good to us, that we want to explore in greater depth, we might consider finding a group that is using that form of meditation as their spiritual practice. Call them, see when they are meeting, and ask if they are open to new people attending their sessions. Meditating in a group is a powerful experience that can feel different than meditating alone. The group energy can create a stronger meditative experience; it is an opportunity to explore the benefits of meditating with other spiritual seekers.

Creating a Meditation Practice

Meditation is called a *practice* for a reason. It takes time, perseverance, and patience to develop any skill. Whether we are learning to play an instrument or a sport, or learning a foreign language, we need to practice in order to develop this new ability. The same is true of meditation; the process of learning to meditate needs to unfold gradually, just like any skill we want to develop.

In India, there is an expression that meditation is similar to making dye-fast cloth. You dip the cloth in ink and then you put it out in the sun to dry. Then you dip it in the ink again and put it out to dry. It is this process of dipping into our thoughts and then bathing in the warmth and light of the sun, the object of meditation, that allows the process to take us to a place that is transformative, that is dye-fast.

In his book, *Torah, Tarot & Tantra,* author William Blank describes the benefits of staying with a meditation practice:

> After a while at this practice, interesting things begin to happen. You may find that you are more relaxed and happier, or that you have more energy and are more creative. You may be able to better express your emotions, or perceive sensory images. Your dreams may become more vivid and easier to remember. Your intuition may become clearer and more accurate. Meditation is not a panacea for all life's problems, but it is a powerful tool for spiritual growth. (pp. 150–151)

Meditation facilitates this deep inward journey, revealing the wisdom of the soul and the transformational process of communicating with the Source. It clears the mind and opens the heart, enabling us to experience peace and love for ourselves. For it is only by loving and accepting ourselves that we can truly love and accept others. As the poet William Wordsworth said, "Beauty lies in deep retreats."

Adam's Experience of Meditation

Adam, now twenty-nine years old, is a creative, mature, and wise young man with a busy schedule. He found a way to listen within and connect to a deeper part of himself. Here is his story:

For me, the process of learning to listen within really began as a process of learning to stop listening within to my mind. I am lucky to have been raised in a family that supports spiritual investigation, and my aunt especially fostered this exploration and growth. I suppose much of this growth started with a simple but consistent feeling of restlessness. I was a happy seventeen-year-old, living a blessed life, and yet I could not shake a certain inner irritation—nor could I shake my eagerness to confront the source of the impatience. My aunt recommended a practice of confronting, called meditation. It was a word I'd heard before, usually associated with cross-legged hippies named Moondawg and airy-fairyness. Of course at the time, I was seventeen and a wannabe hippie, so the prospect of meditation sounded fairly enticing.

After cautiously testing the waters, I skipped the easing-in process and cannon-balled into the pool of meditative inquiry. My first major experience with meditation came in the form of a weeklong silent meditation retreat, somewhere in the Catskill Mountains. I found that once the external noises (conversations, television, traffic) had been stripped away, I was left with what could only be the source of my irritation: internal noise. The profundity of the outward-seeming silence of the retreat was matched only by the depth of inner chatter at work in my own mind. I spent hours attacked by pieces of my brain that could only criticize, got lost in fantasies of lust or violence. I explored bramble-patches of my mind that I'd always assumed were inextricably part of "me." What I learned, after a few days of "shutting down," is how distracting these parts really are, and how to rid myself of them, if only for a few moments.

Once these voices had been discerned, monitored, and quieted—transformed into less grisly versions of themselves—the only thing that remained was: This. This moment. And This One. An incredibly deep and speaking silence, which carries with it the incredible weight of Knowing. I began learning to listen to This—a deeper whisper.

In Practice:
Developing a Meditation Practice

When we first begin to meditate, it helps to set aside time each day to develop a disciplined meditation practice. Learning to meditate is like learning any new art. We need patience, compassion for ourselves, and perseverance. Developing the ability to quiet the mind in order to experience the Inner Self may take a good deal of practice and time because, after all, considerable time has been spent with the mind focusing on thinking thoughts.

Preparation

It is also helpful to set aside an uncluttered, comfortable, quiet place for meditation, and to use it regularly. A special blanket or shawl and a cushion or chair to sit on, used just for meditation, is also helpful. These things allow the energy of meditation to accumulate, and so make meditation easier. The olfactory sense is one of the strongest senses, which is why many people use incense as part of their meditation practice. After a while, just the smell of incense can bring us into a state of meditation. It is also beneficial to meditate at the same time each day. The best time is early in the morning, between 3:00 and 6:00 a.m., because that is the quietest time of the day, with the fewest distractions. However, since that is not possible for most of us, any time that is convenient is fine, as long as we can be consistent. Different people do it at different times. I have one friend, a therapist, who meditates in between clients. Another friend does a walking meditation on a treadmill in the gym.

Time

Meditation can take place in one longer session, or it can be broken up into two shorter sessions, one in the morning and the other in the evening.

It is helpful to use a timer so that you do not need to pay attention to a clock. The amount of time spent in meditation can vary. It is best to start with a shorter meditation, and as you begin to feel comfortable, the amount of time can be increased. Beginners can start with a five-minute meditation, although I recommend beginning with a fifteen-minute meditation. Experiment with lengthening your meditation periods gradually, until you can meditate for twenty minutes, and then eventually forty-five minutes. I have found that meditating for forty-five minutes works the best. It can take thirty minutes—often longer—just for the mind to quiet, so ending the meditation too soon will not allow us to experience the nectar of meditation.

Candle Meditation

Some people find that keeping their eyes open during meditation is more comfortable than meditating with their eyes closed or semi-closed. So, if we prefer to keep our eyes open, a candle meditation can be a comfortable way to begin. Like the other techniques, focusing on a candle can facilitate a state of centering and quieting the mind. Light symbolizes consciousness. The flame of a candle is a powerful symbol, representing the flame of the spirit that resides within each of us. Candles not only light our way in the physical world, but they also light our spiritual path as well. Thus a candle can be a perfect object to use in the practice of meditation. To begin this practice of gazing at a candle, set the timer for five minutes.

Using the guidance I've given in the sections on "The Breath," "The Posture," "The Attitude," and "The Object of Meditation," I invite you to take time to try the different meditation practices that I've described in Appendix F. Try each one for a number of days or a week in order to discover which one feels like "home" to you. Repeat the practice as often as you like, but resolve to do it at least once a day.

You'll find a list of numerous books on different traditions of meditation in the Bibliography, as well as in Appendix G.

10

Accessing Our Intuition

The intuitive mind is a sacred gift and the rational mind is a faithful servant.
We have created a society that honors the servant and has forgotten the gift.
——Attributed to Albert Einstein, *The New Quotable Einstein*
(Alice Calaprice, ed.)

By using tools such as meditation, diaphragmatic breathing, yoga, and guided imagery, we quiet the mind so we can access our intuition. Intuition is the direct channel to our Inner Self and the Source. The word intuition is derived from the Latin word *intueri,* which means "to see within." It is the act or faculty of acquiring direct knowledge or wisdom without the use of rational processes. When the mind becomes quiet, the intuitive channel opens to connect the personality plane to the higher spiritual planes of consciousness. To experience intuition, we have to be fully in the present. I describe intuition as a sense of inner rightness, a precious gift that unfolds naturally as we journey along the spiritual path.

> *When I returned from being with Baba Muktananda at the Siddha Yoga meditation center in India in 1979, I stayed for a short time with my parents in New Jersey. One day, as I was driving over the George Washington Bridge, I suddenly heard a voice in the car. First, I looked behind me to make sure that no one had secretly climbed into the back seat. Whew! I felt relieved that there wasn't anyone else in the car, ready to jump me. Then I checked the radio, thinking that the voice must have come from there. When I realized that the radio was off, I really got scared, because, as a psychologist, I know what they*

say about people who hear voices! The voice was neither masculine nor feminine—it was androgynous and coming from outside of me. As I got off the bridge, this voice was telling me when and where to turn so that I effortlessly negotiated the streets of New York City. The voice stayed with me for the next few days, guiding all my decisions. It was so loud that I thought everyone around me could hear it, but no one seemed to notice. The more I heard it, and listened to it, the stronger it became. After a few days, rather than hearing it on the outside, I began to feel the voice inside me as a sense of inner rightness that guided my decisions. The voice became a trusted friend. My intuition was born.

After this short visit, I returned to San Francisco, where I was working on my doctorate, and was one of the leaders of the Siddha Yoga meditation center of San Francisco. Two years later, my friends Ruth and Marilyn joined me in running the center. We decided to organize a major program for Swami Muktananda where he would speak at the Palace of Fine Arts in San Francisco on March 4, 1981. Ruth, Marilyn, and I each coordinated different aspects of the program. As the overall coordinator, I had hundreds of decisions to make in order to pull off such a huge event. I decided to try trusting my intuition. I could hear my mind saying, "Are you nuts? This is a huge responsibility and you're not going to trust me?" I reassured my mind that things would turn out okay. Somehow I knew that.

Using our intuition to make decisions is a very efficient process. The mind, conversely, often goes back and forth looking at all the possible options before making a decision, and this takes a lot of time. Whenever there was a major problem, I would certainly take into account whatever my mind had to say. But for the most part, I handled my responsibilities in coordinating this huge event by listening to my sense of inner rightness, my intuition.

The theme of Baba's talk was "Who Is a True Psychologist?" We weren't sure we would fill the Palace of Fine Arts, which holds one thousand people. Still, we agreed that it would be smart to set up big monitors outside, just in case more people showed up. That day three thousand people came to hear Baba speak! Due to the overwhelming turnout, we asked if those people in the audience who had already had an opportunity to be with Baba would mind giving up their seats, so that others could also have that experience. It was amazing what happened next: People willingly and graciously gave up their seats, and everyone who wanted to get into the hall was able to see Baba in person. The Palace of Fine Arts is located in a beautiful setting, with swans swimming in the ponds surrounding it, so everyone on the outside enjoyed the scenery and had a wonderful experience watching Baba on the large monitors outside. The day was magical. The program went off smoothly, without any problems. It cemented for me the power and gift of trusting my intuition.

We've all had some intuitive experiences in our lives. Maybe when we were quietly watching a sunset or sitting in front of a fireplace, for instance, we suddenly had a realization about something or someone we weren't even thinking about. As a matter of fact, we weren't thinking about anything at all, and that's what created the fertile ground for intuition to flow through our conscious awareness. Some of us might say to ourselves, "Well, she might have great intuition, but I'm not sure I do." But we all do. We are all born with it. We come into this world with an abundance of love and trust, with the capacity to act directly from our intuitive center. However, over the course of our lives, we are trained to close down and suppress this core process. Rather than encouraging the use of our intuition, we have been conditioned to disregard it.

Indeed, raised in a patriarchal and rational society, we are taught to worship the mind. Descartes summed it up: "I think, therefore I am." We have also learned to focus on external events, such as what we accomplish, as a way of finding validation and happiness. We need to learn "to be" in order for our intuition—the still, small voice—to be heard. Access to our intuition is often blocked because we lack the tools with which to listen to and differentiate between our intuition and the voices of the myriad subpersonalities that exist within us. Modern society is just beginning to recognize intuition as a sound approach to gaining information.

As Rabbi David Cooper writes in *God is a Verb: Kabbalah and the Practice of Mystical Judaism,*

> People who dwell in the realms of intuition have no difficulty discussing souls, where they come from, where they go ... Those who are drawn more to rational, analytical foundations of reality are more challenged by these ideas.

But there is no right or wrong way to explore the mysteries of life and death. If the holistic model is correct, each of us is connected to the center of creation in her or his own way. We need simply to discover the inner language that helps us communicate with the hidden parts of the soul. (p. 39)

I think, therefore I am.   *I don't think, therefore I am.*

Being connected to our feelings strengthens our intuitive faculties. Because of this, I believe it is easier for women to get in touch with their intuition, because in our culture men are more heavily conditioned than women to be unaware of their feelings. Even when men are aware of feelings, they are trained not to express their emotions or vulnerability for fear of being considered weak or out of control. It's sad that many men don't realize that it's a sign of real strength to be able to express their feelings.

Women, too, are negatively conditioned to be the servers of society without considering their own needs. How often do most women stop and ask, "How am I feeling? What do I need?" Generally speaking, "I" is not in a woman's vocabulary and if it is, she is called selfish. As a psychologist, I've worked with countless women who feel unhappy and unfulfilled in their lives, and it's no wonder. Many women keep giving and giving and never stop to take the time to fill up their own wells or ask for what they need from others. Negative societal conditioning and the stress and demands of modern life are not conducive to taking time to identify and understand our feelings, quieting the mind, and cultivating our intuition. By taking time alone or being in the company of others who are also trying to learn how to focus inwardly, we will create the conditions that will allow ourselves to be guided more and more by our intuition.

The more we trust our intuition, the stronger it will become—because if we don't use it, we lose it. Intuition is like a faucet. If we open the valve, it flows. The more we listen to and honor intuition in our lives, the stronger the flow.

My friend and colleague Robert Gass enriched my own perspective on intuition over twenty-five years ago. After all these years, it's hard for me to remember which ideas are his and which are mine, so Robbie, wherever you are, I wanted to give you the credit that you so richly deserve.

Connecting to our intuition, however, requires discipline. We need to relax the body, quiet and open the mind, gain self-awareness of our personality traits, and develop sensitivity and trust in the Inner Self. The goal of this discipline—which for me came through meditation, Siddha Yoga, Voice Dialogue work, and Jewish spirituality—is to guide us toward a paradigm shift of consciousness from an identification with our outer personality, to a realization of our inner essence, or our soul or Inner Self. As I have said, there are many different paths up the mountain, so we need to find the one that feels most familiar in order to develop a discipline that will allow us to do our inner work of becoming more conscious. Lasting transformation happens through heightened awareness.

The Character of Intuition

Intuition often comes unexpectedly, in a flash of insight. Because it is fleeting and so easily forgotten, I suggest writing down any "intuitive hits" so that we don't forget them. They often come to us from a level of consciousness other than our normal awareness—the ethereal realm. This is the realm where certain dreams come from as well. Some of us may have had the experience of having an important dream, and thinking that we'll remember it in the morning. But when we wake up, it's gone, which is why I also tell people to write down their dreams. If we don't write down our intuitions, they will vanish as quickly as they came. We've all heard the expression "in one ear and out the other"—well, that is the fleeting nature of intuition. But intuitive rightness can also have an emotional punch that brings a profound feeling of inner certainty, calm, and resolution. Intuition can also come as a word, an image, a puzzle, or a feeling of quiet strength; it often requires a symbolic, rather than a literal, interpretation.

For this reason, we need to learn to discriminate between our mind and our intuition. It is helpful to know that when we ask a question and want to get an intuitive answer, the first answer we get is usually the clearest. However, there are times when the first answer *isn't* the clearest. Inner knowing feels different than a response from the mind: calm and resolution come with the intuition, and the intuition is often symbolic rather than literal. Our intuition doesn't speak in the dogmatic or hyper voice of a preacher or a salesperson; it is not critical or judgmental, self-aggrandizing or highly dramatic. If that is what you are experiencing, it is more likely a subpersonality disguised as your intuition.

A friend of mine named Lauri told me about an experience she had with her intuition. She lives in Canton, a section of Baltimore that has restaurants with outdoor dining and bars overlooking a running path and the water. As Lauri told me the story, she would often go to one of the outdoor bars with her husband, where they would watch the boats and the runners. She was impressed with the runners' legs and bodies; time after time she would sit at the bar and enjoy watching them. This went on for months, until one night she heard an inner voice say, "Get off your bar stool and get some Nikes." It was said quietly, without any judgment. It was so quiet, it didn't totally register—until the very next day. "A friend of mine came down for lunch and said she was signed up for the Baltimore 5k in six weeks and said to me, why don't you sign up with me. I said to her: What? I've never run before in my life! After a minute I remembered the voice and thought, this is twice in two days now, so step outside of your box and just do it." This time she realized what was happening— her intuition was giving her a message. Listening to the voice, she went out and bought her first pair of Nikes, and started running on that very same running path. After that first 5k run she went on to do a 10k, a ten miler, and then a half marathon. Becoming a runner was the last thing in the world she would have thought of doing, which is how she knew it wasn't her mind or any of her subpersonalities—it was her intuition guiding her. Lauri now has a runner's body and feels better then ever. Lauri says, "Running has completely transformed my life, mentally and physically, and this year I will enter the Marine Corps marathon. Through running, I was able to lower the dosage of my blood pressure medication and completely come off of my thyroid medication as well as handle stress remarkably differently!"

This is the experience when we learn to discern the difference between our mind and our intuition. We benefit from following our intuitive wisdom in ways that we could never imagine.

It's also important to recognize that our intuition doesn't necessarily give us an answer immediately. The time when we can receive guidance from the Transpersonal Realm is when our mind is quiet and not focused on our problems. This may happen hours or days after we first pose our question, and at times when we least expect it. Making a space for our intuitive channel to open is another reason why meditation is so important.

> *When I was in practice in New Hampshire in the 1980s, I was leading "Our Intuitive Wisdom" and "Inward Bound" groups with Essie Hull, PhD, a wonderful friend and a gifted therapist. One of the women in our groups, Kay, was going through a divorce and was isolating herself from her friends and feeling depressed from the divorce. Kay was an introvert and very shy. For one exercise in the group, we suggested that the participants meditate for a few moments and then ask themselves the question, "What am I needing right now?" Afterward, we led them through the process of receiving an answer to their question by opening to their intuitive wisdom. The whole group did the exercise; yet Kay was feeling upset that she didn't get an answer to her question. The next week, a different Kay came back to the group. She was animated and excited to share how, after the last group, she'd been in the shower, when suddenly she'd felt this strong intuitive sense that she was supposed to have an impromptu party. At first, she'd been horrified at the idea, because it was so far outside her comfort zone. Making a decision to listen to her intuition, however, she told us that she'd thrown a party that had gone so well it had brought her out of her depression. She concluded by saying that she no longer felt the need to isolate herself.*

Resources on Intuition

In *The Intuitive Edge,* Phillip Goldberg beautifully describes how our intuition guides us:

> Sometimes with declarative force, sometimes with gentle grace ... More like a sense of direction than a map, it can be ill defined or quite explicit. It might operate on minor, localized situations, nudging us toward this or tugging us away

from that. Or it might manifest itself in larger
issues, such as a sense of "calling," for example,
that overpowering certainty that we are meant
to follow a particular vocation or accept some
mission. Such compelling attractions can often
be justified logically, but they are never logically
derived. Rather, we feel like an iron filing drawn
quite irresistibly to a magnet. (p. 54)

Frances Vaughan reinforces what I have experienced. In *Awakening Intuition,* she writes, "The regular practice of meditation is the single most powerful means of increasing intuition." (p. 177)

Through tools like meditation, we filter out the noise and distractions of everyday life and quiet our minds, which are often preoccupied with events of the past or worries about the future.

After five days at a weeklong silent meditation retreat, I had a powerful experience where I heard the words, "God is in the present." That truth is the basis for this stage of learning our soul-wisdom, for the awakening of our intuition. We must quiet the mind and be in the present to experience our soul and the presence of the Divine. Only with a quiet mind can we hear the voice of guidance from the Transpersonal Realm that we experience as inner knowing.

Intuition can also convey a message with wit and humor.

I had been thinking about a man I'd been dating for several months, wondering where the relationship was going and whether I should talk to him about my questions, or just relax and let it unfold. The question was in the back of my mind, as I was going about my day. When I sat to meditate, I wasn't thinking about him or any questions in particular. Toward the end of the meditation session, I had a vivid image of a big hand coming over my head from behind me and putting ice in a large glass, which represented me. When my mind grasped what the image meant, I laughed in recognition of having been given the answer to my earlier question. My intuition, with its inimitable sense of humor, was letting me know that I needed to be cool about the situation. By taking the time to meditate and quiet my mind, I was able to receive the answer from my intuition. Experiences like that strengthen our connection and faith in our intuitive knowing. After receiving such intuitive guidance, like this big hand pointing the way for me, I am convinced that there is a higher guidance available to each of us. We can all learn to cultivate and access our intuition.

The Steps to Accessing Your Intuition

Step 1: Be confident.

Step 2: Quiet the mind by using the tools you are comfortable with for breathing, relaxing, and getting centered.

Step 3: Ask a question that is as specific and as clear as possible and be patient. Wait for an answer. Intuition doesn't always answer right away. It often comes when you're least expecting an answer, which can be hours or days later.

Step 4: Be open to receive any intuitive guidance.

Step 5: Evaluate whatever guidance you receive. Be conscious if your intuition sounds like it might be the voice of one of your subpersonalities. Discernment is one of the most important spiritual attributes. You need to be able to differentiate between the voice of your intuition and the voice of the mind or a subpersonality.

Step 6: If it feels appropriate, honor your intuition by following through with what you have been given.

A Client's Experience of Accessing Her Intuition

From the time I was a small girl, I always knew that there was more to reality than just the physical realm. For instance, I could sense when something bad was going to happen—I was aware of my grandmother's impending death three days before she passed on, and I knew the last time I saw my father that it would be the last time I'd see him before he passed away unexpectedly from a heart attack. These and many other powerful experiences caused me great anxiety. So, I learned early on to suppress my intuitive capabilities. As a young adult, neither the language of academics and religion, nor any words I could come up with, could explain this sense of "knowing" that was perched on the tip of my consciousness. Unable to understand it myself or articulate my experiences openly to family members, teachers, friends, or college professors, I became frustrated and buried this sense of "knowing" beneath layers of my projected sense of self. Instead, I surrendered to a sort of unconscious existence that involved adapting to the sociocultural norms that appeared acceptable to everyone, including myself.

I graduated from college, married, raised four children, lived in a nice house, and drove nice cars. I volunteered, sat on boards, raised money for schools, and embraced the social hierarchy of an affluent community.

Unfortunately, years of repressing my intuition became counterproductive and wreaked havoc in my life. I felt awkward, anxious, and began to withdraw socially; eventually, I became seriously ill.

In order to save my life, I sought the help of a trusted and devoted transpersonal psychotherapist. While in therapy, I realized that what had made me so sick was a lifetime of complete disconnection between the self I projected onto the world and my true core. Instead of honoring my heightened perceptions of reality, I suppressed them to the point of stifling my Inner Self. Without having access to my intuition, it was impossible for me to function in healthy ways. Eventually, this made me physically ill. I needed to relearn how to pay very close attention to and trust my voice within, my intuition. I had to learn to be open and receptive to this gift, rather than changing this very natural part of who I was.

This called for me to undergo a specific process. What I learned in therapy was that before I could begin to trust my intuition and use it as an effective tool in my life, I needed to heal the old wounds, disengage faulty defense mechanisms, and separate from irrational ways of thinking that I had developed to protect myself. This was the hard work of therapy, but an enlightening process that I preferred to think of as clearing a path back to the heart and soul of my true self.

After years of psychotherapy, reading self-help books, participating in workshops, and even going back to graduate school to become a psychotherapist myself, I came to understand intuition simply as a way of integrating information from all our senses with already-learned life experiences. This provides ways of obtaining information from a more expanded consciousness. The process of tuning in to and trusting my intuition was liberating, exhilarating, and enlightening.

Now, when something is happening intuitively, I usually notice a tense, tightening sensation, either physically in my body or sometimes in my mind. Sometimes I hold my breath or I get goose bumps. That is usually a sign that something is going on. I have learned to pull down the menu of feelings and use the "Checking-in" process to see if I can put a name to my reaction. I usually know right away, but sometimes I need to find a quiet place, clear my mind, and meditate before insight arrives. When I clear the way for intuition, guidance and answers do appear.

It can still be difficult for me to trust my intuition at times, due to my own natural tendency to put my faith in the experts of the world in science, psychology, statistics, and medicine. It's sometimes difficult to be part of a culture that has a tendency to discredit intuitive experiences and embrace only empirical data and logical analysis. But I know intuitively that the gifts I have been given are for a purpose that is greater than me, and I trust that. It seems that the most important gifts in life are the ones that are placed deep within our hearts and souls, and the greatest journey in life is the one inward to discover them.

In Practice:
Listening to Your Intuitive Wisdom

The way to access your intuition is simply by calling on it and asking it for guidance in your life. The tricky part is to become quiet enough so you can hear it when it answers!

1. *Take a moment and think of a situation in your life about which you would like more clarity. Maybe there is an issue that is unresolved, a choice you need to make, or a situation with a friend or a family member that you would like to understand more fully or feel better about. Write about this situation or issue.*

_____

_____

_____

_____

_____

2. *Now think of a question that you would like answered regarding this situation or issue in your life. If you can't think of a question, an important all-purpose question that is helpful to ask is this: "What do I need right now?"*

_____

_____

_____

_____

_____

3. *Take a few deep breaths. Breathing is the secret to relaxing the mind and the body. Focus on your body and become aware of any places where you are feeling tension or tightness. Breathe into these places and allow them to relax. Take another deep breath, and on the exhalation allow more tension to flow out through your fingertips and your toes. Feel your body relaxing and getting heavier, sinking into the chair, or whatever you are sitting on, as you allow it to totally support you.*

In a moment I am going to ask you to stop reading this page and close your eyes, as it's much easier to block out the external distractions and relax the body and the mind with your eyes closed. Remember to have patience, as you may get your best answers hours or a day later, or even in a dream.

Be confident and know that you can cultivate a connection to your intuition. You just have to remember what you learned in kindergarten when you were taught how to cross the street:

"STOP, LOOK & LISTEN."

STOP the mind,

LOOK inside, and

LISTEN to your intuition.

Who knew that even back in kindergarten you were learning about the transformational journey!

4. *Now close your eyes, take another deep breath and silently ask your intuition the question you thought of in #2. Try not to think of an answer with your mind. Remain quiet and patient and allow any answers to bubble up to consciousness from within.*

5. *Remember to write anything down that you receive from your intuition. As in your dream states, your intuitive answers come from the ethereal plane and can easily be forgotten when you come back to your normal state of consciousness.*

11

The Gift of Faith

The sole wisdom of our soul's wisdom is to have faith.

—Abby Rosen, PhD

"Bidden or Not Bidden, God Is Present" is the inscription on a plaque that sits on my fireplace mantel. It was given to me by a client a number of years ago. As I was writing Chapter 10 on intuition, I looked at this wise statement and realized that this is the essence of faith.

Through the course of our life's journey, the most important gift we are given is faith. Faith provides us with a sense of being guided by a higher wisdom. Once we develop faith, we realize that events may be happening for a reason, and exactly at the time they are supposed to happen—even if we can't understand the reasons or timing of these events. Faith allows us to relax and stay conscious, so that we can learn our life lessons and develop our soul-wisdom, even when faced with life-threatening illness, unemployment, or other life challenges. The more we accept the journey and feel the awe that comes from faith, the more we can find the strength to face our fears. Faith leads to inner peace, compassion, wisdom, and even joy. The more we feel these states rather than fear, the more at peace we are, and the more compassionate, loving, and wise we become.

Sharon Salzberg, writing from deep inside herself, says the following about faith in her inspiring book, *Faith: Trusting Your Own Deepest Experience:*

> Faith enables us to get as close as possible to the
> truth of the present moment, so that we can offer

> our hearts fully to it, with integrity. We might
> (and often must) hope and plan and arrange and
> try, but faith enables us to be fully engaged while
> also realizing that we are not in control, and that
> no strategy can ever put us in control, of the
> unfolding of events. Faith gives us a willingness
> to engage life, which means the unknown, and
> not to shrink back from it. (pp. 87–88)

Faith is defined as "A belief in, devotion to, or trust in somebody or something, especially without logical proof." I have a pillow in my therapy office that has a saying from the Bible: "Faith is being sure of what you hope for and certain of what you do not see." Like intuition, faith is based on something other than logic and reason. They are both beyond the mind's knowing or understanding. Gaining access to intuition and faith is central to the spiritual journey, especially if we are to do the work that leads to lasting transformation. Only when we are willing to travel the road that goes beyond the mind are we able to receive these truly powerful gifts of intuition and faith.

Self-Effort and Grace

Grace is another gift that we receive on the journey of transformation. The dictionary defines grace as "the infinite love, mercy, favor, and goodwill shown to humankind by God." One of Baba Muktananda's important teachings was that life is like two wings of a bird. The first wing is self-effort. The second wing is grace. Our job is to persevere, to focus on doing self-effort, to try our best without focusing on the outcome. The Universe will then bring forth grace, so the bird will take flight. This has become a philosophy that I use to guide my life, as it always seems to prove true.

We can have faith that grace will appear, and that the highest good for our life will unfold. As Jean-Pierre de Caussade, author of *Abandonment to Divine Providence,* said, "Listen to me: let your hearts demand the infinite. For I can tell you how to fill them … Your faith will measure it out to you; as you believe, so you will receive." (p. 41)

One of the most amazing experiences I had of honoring my intuition, having faith, and doing self-effort, so grace will appear, began with a dream. I had been leading Voice Dialogue retreats at a beautiful retreat center in Maryland for a number of years. Barbara, the owner, told me that I would no longer be able to hold retreats there because she had decided to sell the center. Knowing I am Jewish, she said I might even know the rabbi who was thinking of buying the center. I said, "Really? Who is it?" It turned out that it was Rabbi David Shneyer, who has been a friend of mine for a number of years. I immediately called him and said, "What's up? I hear you're about to buy a retreat center." Rabbi David had long dreamed about creating a spiritual retreat center that would be a place of natural beauty and peace for people of all spiritual traditions. I asked how I could help. The Universe answered my question by speaking to me through my dreams.

Not long after I'd spoken with Rabbi David, I dreamed that Barbara was very upset and frustrated over the sale of her center. I awoke from the dream wondering what that meant, so I called Barbara to see how things were going. She shared with me how upset and frustrated she was with the negotiations, and said that she was even thinking of selling it to another group. I had an intuition that Barbara and David needed to talk directly, rather than going through the realtors. Asking her if she would hold on, I dialed David's number to set up a three-way conference call. Once they were able to speak directly, the negotiations continued unimpeded. A few weeks later, I had a second dream where Barbara was upset again. Communication had broken down, and the realtors weren't even speaking to each other. After another intervention where Barbara and David were able to talk with each other, the negotiations were finally completed and the sale of the property went through. Each of us was very grateful for those dreams. Because I was the only person who knew both Barbara and David, the Universe had used me to help the two of them connect, so that the Am Kolel Sanctuary and Renewal Center could be created. Rabbi David calls me the midwife of Sanctuary. He and Dr. Gilah Rosner, Sanctuary's retreat manager, have created a sacred place that is a gift to our community and to our world. Joyous events and spiritual groups from many different traditions now come to enjoy the twenty-eight acres of peace and beauty.

It is experiences like this that have helped me to "keep the faith." I had never before had a prophetic dream. What if I had ignored those dreams, or what if I had not trusted my intuition? What if I had not acted in faith by making those phone calls? For me, this experience beautifully illustrates the flow of listening to our intuition and having faith that, by making the self-effort, grace will appear. If there had been a change in any step along the way, things might have turned out quite differently.

When Grace Doesn't Happen—Or Does It?

Sometimes we get frustrated or critical with ourselves, and angry with God that what we want to happen isn't taking place on our timetable. Yet I discovered that when I looked back on a situation that didn't seem to work out the way I wanted, I realized in hindsight that what had occurred was really for the best, and I even felt grateful.

The beach house that I am sitting in at this very moment is a perfect example of learning this soul-wisdom. I love expansive views of the water, and I would frequently take trips to the water specifically to write. Finding a beach house with an expansive view where I could give retreats and write by the water had become my dream. Five years ago I was involved in trying, for the first time, to buy a beach house with some good friends. After much energy was spent finding a place and negotiating to buy the house we'd finally found, someone came in at the last minute and offered to buy the house without an inspection or any of the repairs that were needed. He won the bid—and there went my dream. I was disappointed, yet this lesson of trusting the mysterious hand of fate wasn't new to me. Three years later, after many more trips to the ocean to write and play, a client told me about a beach in Delaware that was beautiful and secluded. I rented a house on this beach; this in turn led to looking for a beach house at this new location with my sister, Diane, and my brother-in-law, Barry. By this time the real estate market had plummeted, and we were able to buy a beautiful house for substantially less than the first beach house. Our new vacation home turned out to be bigger than my first choice. It was built on a much quieter beach, was closer to our homes, had an unobstructed view of the water, and even had an indoor hot tub and fireplace. Even though it had seemed as if the force of grace wasn't in effect during my first attempt to buy a beach house, the beautiful setting of the house that I eventually bought with my sister and brother-in-law made it clear in retrospect that grace had been at work all along. In the end, losing the first house to the other man's bid saved us from what could have been a costly mistake. What had seemed like a loss led instead to the fulfillment of my years-long dream of owning a beach house. Writing, giving retreats, and sharing this place has been such a gift. I often walk down the beach and look out over the water, observing the majesty of the snow geese as they lift off and fly overhead in their "V" formations, demonstrating their faith in each other and shared leadership as they take turns being at the point of the "V."

After a while, recurring situations like this can't help but forge a stronger sense of faith. Now when I feel disappointed about something, I just remind myself of this soul-wisdom, and have faith. Life then becomes much more "grace-full."

Power and Control Versus Higher Consciousness

From my experiences as a psychologist and from my spiritual experiences on this journey of transformation, I have developed a theory of sorts. By "theory of sorts," I originally meant that it isn't a big psychological or spiritual theory. As I reread the term, however, I realize that it is truly a theory of "sorts" because it helps to sort out a person's consciousness. I have found that there are two major tracks in life. One track is about power, control, and materialism (the power-and-control track); the other is about higher consciousness (the consciousness track). Our world is dominated by the power-and-control, materialistic worldview of "Whoever dies with the most toys wins." The other track is the road less traveled, an inner road that takes us beyond the materialistic, power-and-control focus to an awareness of life's emotional, energetic, psychological, and spiritual consciousness. This second track offers deeper connection and inner joy. If we do the inner work, one of the blessings of the higher consciousness track is faith. In the following story, we'll see how being on the power-and-control track can derail a life and destroy a marriage, and how commitment to the consciousness track, along with faith, can save it.

A few days ago a young couple called for an appointment because they were in crisis. I had seen Mara five years ago. Even back then, I found her to be an exceptionally conscious, wise, and aware young woman. Since then she had married Scott; they now had a one-and-a-half-year-old son who is the joy of their lives. Recently, on a business trip, Scott ran into an old girlfriend and had an affair. Scott didn't tell Mara, but she found love letters to the woman "hiding in plain sight" on their joint e-mail account. You can imagine Mara's distress and Scott's shame at the time they called me. When I saw them, they had already done some excellent work on discovering what was really happening in their relationship.

Although theirs was basically a solid relationship, Scott and Mara had been losing touch with each other, as they had both become extremely busy. Mara was pursuing a doctorate, and Scott had begun coaching and taking on extra responsibilities at work. Mara could feel their disconnection; initially, she suggested that she take time off from her doctorate program. However, they both decided that this wasn't a good idea. Rather than picking up some of the slack in the home that occurred because of Mara's studies, however, Scott selfishly got busier doing things that he wanted to do. After all, if she could make her interests a priority, so could he! He was operating on the power-and-control track. Mara sensed that they were once again losing their connection, and tried without success to create opportunities for connection and intimacy.

In describing why he chose to have the affair, Scott said he had a need to once again feel that he was a powerful and desirable man. He was thinking about his own needs and not his betrayal of his wife or the needs of the family he had cocreated. He clearly still loved his wife and was not interested in continuing the affair—yet his judgment and choices failed to reflect the responsibility and wisdom that are part of the consciousness track. Growing up with hypercritical parents had lowered Scott's self-esteem. His father (and role model) had also had affairs. These were underlying factors in Scott's betrayal. His behavior was a purely unconscious manifestation of the need for power and control. Scott's work is to learn how the judgment and choices of the power-and-control track can be replaced with 2 percent of the sensitivity, responsibility, and wisdom of the consciousness track, which is the energy that Mara expresses.

Mara also grew up with anxious and critical parents, and even though she has long been on the consciousness track, she still has important work to do to claim what she has disowned—a feeling of empowerment and a sense of being entitled to express her needs. In other words, it is important for Mara to incorporate 2 percent of the power-and-control energy that Scott expresses in order to be comfortable saying no, setting boundaries, and expressing her own needs. This will be a preventive health measure for her life and her marriage.

After the affair had taken place, Mara was able to share her despair, anger, and hurt. Despite everything, she still loved Scott and had faith that their relationship could be healed. Even more importantly, the compassion and sensitivity that Mara expressed in relation to Scott's emotional history was amazing! Never having experienced such profound love and integrity growing up, Scott was deeply moved by Mara's inner strength, spirituality, commitment, and faith. He remembered that this is what initially attracted him to her. His intense love and appreciation for her motivated Scott to save the marriage, and to make the commitment to move onto the higher consciousness track.

I felt honored to be a guide for Scott and Mara on this very precarious course to healing their relationship—something that could only happen through the healing of their own hearts and souls. Their crisis created an opportunity, or what I call a "crissitunity," for deeper work to be done as together they build a stronger foundation for their relationship. I have faith that as they become more conscious individuals, learning their life lessons and deepening their soul-wisdom, their relationship will grow stronger, deeper, and more secure for themselves and for their new baby, who is a light in their lives, moving them farther from the darkness that was lurking in the shadows.

Discernment

For those of us who believe in the "Divine Source of all," faith includes believing in a force that is greater than we are. However, many people who embrace a spiritual path don't hold a belief in a higher being or deity. Regardless of our beliefs, it is important along the journey of consciousness to move from blind faith to questioning, plumbing the depths of our souls, and then, finally, trusting our own experience. Baba would continuously tell us, "Don't believe a word I say. Trust your own inner experience." Along the journey we need to develop discernment. I know I've mentioned this before, but discernment is so important that it deserves its own section. It is through questioning, then confirming what we learn, that we stand firmly on the grounded truth of our own experiences. Only in this way can we develop a faith that we can trust.

Religion Versus Spirituality

Higher consciousness or spirituality doesn't necessarily involve religion; neither does faith. People who are deeply religious may embrace a higher consciousness, but this is not always the case. Some people who are religious may still be on the power-and-control track. After all, many wars have been fought over religion. On the other hand, whenever I meet a fellow spiritual traveler, it doesn't matter which spiritual path they are on, we have an immediate connection. There is a mutual feeling of trust, knowing that we are working on ourselves, and trying to become more openhearted, less defended, and more compassionate. We are engaged in the journey of learning our life lessons, caring about other beings and the planet, and using whichever tools our spiritual path suggests for quieting our mind and connecting to our soul's wisdom. Along the journey, an understanding develops that intuition, faith, grace, gratitude, and honoring a Higher Source are what is of true importance.

If you have gotten to this chapter, then you are embarking on or have already been on your own journey of higher consciousness. You are a fellow traveler, and I am honored that you are reading this book. May my words help you travel further up the mountain on your journey of transformation, higher consciousness, and faith. All the spiritual paths leading to higher consciousness merge at the top of the mountain. Yet even along the way, those who are on parallel paths recognize the oneness of each other's souls.

A Client's Experience: A Question of Faith

This is my story of being a loving, trusting, caring, spiritual person and my descent into total darkness and despair:

I was the youngest in a family of four with twelve years between my next oldest sibling and me. Early in my life, there were dramatic changes in my family. We had to move to a new town, far away from the people and structures that had allowed me to feel safe and secure. Then my father fell seriously ill, and died only a year later.

The dysfunction in my family made it impossible for me to cope with all of these changes. I experienced a loss of trust that began within my broken family, and later spread as I became isolated from all my friends. I began living a haunted life of fear and darkness. To the outside world, I did not have any problems. But I was merely going through the motions. Behind closed doors, I was living a nightmare—hating my life and not connecting with people. I felt as if I had lost my purpose. Everything that mattered to me was gone. I was in total anguish.

It felt as if one day I was living my life, and the next moment I had fallen into a chasm, where I lived for years plunged in darkness. With the birth of my niece, I began to climb out of this despair and reconnect to life once again After she was born, I began to care about her—and then I began to care about myself. The slow process of recovery had begun.

Shortly thereafter, three wonderful professional women came into my life and facilitated my step-by-step recovery and journey back to wholeness.

The first was my longtime family doctor, who knew me well enough to see through the front I had put on and to recognize my despair. During a routine visit she said to me, "You're too good to be this unhappy. Let me call someone I know who can help you." Because I had not had positive experiences with therapists in the past, I resisted the idea. But she took it upon herself to make the call on my behalf. This call introduced me to my new therapist, the woman who changed my life. Once I chose to enter therapy, I began to feel the despair and loss of spirit that had burdened me for thirty years begin to lift.

Through the compassion and feeling of safety that I experienced in our sessions, I revealed my fear that I would never emerge from this darkness; that my faith in God, my spirituality, had deserted me. I did not know if I could ever believe again. I felt bereft, as if my own spirit had abandoned me. My therapist's response to this—"I will just have to have faith enough for both of us, until you can believe again for yourself"—was a lifeline for me.

Over the next two years I experienced a spiritual awakening. My inner source came back to life, and I began to reconnect to my spiritual journey. My therapist suggested that I attend a church, which I still go to regularly. I began to associate with my life, rather than disassociate. I began to find a renewal of energy, connection, and faith in spirit and myself.

My therapist had engaged an art therapist to facilitate an expressive women's therapy group, and she suggested that I join it. My interaction with this gifted and talented therapist and our group of special women further enabled me to develop my trust and faith in myself, others, and Spirit.

The insight, love, and belief in me that came from these three women provided the secure space I needed to reintegrate my life and my faith, and to feel whole and secure in the world again. I continue to struggle to have inner peace and security, but when I do despair, Spirit has a way of knocking on my door to remind me that "Spirit does exist, and I am here for you," telling me to have faith. Today I have an abundance of friends and love in my life. I have breathtaking spiritual moments. I no longer carry the fear of falling into that chasm. I have experienced a "lasting transformation." For within my life, Spirit and faith are present. I know this.

In Practice:
Transpersonal Inspiration and Psychological Mountain Climbing

Roberto Assagioli, the founder of psychosynthesis, gives two different means by which energies from the superconscious, or the higher Transpersonal Realms, can be drawn down and experienced in normal consciousness. Accessing the higher Transpersonal Realms of Consciousness and experiencing the Higher Self or the Inner Self allows for the strengthening of faith in our lives. The first way involves the inflow of higher elements into the field of consciousness in the form of intuitions, inspirations, creations of genius, and impulses to humanitarian and heroic action. Assagioli describes this as the descent of the higher elements, or transpersonal inspiration.

The other way is ascent, or establishing contact with the superconscious. This is done by raising the conscious "I" to higher levels, thus expanding the area of consciousness to include the content of the superconscious and contact with the Spiritual Self. Assagioli calls this latter way "psychological mountain climbing." The following exercise, adapted from Assagioli's book, *Psychosynthesis,* uses both of these approaches.

1. *Place a pen and a piece of paper near you. Get in a comfortable position and close your eyes. Slowly take a few deep breaths and as you exhale let any tension that you feel in your body flow out with your breath. Allow your body to relax as you concentrate on your breath.*

2. *Now think of an area in your life in which you are having difficulty. Imagine that you are in a meadow. It might be a meadow that is familiar and special to you, or one that you create in your mind. In the meadow is an amphitheater, and inside the amphitheater is whomever or whatever is causing you difficulty. Spend a few minutes thinking about the conflict; then*

communicate to the other person or thing that you will return in a little while. Walk out of the amphitheater into the meadow.

3. Walk through the meadow, feeling the grass under your feet and hearing the birds, or the sound of water flowing and the breeze rustling through the trees. Let yourself experience the beauty of nature. It is a sunny day, and as you walk through the meadow you see a mountain. As you approach the mountain, you can see a path that leads from where you are up to the mountaintop.

4. Begin to climb the path toward the summit. This may require some effort; you can feel the strain in your legs and throughout your body, but it is not too difficult. As you climb higher and higher, let yourself experience the increasing sense of elevation and expansion. Notice what is around you. It's a beautiful, clear, sunny day. You stop at a resting place.

5. Now turn around and look at the meadow in the distance. From where you are on the mountain, you can see the amphitheater. As you look down, you can see the stage and yourself on the stage together with the other person or the other thing that is involved in the conflict in your life. From your place on the mountain, what do you see as your part in the play unfolding on the stage in the meadow below? What do you understand about the lessons you are learning in the play of your life? How does the play evolve as you watch it from partway up the mountain?

6. Now continue to climb up the mountain, and as you look up, you can see that at the top of the mountain there is a clearing. At its center is a temple—the temple of silence. As you approach the clearing at the top, you sense the stillness and the energy of silence radiating from the temple.

7. Enter the clearing that surrounds the temple and let your body fill with the silence, so that it becomes quiet and relaxed. Then move slowly toward the entrance to the temple. As you enter the

temple, allow the energy of silence to permeate your feelings, making them calm and serene. The area at the center of the temple is open to the sky. As you reach this area, silence infuses your mind, so that it becomes still and at the same time clear and alert.

8. *At the very center of the temple, a beam of sunlight is shining down. It is from this central light that the energy of silence is radiating. Walk into the sunlight and allow silence to fill your whole being. Turn toward the sun and open yourself to the energy coming from above. Let yourself experience its radiance. Take as much time as you like to do this.*

9. *Suddenly, in the center of the sunlight, appears a very wise old being, whose eyes express great love for you. Perhaps this being has something to tell you. Or you may have something you would like to ask this wise one.*

10. *From the temple, you can see the amphitheater below in the meadow. In the presence of the wise old being, take time to look at the play of your life that you left there. Engage the wise old being in conversation. Use this being's presence and guidance to help you understand whatever questions, direction, or choices you are currently dealing with in the amphitheater below. Take all the time you need in this exchange.*

11. *As you feel the sun warm you and fill you with the energy of silence, ask the wise old being for a word, phrase, or image that you can reflect on. Focus on the quality, the meaning, the function, and the value of the insights the wise old being has given you for your life. Open yourself to this word, phrase, or image and feel it to be almost living and breathing within you.*

12. *When you feel ready, open your eyes and take time to reflect on and write down your experience.*

12

Repairing Our World: From Self-Serving to the Serving Self

Everyone has a purpose in life… a unique gift or special talent to give to others. And when we blend this unique talent with service to others we experience the ecstasy and exultation of our own spirit, which is the ultimate goal of all goals.

—Deepak Chopra, *The Seven Spiritual Laws of Success*

Repairing Our World

Until now, this book has focused on the inner work of transformation of the self through learning our life lessons, creating healthy relationships, and deepening our connection to our soul's wisdom. Now we begin to look outward to discover the ultimate purpose of our lasting transformation— to be of service in our world. *Tikkun 'Olam* is a Hebrew phrase that means "to heal or repair the world by making it a better place." This is one of our most important jobs as human beings. All the great spiritual traditions speak of being of service as integral to life's purpose. Tikkun 'Olam teaches us that to be of service means finding ways to give to others and to care for the Earth. Ways to repair our world come in as many shapes and sizes as there are human hearts beating. Each person's contributions are unique. Finding and cultivating the distinctive gifts and talents through which we can contribute to the repair of our world is a process that flows effortlessly for some; for others, however, it may be the result of years of searching and struggling. The stepping-stones that have been laid out in this book—openheartedness, vulnerability, intuition, self-effort, and faith—provide significant help and guidance in finding our unique way of being of service in the world. For most of us, aligning with our life's purpose is a process that goes hand in hand with the behavioral changes and transformation of our relationships to our self, each other, and our world. This is accompanied by a deepening awareness and a healthy connection to our heart, our soul, and our Source.

From Self-Serving to the Serving Self

If you haven't reached the stage of connecting with the Serving Self in repairing our world, don't feel guilty. The evolution of consciousness unfolds gradually; it begins with an outer-directed, ego-driven focus on serving one's own needs and desires. This stage is essential because we all need to develop a strong sense of self-esteem before we can transcend the ego, or the small self, and focus on serving something greater than our own needs. During this stage, it is crucial for us to focus in a healthy way on fulfilling our own needs in life. Even if most of our time goes toward making a living, and feeding and clothing ourselves and our family, this is precisely what we should be doing to repair the world.

We live in extraordinary times. Many people can't find jobs; others are chronically ill and unable to work. But if we feel frustrated because we are struggling to make ends meet, it is important to know that survival and safety needs *have* to come before our ability to serve others. We have to serve ourselves and our families before we can serve the larger world. Sometimes, for example, moms come into therapy feeling frustrated that they have to put their careers on hold while they are bringing up their children. Yet being a good parent is one of life's most critical services and meaningful tasks. Whatever stage of life we are in, what matters most is right consciousness, or honoring whatever we are focusing on with our full presence. As we put self-effort toward whatever needs our attention at the present, grace comes in and guides us toward the next step on our life's journey.

The psychologist Abraham Maslow first proposed the theory of a "hierarchy of needs" in a 1943 paper titled "A Theory of Human Motivation." This pioneer in the field of humanistic psychology taught that our basic survival needs for food, shelter, and clothing have to be met before we are able to focus on needs for safety and security, which have to be met before we can focus on social needs, or a sense of belonging. And each rung on the ladder leads to the next level of needs being met until we get to higher-level needs of self-esteem and self-actualization.

Self-actualized people are those who have been able to manifest their potential; this includes realizing that they are more than the limited identification with their ego. In his book *Motivation and Personality*, Maslow describes the shift that occurs when people transform their focus from being self-serving to becoming self-actualized, or what I have named the "Serving Self": "Most people, when thinking of problems in their life," he wrote, "focus on what affects them and their own problems and issues. Self-actualized persons focus not on themselves, but on some greater good" (p. 210). This doesn't mean that self-actualized people don't focus on themselves or their own needs; however, they also have an awareness of and desire to serve others. What is important is creating a bridge between the self-serving ego and the serving Self.

For many, the first step on the bridge that leads from the self-serving ego to the serving Self begins with the social need to feel a sense of belonging and acceptance—the third stage of Maslow's hierarchy of needs. In addition to belonging to a neighborhood or community, this stage can also be fulfilled by joining an organization or movement that has the larger goal of making the world a better place. Membership in such a group can lead to service-oriented activities as a way to give back. This third stage of development typically unfolds as a natural outgrowth of spiritual development, which leads to self-actualization and a shift in focus toward the "greater good."

For others, due to psychological wounds and emotional immaturity that stems from not getting one's healthy developmental needs met while growing up, the focus on one's self remains self-serving. We all have wounds—it is part of the job description of being a human being—so I am not talking about the vast majority of those who come to counseling. However, the wounds and the traumas that some people experience in their lives can create a significant blockage in their development. These people do not have the psychological and emotional maturity necessary to be a healthy adult. Unless they do some inner healing work, they won't grow to realize that life is about much more than gratifying one's own needs. Indeed, for those who have reached a developmental impasse in the evolutionary process of transitioning from being solely ego driven, reparenting and birthing the authentic Self through counseling has to occur before they can respond to the call to serve the greater good.

In her insightful thesis, "Building Bridges and the Process of Counseling," Debbie Kidwell, a licensed professional counselor, describes the process of creating the bridge from self-serving to the Serving Self. According to Debbie, "Just as the traveler reaches an impasse in his journey and may need the help of a bridge, a client may also reach a block in the road of life and might need the help of counseling. With problems as potential for healing and growth, the client reframes his existence and lives with new meaning in his life. Viktor Frankl describes this reframing in *Man's Search for Meaning* as 'the call of a potential meaning waiting to be fulfilled by him.' (p. 166)"

Be the Change You Want to See: Make a Difference, Take Action

As we reach the mountaintop on the journey of transformation, we find ourselves standing on a plateau that allows us to see the "big picture." As a result of this expanded view, we arrive at the stage where we realize that our purpose for being here on planet Earth is to help each other and repair the world. Today, more than ever, society is in desperate need of this kind of regeneration.

But in a world where the news media constantly display the horrors of war, poverty, natural disasters, pollution, global warming, and terrorism, it is easy to feel powerless and helpless. The dishonesty of some of our politicians, the violence in our schools, and the breakdown of our families all point to a breakdown in our society. As Ruth Messinger, president of the American Jewish World Service, reminds us in her letter to the Partners in Social Change, "Faith can transcend our powerlessness, both real and imagined, and given the will to change we can overcome the most formidable challenge … Do not think for a moment that you can't make a difference in the world. When you join together with other concerned people, you can."

> *An example of what Ms. Messinger describes so movingly is exemplified in the story of a good friend of mine, Barbara Feuer who, together with her friends Betsy, Fiona, and Robyn, helped to organize Womenade/ Carderock. In doing this, they were inspired by Washington Womenade, a group of women friends who, in 2001, banded together to raise money for low-income women and their children. They invited all their female friends to attend delightful potluck dinners, to which they were asked to bring a dish to share, along with a check to maintain a fund for needy women and their families in Washington, D.C. This idea was started by a small book club, and it has grown to have a very significant impact. Last year they raised twelve to thirteen thousand dollars!*

Mokichi Okada, a poet, artist, mystic, and spiritual teacher who was also a husband and father, wrote this poem about our responsibility to help repair our world:

> Born as human beings it is our duty
> to strive our utmost
> for peace in the world
> and the happiness of others.
> Those who love humanity
> and help people in need, are
> always loved and protected
> by God wherever they may go.
> A person who strives constantly
> to help others and better the world,
> is like a diamond buried in the sand.

Learning our life lessons and our soul-wisdom is what helps us to become diamonds, sparkling with all of our glistening facets. Along the path of our life's journey, we sometimes encounter difficult challenges. Yet those challenges generate the intense heat and pressure that are important aspects of learning our life lessons and soul-wisdom. In Sanskrit, this is called *tapasya*, which is the process of applying the intense heat and pressure that is essential to transforming coal into diamonds. I have found this concept helpful to remember, especially when I face situations that are challenging. When we trust the process of *tapasya*, it allows us to survive these challenges with greater faith in our life's journey, leading us closer to our unique form of service in repairing the world.

When Ruth Berlin was living in Los Angeles in 1990, she and her son Jesse were poisoned by the city's aerial spraying of a pesticide for fruit fly eradication. After moving to Maryland and starting InnerSource with me in 1992, she went on in 1994 to create The Maryland Pesticide Network, a coalition of twenty-five organizations concerned about the impact of pesticides on public health and the environment. In 1998, The Maryland Pesticide Network was instrumental in passing a law that changed pest control in Maryland schools from using pesticides preventively, to using pesticides as a last resort. As a result, the law today mandates that school districts must notify parents and school staff members twenty-four hours before pesticides are applied in and around schools; parents must also be informed of a pesticide's potential adverse health effect. This law led to similar laws in many other states and to the federal School Environmental Protection Act being debated in Congress. "Looking back," said Ruth, "I believe that the pesticide poisoning that profoundly impacted my son and me happened for a reason—it propelled me into doing what I'm still doing twenty years later." In suffering through the extreme pressure of that situation, the "tapasya" that was one of life's biggest challenges for Ruth and her son, she made a major contribution to repairing the world.

Finding Your Purpose

Finding your purpose does not necessarily mean finding a single, grand, overarching reason for living. Whether others would view your purpose as large or small is irrelevant. For each of us, what we "do" in life is the external manifestation of our inner purpose, or our soul's calling. Your inner purpose is to be the most conscious person you can possibly be, and to manifest your soul's calling, whatever that is, so that the life you are living brings out your highest potential. As Martin Luther King Jr. said to a group of students in Philadelphia on October 26, 1967: "If a man is called to be a street sweeper, he should sweep streets even as Michelangelo painted, Beethoven composed music, or Shakespeare wrote poetry. He should sweep streets so well that all the hosts of heaven and earth will pause to say, here lived a great street sweeper who did his job well."

Often our soul speaks to us in the language of our dreams and desires. When we align our inner purpose with our passion, as well as our natural abilities, acquired skills, and needs, we will find ourselves doing what we are meant to do; we will be who we are meant to be. We can turn our abilities, proclivities, passions, and dreams into a reality that can be our vehicle for making our world a better place. This is reflected in the Buddhist concept called right livelihood: This means that we are doing in the world what we are meant to do, what comes naturally to us, what we love to do, and we are making a living doing it.

Right Livelihood

One of my most rewarding experiences in therapy is helping clients find the way to their right livelihood. Our lives provide a map that directs us. It's as if the Universe leaves a trail of cookie crumbs and we just need to learn how to follow where they lead us. The crumbs could come from significant experiences that we had growing up, our special talents, wounds that we incurred along the way, or training in a career that didn't work out—but that may be pointing the way to a new direction that could be right for us.

> *A great example of having a significant experience and a physical wound that led to right livelihood happened to my brother-in-law, Barry. When he was a teenager, he was very active in sports. Then one day, when he was playing with some friends, he got hit in the head with a metal horseshoe. He had a depressed skull fracture and was partially paralyzed for a while. He wasn't allowed to play sports without a helmet, and he would often get headaches. While he was recuperating, his mother bought him a paint set so that he wouldn't be bored. He gradually got more and more involved in painting, and over the years his passion for art led him to a successful and fulfilling career as an artist, author, poet, and director of painting at the Maryland Institute College of Art in Baltimore. His right livelihood is reflected in the beautiful cover for this book.*

Events in our lives happen. We don't and can't always know what the reason or meaning is at the moment they happen. This is why it is so helpful to have faith and trust that there is a method to what often seems like madness. If we can stay in the present moment and open ourselves to our life lessons and soul-wisdom, we will be able to experience Presence operating in our life.

A metaphor I use for finding right livelihood is a sailboat. It is important to create an intention for our inner purpose, a focus that feels meaningful. Then it is important to express that intention to the Universe. It is helpful to take the time to meditate, so that we can stay in the present and quiet our minds, allowing our intuition to flow into our consciousness. By taking steps that feel intuitively right to us, and by focusing our self-effort in a particular direction, we are putting up our sails, so that the wind can move us in the path that the Universe wants us to go. The word for wind in Hebrew is the same as the word for spirit—*ruach*. Be receptive and watch closely how the Universe guides us—through the people we meet, the dreams we have, and the messages that we receive in a myriad of ways. Have faith that grace will appear and spirit will guide us toward our right livelihood. As I mentioned in Chapter 10 on intuition, it is important to put in the self-effort to follow through with any "intuitive hits" that we get along the way, so that the grace will continue to flow.

"The Healing Prayer" that songwriter Debbie Friedman put to music is based on a Jewish prayer for people in need of healing. As I was reading the prayer, I realized it is also a beautiful intention for right livelihood:

> May the Source of strength
> Who blessed the ones before us
> Help us find the courage
> To make our lives a blessing
> And let us say, "Amen."

When we pray, we are asking to be guided to what we can do to heal the world and make it a better place. If we can find our path, our right livelihood, and the courage to walk it, our lives become a blessing.

The Interconnectedness of Who We Are

As we deepen our connection to our self and our soul, as we have faith in and experience of our Source, and as we find our right livelihood, a natural sense of interconnectedness becomes part of our consciousness. In one of my favorite books, *Ask and It Is Given: Learning to Manifest Your Desires*, authors Esther and Jerry Hicks make this point beautifully:

> No one connected to Source Energy would ever cause harm to another. They lash out in their defensiveness, or in their disconnectedness, but never from their state of connection. If everyone understood the power of their own Being, they would not seek to control others. Any feelings of insecurity and hatred are born from your disconnection with who you are. (p. 105)

Therefore, as this sense of interconnectedness is experienced, there is a realization born in the heart of our responsibility to take care of our world.

To make our world a better place, we have to learn how to be in relationship with people with whom we don't experience that sense of interconnectedness. All too often, our relationships do not result in the awareness of interconnection or in healing. Instead, we get locked into painful relationships with people with whom we may experience a great deal of conflict. Why does this happen?

In Chapter 6, "The Higher Purpose of Relationships," we learned that although the psyche disconnects from the behaviors of those who have harmed us or who were unseen by us, the pain from such experiences gets pushed into the unconscious and gathers there as disowned energies. Despite our attempts to run away from the buried pain, we nevertheless attract to us energies that we disowned or lessons that we never learned. We attract these energies in the form of an "other"—the people or even animals with whom we come into relationship. To make matters worse, we often project our shadows onto others, rather than facing them within ourselves. Thus, relationships can be an opportunity for seeing and healing what is in our shadow. But until we are able to pull our shadows into the light of consciousness, thereby transforming them, we will attract adversarial relationships over and over again. This is true for nations, as well as for individuals.

Sarah Yehudit Schneider, one of my most important teachers, offers us a spiritual perspective on disowned energy and conflict in her book, *You Are*

What You Hate: A Spiritually Productive Approach to Enemies. In this case, an "enemy" can mean one with whom there is any degree of conflict.

> Enemies hold fallen slivers of our souls, estranged sparks that we do not recognize as pieces of our very own selves. They have chosen us as their opponent because they are trying, in their deluded way, to connect back to their root, which really is us. The spark of ourselves inside the enemy must be recovered...We cannot complete our life mission until we have collected all the scattered pieces of ourselves, including those currently embedded within our enemy's soul. The question becomes: How do we both protect ourselves and reclaim our sparks? What is the most spiritually productive way to succeed at this paradoxical mission? (pp. 116–117)

Sarah Yehudit answers this question via the teachings of nineteenth-century Kabbalist and Hasidic master Rabbi Yitzchak Yehuda Yechiel Safrin, the Komarno Rebbe. His is a truly enlightened strategy that balances self-protection and generosity of spirit, protest and acceptance, street smarts and idealism, and intolerance for evil and compassion.

> "What is the most spiritually productive way to deal with the enemy?"—it is not a sentence, it's a journey, a multi-millennial trek that is guided by practical considerations, ethical imperatives, and spiritual principles...R. Safrin (building upon... the Book of Job) suggests a no-risk practice that is easy to incorporate into any action-plan: In addition to praying for ourselves, and praying for the planet, and praying for the messianic golden age, we must also pray for our enemies' spiritual redemption—*teshuva*—that they should right their ways and see the Light (which is exactly what we seek for ourselves). (pp. 258, 260)

Rabbi Safrin alludes to the biblical story of Job, who demonstrates how to deal with our adversaries. Job's friends attacked his character and acted more as enemies than as friends. Yet Job was transformed through his misery and torment from his "friends." Sarah Yehudit offers us a spiritual point of view of transformation through this story. "What is the proof of Job's transformed self? ... that is the fact that he prayed for those very ones who judged him most harshly and caused him emotional anguish throughout his travail" (p. 258). Holding this vision of Job can give us an image to aspire to on our journey of transformation.

Although it might seem quite radical to pray for our adversaries, the Buddhist metta practice of lovingkindness that I mentioned in Chapter 9, Voice Dialogue's technology of working with our disowned energies that I mentioned in Chapter 6, and Sarah Yehudit all teach that this approach is relevant in both personal and communal situations. It seeks the spiritual transformation of hatred and conflict, not merely their containment. As we enter the light of consciousness and interconnectedness, we pray for our enemies' spiritual redemption.

This approach is not only useful in dealing with our enemies, it can also be helpful in dealing with any relationship in which something unconscious lurks in the shadows, including our relationship with our own self. When we learn to have compassion for our shadow selves, whether internal, projected, or embodied in the "other," we learn to "love our shadow as our self"—because it is our self. When we own our shadow, we can begin to transform it. This awareness is the beginning of true peace, an essential foundation of healing our hearts and truly being of service in repairing the world.

In her deep and meaningful book, *Born to Serve: The Evolution of the Soul Through Service*, Susan Trout describes the need to do the inner work of integrating our shadow in order to move forward on our journey of expressing the soul in our lives, and through our service. As she writes:

> Coming to terms with the shadow is the work of the soul's evolution. Self-growth and serving others are inseparable and complementary human activities. We integrate and ground the learning of our personal inner healing work by applying it in service in our daily lives. In turn, our service reinforces our self-knowledge and strengthens our inner healing. Like an infinity sign, the energy of giving continually flows into the energy of receiving and back again. (p. 78)

Abby Rosen, PhD

Deepening Our Awareness and Connection to Our Earth

As Rabbi Arthur Green reveals in *The Jewish Lights Spirituality Handbook: A Guide to Understanding, Exploring and Living a Spiritual Life*, our connection to the Earth includes "the relief of human suffering, the achievement of peace and mutual respect among people, and the protection of the planet itself from destruction." (p. 325)

Ruth Berlin uses a term called Spiritual Activism, which, she says,

> is based on the awareness of our interconnectedness and the consequent need to serve something beyond our personal needs and wants to effect social, environmental, public health, and/or political change. Being a change agent with a spiritual/conscious perspective can provide us with great strength, courage, and inner wisdom. It allows us to transition from an us-them paradigm to a "we perspective" that makes effecting change more powerful.

James Gustave Speth, Dean of the Yale School of Forestry and Environmental Studies, wisely taught his students: "Realizing that we are completely dependent on our ailing Earth is the first step toward solving environmental problems and, as a side effect, solving human problems." Not learning this lesson of healthy dependency is wreaking havoc on our environment, in our communities, and in our world. Caring for the Earth and solving humanity's problems with Earth-centered solutions are essential. Howard Clinebell, in his book *Ecotherapy: Healing Ourselves, Healing the Earth*, says,

> Ecoviolence against the Earth is interrelated with other types of human violence. If one works to stop oppressing the Earth, the motivation to cease oppressing other people should follow. For in responsibly caring for the Earth and becoming educated about its problems, humanity will recognize that everyone is alike in the fact that they live on Earth and are nurtured by it. Differences in sex, race, or income lose their importance upon

184

the realization that humanity's future existence is
at stake." (pp. 260–261)

The desire to become a strong and empowered force for our environment, and for those in the world who are vulnerable, can be a natural extension of learning to value and protect our own vulnerable Inner Child. In this way, the awareness and compassion we develop through the process of aligning our personality's life lessons and our soul's wisdom as we move from self-serving to the Serving Self can directly inspire us to serve in our world.

The horrific times when there is a natural disaster like a tsunami, an earthquake, or a flood are examples of how people around the world can rally to serve those who are most in need. Service-oriented groups, faith-based organizations, and nurses and doctors fly to the devastated area to help with the humanitarian effort to save lives. Others give money to different charitable organizations that support the relief effort; those who can't give their time, energy, or money, pray. These relief efforts are examples of the many different ways there are to be of service, because so many ways are needed to help repair our world.

As we come to the end of this chapter, which brings Stage Two: Soul-Wisdom Therapy to a close, trust that your soul's wisdom knows how to lead you to your unique way to serve—let your "consciousness" be your guide.

Joan Borysenko, PhD, a renowned psychoneuroimmunologist, beautifully sums up this stage of gaining our soul-wisdom on this journey of lasting transformation in *Handbook for the Soul,* edited by Richard Carlson, PhD, and Benjamin Shield, PhD:

> Some tension is necessary for the soul to grow, and we can put that tension to good use. We can look for every opportunity to give and receive love, to appreciate nature, to heal our wounds and the wounds of others, to forgive and to serve.
> (p. 45)

Laura's Experience of Discovering Her Serving Self

My path to right livelihood has been one where I could not always see around the bend, and yet, if I had been able to look down over the landscape of my journey from the air, I would have seen that, for all the creeks and eddies, I was navigating one river flowing back to its source.

I grew up with the message that "suffering makes you a better person," which is a potent axiom to hand to a child who wants to please. I believed it was my job, my purpose, to allow others to hurt me if that's what they needed to do. I believed that by feeling the pain of others as if it were my own, I could be of service. I believed that my willingness to suffer connected me to God. And I think I may have even felt a little moral superiority in that suffering. None of this would look very good on a résumé. Greatest skill? Suffering. Length of time on the job? Birth to Present.

As an adult, I learned what was unacceptable, how to set limits, how to protect and respect myself. But that yearning that was my connection to God remained. I still just didn't believe it was okay to be happy. Happiness was something to be earned by being sad and, clearly, God liked us humble, sad people a lot better than our happy (and audacious) counterparts.

Just as compelling as the message that suffering would make me a better person was the message that self-improvement was the reason I'd been born. Self-improvement involved self-reflection, and in exploring the contradictions between what I felt and what I thought I should feel, I stumbled on the Rosetta stone of writing, and a career was born. I was fortunate. I put it all on the page, and I published. I began to teach others to write as well.

But over time, this right livelihood began to frustrate me. Award-winning stories were still difficult to place. Students showed up, but didn't work. If I was going to spend the next three decades writing stories that were not read and teaching students who would not write, what was the point? So I quit. I didn't know what I was supposed to be doing with my life. I just knew it wasn't this.

And in the year that I quit I faced some life-altering challenges. My son was diagnosed with an incurable illness, living twelve thousand miles away with no health insurance. My youngest child left home, my marriage hit an impasse not of my choosing, and, ironically, in the midst of all this, I faced a medical crisis of my own. Alone and unemployed, I decided to just float for a time.

It was then that I began the real soul work of becoming happy; happy in spite of circumstances, happy from the inside out. It began with learning to believe a new message: God loves happy people.

Could this be?

I looked at my children. Didn't I want, more than anything, for them to lead joy-filled lives? Did they have to earn that desire from me, or was it their birthright? And when I felt joy myself, wasn't I kinder, more loving, more tolerant and compassionate? Maybe it really was okay to embrace joy. Maybe it was okay to be happy just because there was a river to float on, a current moving me somewhere, even if all I could see was sky.

And the happier I became, the more the energy of my joy radiated outward and began to change the circumstances around me. Not transcend those circumstances—transform them. My son's health stabilized, my marriage reached new depths, my own health issues were resolved, and the sadness that had haunted me—the feeling and the belief that the only way to connect to the Divine was through a vigilant and humble sadness—all reversed. I began to see that my joy had a transformative effect in the world, quite literally.

So I began to speak and write about that, and one day a student appeared who said, "Teach me to be happy, too." I was uncertain and afraid to try, but one night I awoke with the realization that I had said to the Universe, "Please, please tell me, what should I do with my life?"—and the Universe had sent me a student. I was waiting for a phone call, when the telegram was right in my hands.

I started teaching others how to do what I did—to find an inner happiness independent of circumstances—and how to allow the Universe to mirror that reality.

I call this practice Learned Happiness. It is gratifying, exhilarating. It requires a rewriting of the story within us. It has become an important part of my right livelihood. I teach happiness to stay fluent in the language of joy.

—*Laura Oliver*

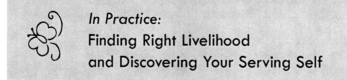

In Practice:
Finding Right Livelihood
and Discovering Your Serving Self

Those of you who know what your right livelihood is are blessed. For those of you who are open to guidance from the Universe and your intuitive wisdom, this exercise is for you.

1. *Make a list of what you would describe as your natural abilities—talents you have that you love expressing. These are the things that you would do whether you got paid or not.*

_____

_____

_____

_____

_____

_____

_____

_____

_____

_____

Example: I have a client who is naturally organized. She gets great pleasure from making order out of chaos. She is also very nurturing and noncritical. I thought that she would make a wonderful personal organizer for people, and connected her with another client who didn't have that organizational gene, and who desperately needed help with her house. They are working together and both enjoying and benefiting from it. The first client is getting paid for what she loves to do and does naturally. She has found her right livelihood.

2. *Name some of the significant experiences you have had in your life, powerful messages that you got and believe in today, and/or particular wounds or hurts that you experienced growing up.*

_____

_____

_____

_____

_____

_____

3. *We move in the direction of our thoughts and images, whether we want to or not, so let your imagination flow by playing with possible paths that may lead to your right livelihood. Meditate and ask the Universe to guide you toward your unique way of being of service in the world. Call out and ask for guidance to help you create a clear vision of how you can fulfill your purpose in serving to help repair the world.*

4. *Allow your intuition to guide you to name two steps that you can envision taking in the next month that would be the equivalent of doing self-effort, so the grace will flow.*

   Write down:

   Two steps toward finding right livelihood and repairing the world:

   1. _____

   2. _____

A Summary of the Journey:
Life's Rules of the Road

How much easier life would be if, like driving, you could find a good map and a clear set of rules of the road. You can! You have a built-in navigational system, which *LASTING Transformation* can help you access. Like learning to drive, transformation takes time, a genuine desire, courage, perseverance, and plenty of life experience to learn from your mistakes and successes. But as you embark on this journey of lasting transformation, you'll acquire a lifetime emergency road service membership to pick you up whenever you're stuck or broken down. An amazing and inspired life is available to us when we learn to balance the outer journey with an "inner-net" that allows us to navigate life, know our true self, learn our life lessons, and tap into our soul-wisdom. The following "Rules of the Road" summarize the journey we have been traveling together through *LASTING Transformation:*

1. Develop a strong sense of self. Value yourself and become your own Inner Nurturing Parent, whose love fosters a feeling of worthiness. (Chapters 1, 2, 3, Appendix C)

2. Get to know your inner world of feelings and learn to express them clearly and constructively. Healthy communication facilitates healthy relationships. (Chapters 3, 4, 5)

3. Take appropriate risks. It's how you find out about yourself and learn to trust your decisions and intuition. Don't let fear keep you from making choices that are right for you. (Chapters 4, 5)

4. Connect with and express your core sensitivity. Vulnerability is the key to intimacy and to accessing your inner wisdom, which is an amazing source of guidance, awareness, and clarity. (Chapters 1, 2, 3, 4, 5, 6)

5. Through relationships, we attract into our lives qualities we've disowned. The "other" manifests the very traits, in their extreme form, that we need a healthy dose of in our own lives. By incorporating just 2 percent of this disowned energy, our lives and our relationships come into greater balance. (Chapters 2, 6, 12, Appendices A, E)

6. Transform negative behavior patterns that cause pain and problems in relationships and in your life. Become aware of defense mechanisms that worked to protect you growing up. As an adult, they often create the very pain they were set up to protect you from. (Chapters 1, 3, 4, 5, 6, 7)

7. Develop a connection with God, or whatever you feel comfortable calling your Higher Power. Make time to quiet the mind so you can listen within, experience your intuition, know your Inner Self, and honor your Soul's calling. (Chapters 8, 9, 10)

8. Life is like two wings of a bird. The first wing, which is our job, is to focus on self-effort, not outcome. Try your hardest. Then have faith that the Universe, the other wing, will do its part, and the bird will take flight. (Chapter 11)

9. Make the shift from "self-serving" to the Serving Self. Find ways to give to others, the society, and the planet. Helping to repair the world is our most important job as human beings. (Chapter 12)

In my meditation this morning, I asked if there was anything else that was important for me to communicate as this book comes to a close. Using the tools that I have taught throughout these chapters, I repeated my mantra and quieted my mind, so that I could open to hear any guidance. After meditating for a while and asking to receive, here are the words I heard, which I want to share with you:

Love yourself, love each other, and love the planet. The rest is commentary!

Tears came to my eyes, yet I had no idea what I was crying about. Using more tools, I "checked in" to see if the tears were tears of sadness, as I was grieving the loss of my father, who had recently passed. But, it didn't feel like these tears were about my dad. I kept bringing down the computer menu of feelings and asking—were they feelings of gratitude or happiness? I kept getting no, no, that's not it. Then suddenly I realized what the tears were—they were deep tears of Love that flowed into feelings of Love for God. I hesitate to use that word, because I know some people have a difficult time believing in God, especially a personal God. Yet as I remember all the miracles that I have experienced and that I've shared throughout this book, I feel grateful. These miracles are a blessing in my life, because these experiences allow me to rest in the faith of that inner knowing.

Another feeling began coming up during my meditation, and again I wasn't sure what was going on inside me. Using the "Checking-in" process, I realized that what I was feeling was awe at this journey of life, which is also the journey I guide my clients on and have shared with you in LASTING Transformation.

I laugh because I am also in awe that, after so many years (as you'll read in the next section), I have finally finished this book. Some things you just don't want to rush into! The process of writing this book has been the experience of a lifetime. It has touched my heart and soul in deeply meaningful and inspiring ways. My prayer is that this book has also touched your heart and soul. Through it, I know I've learned more of my life lessons and soul-wisdom, and I hope you have, too. Thank you, my fellow consciousness companions, for joining me on this sacred journey.

The Inspiration for This Book
and an Inspiration for Our Lives

As a psychologist, I've had the privilege of helping clients learn their life lessons, feel empowered as they learn to communicate more effectively with others, and learn their soul-wisdom as they connect and communicate with the Source, Higher Power, or whatever they think of as God. Repeatedly, my clients would ask me to write a book. Knowing what a difference learning to express my feelings and "talking my own truth" has made in my life and in the lives of my clients convinced me that this book could indeed be a gift to others.

Then something transformative happened that gave me the TLS (tender loving shove) to actually begin writing this book. My mom passed away in November 1990. In February 1991, one of my best friends, Marilyn, was getting married in Los Angeles. She told me about a clairaudient who lives in Los Angeles and who communicates with people who have passed over to the other side. I was skeptical and didn't call him until the night before I was about to fly out for the wedding. He normally has a three-month waiting list, yet he just happened to have a cancellation on the only day I could see him. Given my skepticism, I decided not to tell him anything about myself, so that I would be sure he wouldn't be guessing about me from "context" clues. These events took place right before Valentine's Day. The night before I left, I was staying at my sister and brother-in-law's house. I had gone to the health food store and bought my niece and nephew heart-shaped lollipops. Thinking they were chocolate, they bit into them excitedly— when to all of our surprise they said, "Yuck! These don't taste like chocolate." I realized that, of course, the lollipops weren't chocolate, they were from the health food store, so they must be carob. Well, the lollipops were thrown away, and I left for Los Angeles the next day.

Soon after arriving, I had my reading with the clairaudient. He proceeded to tell me many things that confirmed that he was getting information from my mother. Other souls were present to help her communicate, since this was a new and difficult process. They had to slow down their thought vibrations and communicate with feeling. He told me that my mother had died from congestive heart failure, and that she was no longer in pain. In fact, he said, she looked like she did when she was twenty. She could kick up her heels and dance, which she always loved to do when she was younger. He told me my father's name, and that my mom had been watching over him during his recent trip to Florida. He correctly told me that I had a brother and sister; where my mom grew up; and that my mom and the other souls who were with her were very proud of the work I did, helping to heal the "little kids" within my adult clients. Even though I never thought of my work as a psychologist in this way, that is exactly what I do.

*Then he started laughing and said, "I have no idea why she is telling me this, but maybe you'll understand. She just said, '**Carob is definitely no substitute for chocolate!**'"*

My mind was blown! How could he have known that? After I recuperated from the shock, I laughed, realizing that this comment was my mom's wonderful sense of humor. I felt my consciousness transformed in that moment. It confirmed something I thought had been a possibility: that the souls of our loved ones are still with us even after they pass away, and that my mom had, in fact, been watching over us, as I gave my niece and nephew their carob Valentine lollipops.

I feel like I was given this experience not only to be a comfort for me, but also over the years this experience has been a great source of comfort for my clients, family, and friends. The awareness that our loved ones are still watching over us has helped to ease the grief for many after they've lost a loved one.

This exchange gave even more credence to what the clairaudient proceeded to tell me next. My mother saw my name on the cover of a book. She even described the different chapters of the book, which were identical to the book I had envisioned for years. When I went back to listen to the tape recording from our session, everything was on the tape except for the part of the reading that was about the book. Instead, there was a blank section in the middle on the second side of the tape. My mom had given me the impetus, the TLS to write the book, and now it was up to me to make it my own creation.

As the writing of this book comes to an end, I feel grateful for this precious moment of completing this creation. I am sitting on my screened-in porch, listening to the chorus of birds in the trees surrounding my house in Annapolis, watching the bigger birds swooping on the air currents. I feel touched by nature, as I often do when I am in the palpable presence of the Sacred. Tears well up—tears of recognition. We are all God's creatures dancing on the air currents of our lives.

My prayer is that the magic of the communication with my mother and the transformation of consciousness that began this book have continued through your reading of LASTING Transformation *and into your life.*

Acknowledgments

This book is a community creation. Family, friends, clients, colleagues, and teachers were all so supportive and appeared at the most amazing moments to offer their editing expertise, wisdom, stories, and humor.

I am forever indebted to my teachers, mentors, and clients:

The most significant influence in both my personal and professional development has been Drs. Hal and Sidra Stone. You are extraordinary therapists, and consciousness guides, and an awesome inspiration for a loving relationship that is ever growing and deepening. I have learned so much from each of you about the dance of energy in life. I thank you from the bottom of all of my selves' hearts and the deepest level of our collective soul for the magnificent, magical mystery ride of consciousness that your creation, Voice Dialogue, adds so majestically to my life and to so many lives.

To my mentors and friends, whose deep and kind words of endorsement begin and end this book, thank you for your openhearted support of my work. Joan Borysenko, PhD; Rabbi David Cooper; Stan Grof, MD; Sam Keen; Christianne Northrup, MD; Sharon Salzberg; Sarah Yehudit Schneider; and Bernie Siegel, MD: What you have shared—the love and energy you have put out in your books and workshops—has helped transform our world. I feel honored and embraced by your words as I step out onto a path where you've gone before. Thanks for your inspirational paving of the way.

To all my teachers and rabbis: Sarah Yehudit Schneider, Rabbi David Shneyer, Rabbi Henry Glazer, Rabbala Liebe Hoffman, Rabbi Phil Pohl,

Rabbi Dovid from Israel, and Reb Tzipi Radonsky—your guidance, support, and wisdom in my life are a blessing.

To Swami Muktananda and Gurumayi Chidvilasananda for awakening me to the spiritual path and giving me the gift of my Inner Self.

To my wonderful clients over the years—for without you, this book would never have been written—thank you for sharing your lives with me and for trusting me. For all of you who have written about your experiences—each contributed your experience of awareness, truth, and behavioral change to this book—I am grateful for the sharing of your life lessons and soul-wisdom.

My professional team was wonderful. So many thanks to:

My professional editors: Diana Drew, senior editor with Stella Hart Editorial Services, who has carefully touched each word and concept and has been invaluable and available to answer all my questions willingly and tirelessly. Pythia Peay, who wrote a wonderful book called *Soul Sisters*— you are a soul sister; thanks for your editing expertise, which you did so lovingly and soulfully. Sheryl Sieracki, for your brilliant proofreading; it is clearly your right livelihood. Diana, Pythia, and Sheryl, your caring commitment to my writing this book is extraordinarily appreciated.

Darlene Swanson, for all your hours of consulting and invaluable guidance and information. Pam McNay, my creative assistant who has added much to the manuscript and to the running of my office.

Anne-Marie Esson, for illustrating the wonderful cartoons we created; your artistic experience and vision have been invaluable to this book. To my cartoon consultant, Herb Curkin, your heart and your humor are a joy to me and to so many.

My publishing team has been great: Gerry Shryock, Matt Lawrence, Jenn Handy, Kat Edmonds, Katie Schneider, Chandra Rose, Amanda Koumoutsos, and Lauren Allen. I want to acknowledge and offer deep gratitude to Anthony Schrock, Alan Bower, and Robin Lasek for promoting this book and making a difference in my life.

With excitement and special thanks to Peter Perdoue, Matthew Monroe, Reid Tracy and of course, Louise Hay, for choosing *LASTING Transformation* to launch Balboa Press, an innovative division of Hay House.

Thanks to Connie Reider, Tommy Price, Maarten Maarschalkerweerd, and Sheldon Green for your creative magic in my life.

This book is a family affair.

My deepest thanks to: My sister Diane Nemett—your continued commitment to be with me each step in the writing of this book and in my life is a blessing. Thank you for your guidance, support, wisdom, and love. Our relationship with each other and with Marc, who is such a good human being and a wonderfully supportive brother, is a gift I am grateful to Mom and Dad for every day.

My brother-in-law Barry, whose incredible artistic talent graces the cover and the inside of the book. Your vision and wise counsel have made such a difference in this book and in my life.

My niece Laini, for formatting the covers of this book. You add goodness and beauty to all you touch. Your artwork on the inside of the book, and your patience, professionalism, and detailed attention to the artistic design of the book cover are a heartfelt gift.

My nephew Adam, for creatively writing your awesome "out there" experience of the "in there" meditation program we shared. Thanks for having the courage to take the road less traveled. Thanks to you and Kate Lynn for the thoughtful gifts of my writing muse and tea, which got me through many long nights of writing.

The rest of my wonderful family—Joyce, Josh, Mandy, Sydney, Leah, Kate, Ella, Todd, Kristy, Aiden, Heather, Jason, Will, Evie, Marilyn, Jody, Larry, Mia, and Brooke, for your constant support and loving presence in my life.

Miriam, my friendsis, for your holy heart, your gift of wordsmithing, and the depth of your support and love.

My friends and colleagues gave so much to this creation:

Gilah Rosner, whom I am officially hereby naming as the midwife of *LASTING Transformation*, for all the hours we spent at the beach house and through the snowstorms, editing and creating clarity for the concepts I share here. Thanks for your partnering in the beach retreats, your amazing cooking, and your healing herbal remedies that kept me happy and healthy through the writing of this book. I so appreciate your caring heart and deep soul.

Ruth Berlin, for your friendship through the years and for your commitment to and valuable critiques of the manuscript. I am grateful for all we've shared—from our Siddha Yoga Meditation Center with Marilyn in San Francisco to InnerSource. Ira Rifkin, your feedback and your experience as an author have also been invaluable.

Marilyn, your friendship has made a major difference in my life. Thanks for introducing me to Brian, an amazing clairaudient, whose reading with my mom was the genesis for this book, and for introducing me to Hal and Sidra. What would Ruth and I do without our Treveni's memory?

Rona Warner, for the goodness of your heart to help me with whatever I needed, whether it was finding pages for quotes or your helpful editorial comments. Thanks for your heartwarming and soul-touching enthusiasm after reading the manuscript. Steve Warner, thanks for your caring, your wonderful soup, and Rona's and my weekend away.

Barbara Feuer, Marteen, Alex Rietveld, and Elsie for your friendship and all your love and support. Barb, thanks for your wonderful editing. Marteen, the subtitle of the book changed when you told me that men wouldn't buy a book with therapy in the title; what was I thinking? Alex, you are so perceptive and amazing—I love being your fairy godmother! Elsie is our poster-dog for the beach house!

Jane Myerow, your friendship, like your feedback, has been a constant source of unconditional love and wisdom. Your ability to speak truth, coupled with your delightful sense of humor, is a joy and an inspiration in my life.

Thanks to my wonderful InnerSource staff community for your continued support and encouragement, and for joining me on a journey of sharing an approach to health and healing that is integrated, creative, and collaborative: My committed and caring assistant director, Mary Strueber, LCPC; Mindy Allanson; Kim Dumbroski, LCSW; Sharon Riley Jawish; Jamie Lapin, CFP; Diane Nemett, PT, DO (MP); Howard Pressman, MD; Margery Silverton, LCSW-C; Jack Vaeth, MD; Alan Weiss, MD; and Mary Lee Zetter, LCSW-C.

Dale O'Brien, who since InnerSource's inception almost eighteen years ago, has been guiding me, my clients, my family members, and my friends in the timing and rightness of business decisions, relationship choices, and geographical appropriateness. Thanks, Dale, for astrologically reading the timing for my dad to give up smoking—he did, which made your reading brilliant. It probably gave us many more years with him.

Thanks to those who read all or parts of the manuscript: Spencer Adler, for your awesome encouragement over the years. I am so grateful for our similar way of seeing and sensing life, and your crazy sense of humor; Charna Rosenholtz, my Mussar buddy—let us continue exploring; your brilliance is dazzling. Francesca Giamo, I love sharing our spiritual insights; thanks for reading the galley. Debbie Kidwell and Laura Oliver, your contributions were invaluable. Helen Claire, Jan Earnest, Rose Glazer, Jim Mallon, Bev and Stan Martin, Betty O'Brien, Simcha Raphael, Camilla Schwarz, Lynn Schwartz, Jay Stearns, and Dorothy Whitaker for your caring input into the book. Essie Hull (aka Thelma—or were you Louise?), I treasure your friendship. Robert Heller for your deep heart and caring support over the years. Judy Billage, your sense of fun makes my life richer.

To all my Voice Dialogue colleagues and those on our Thursday Voice Dialogue Community calls, thanks for your input and support. Thanks to Ann Dobbertin, for your partnering on our Voice Dialogue retreats; Alice Simmonds for your heart and home; and Dorsey Cartwright and Donna Armstrong for your support and resources.

Thanks to our beach support staff, Kath Johnson, Laura and Rodney Hufford, and Laura Mestro, for making the beach house dream a reality, so we can have Tools for *LASTING Transformation* retreats there, and for Bob and Cathy Hodges and Jane Cluesman and your crew for keeping the beach house going so I could write this book.

Lastly, and mostly, to the Divine Source of All: Thank you for the depth to which you touch my heart and soul, and for all the miracles you have showed me in my life, some of which I have shared throughout these pages. May this book serve as your emissary—opening those who read it to an enlightening experience of the wisdom and love of their InnerSource and your Divine Oneness.

Credits:

Cover painting and Stage One artwork: Barry Nemett,
    Maryland Institute College of Art, Baltimore, MD
Cover design and Stage Two artwork: Laini Nemett,
    www.laininemett.com
Cover design and layout: Lauren Allen, Chandra Rose
Creative Consultants: Pamela McNay, www.bigblueheaven.com;
    Alan Bower, abower@authorsolutions.com
Design Consultants: Jenn Handy, Amanda Koumoutsos
Design of interior layout: Katie Schneider, Robin Lasek
Editors: Diana Drew, graydrew18@aol.com, www.stellahart.com;
    Pythia Peay, pythiapeay@gmail.com, www.pythiapeay.com;
    Sheryl Sieracki, sherylsieracki@gmail.com
Illustration cartoons by Anne-Marie Esson,
    www.annemarieesson.com
Photograph by Connie Reider, connie@conniereider.com,
    www.conniereider.com
Stylist: Tommy Price, tommy.rma_macys@yahoo.com
Timing Specialist: Dale O'Brien, docchiron@yahoo.com,
    www.docchiron.com

Bibliography and Resources

Aron, Elaine N. *The Highly Sensitive Person: How to Thrive When the World Overwhelms You*. Bridgewater: Replica Books, 1999.

Assagioli, Roberto. *The Act of Will: A Guide to Self-Actualization & Self-Realization*. Wellingborough: Aquarian Press, 1994.

———. *Psychosynthesis: A Collection of Basic Writings*. Amherst: Synthesis Center, 2000.

Barks, Coleman. *Rumi: The Book of Love: Poems of Ecstasy and Longing*. San Francisco: Harper One, 2003.

Blank, William. *Torah, Tarot, and Tantra: A Guide to Jewish Spiritual Growth*. Ft. Collins: Sigo Press, 1991.

Borysenko, Joan Z. *Inner Peace for Busy People*. Carlsbad: Hay House, Inc., 2001.

———. *It's Not the End of the World: Developing Resilience in Times of Change*. Carlsbad: Hay House, Inc., 2009.

Borysenko, Joan Z., and Gordon Dveirin. *Your Soul's Compass: What is Spiritual Guidance?* Carlsbad: Hay House, Inc., 2008.

Bradshaw, John. *Homecoming: Reclaiming and Championing Your Inner Child*. New York: Bantam, 1992.

Calaprice, Alice, ed. *The New Quotable Einstein*. Princeton University Press, 2005.

Carlson, Richard, and Benjamin Shield, eds. *Handbook for the Soul*. New York: Little Brown and Company, 1995.

Castle, Miriam Millhauser. *The Breath and Body of Inner Torah*. Southfield, Targum Press, 2009.

———. *Inner Torah: Where Consciousness and Kedushah Meet*. Southfield: Targum Press, 2004.

————. *Practical Inner Torah: A Guide to Going Within*. Southfield: Targum Press, 2007.

Caussade, Jean-Pierre de. *Abandonment to Divine Providence: Classic Wisdom from the Past on Living Fully in the Present*. Translated by John Beevers. New York: Doubleday, 1975.

Chödrön, Pema. *Noble Heart*. Audiobook CD. Boulder: Sounds True, Inc., 2004.

————. *The Places That Scare You: A Guide to Fearlessness in Difficult Times*. Boston: Shambhala Publications, Inc., 2001.

Chopra, Deepak. *The Seven Spiritual Laws of Success: A Practical Guide to the Fulfillment of Your Dreams*. Novato: New World Library, 1994.

Clinebell, Howard. *Ecotherapy: Healing Ourselves, Healing the Earth*. New York: Routledge, 1996.

Cooper, Rabbi David A. *Ecstatic Kabbalah*. Audiobook CD. Boulder: Sounds True, Inc., 2005.

————. *God Is a Verb: Kabbalah and the Practice of Mystical Judaism*. New York: Riverhead Books, 1997.

————. *Renewing Your Soul: A Guided Retreat for the Sabbath and Other Days of Rest*. New York: Harper Collins, 1995.

De Pree, Max. *Leadership Is an Art*. New York: Broadway Business, 2004.

Estes, Clarissa Pinkola. *Women Who Run with the Wolves*. New York: Ballantine Books, 1996.

Fadiman, James, and Robert Frager. *Essential Sufism*. New York: Harper One, 1999.

Frankl, Victor E. *Man's Search for Meaning: An Introduction to Logotherapy*. New York: Washington Square Press. 1996.

Glazer, Rabbi Henry. *I Thank Therefore I Am: Gateways to Gratefulness*. Bloomington: Xlibris Corp., 2008.

Goldberg, Philip. *The Intuitive Edge: Understanding Intuition and Applying It in Everyday Life*. Los Angeles: Jeremy P. Tarcher, Inc., 1983.

Gray, John. *Men Are from Mars, Women Are from Venus: The Classic Guide to Understanding the Opposite Sex*. San Francisco: Harper Collins, 1992.

Green, Rabbi Arthur. "Tikkun 'Olam." In *The Jewish Lights Spirituality Handbook: A Guide to Understanding, Exploring and Living a Spiritual Life*, edited by Stuart Matlins. Woodstock: Jewish Lights Publishing, 2001.

Grof, Stanislav. *The Cosmic Game: Explorations of the Frontiers of Human Consciousness*. Albany: State University of New York Press, 1998.

———. *Psychology of the Future: Lessons from Modern Consciousness Research*. Albany: State University of New York Press, 2000.

Hartranft, Chip. *The Yoga-Sutra of Patanjali: A New Translation with Commentary*. Boston: Shambala, 2003.

Hicks, Esther, and Jerry Hicks. *Ask and It Is Given: Learning to Manifest Your Desires*. Carlsbad: Hay House, Inc., 2004.

InnerSource, Inc., A Center for Psychotherapy and Healing, Annapolis, MD. For a referral to an InnerSource practitioner or a listing of *LASTING Transformation* workshops, please contact Abby Rosen at 410-269-6298, ext. 1. For a description of InnerSource practitioners and services, go to www.innersource-inc.com.

Kaplan, Aryeh. *Meditation and Kabbalah*. Lanham: Jason Aronson, 1995.

Keen, Sam. *Fire in the Belly: On Being a Man*. New York: Bantam, 1991.

———. *In the Absence of God: Dwelling in the Presence of the Sacred*. New York: Harmony Books, 2010.

Kidwell, Debbie. "Building Bridges and the Process of Counseling." Debbie Kidwell Counseling Services. www.debbiekidwelltherapy.net.

Kornfield, Jack. *After the Ecstasy, the Laundry: How the Heart Grows Wise on the Spiritual Path*. New York: Bantam Books, 2000.

Kübler-Ross, Elisabeth. *On Death and Dying*. New York: Scribner, 1969.

Luzzatto, Rabbi Moshe Chaim. *The Knowing Heart: Da'ath Tevunoth*. Translated by Rabbi Shraga Silverstein. Jerusalem: Feldheim Publishers, 2003.

Maslow, Abraham. *Motivation and Personality*. San Francisco: Harper Collins, 1987.

Matt, Daniel Chanan, ed. *Zohar: Annotated & Explained*. Woodstock: Skylight Illuminations, 2005.

Morinis, Alan. *Everyday Holiness: The Jewish Spiritual Path of Mussar*. Boston: Trumpeter, 2008.

Muktananda, Swami. *Light on the Path*. South Fallsburg: SYDA Foundation, 1994.

———. *Mystery of the Mind*. South Fallsburg: SYDA Foundation, 1992.

———. *Play of Consciousness*. South Fallsburg: SYDA Foundation, 1994.

Northrup, Christiane. *Mother-Daughter Wisdom: Understanding the Crucial Link Between Mothers, Daughters, and Health*. New York: Bantam Dell, 2006.

――――. *The Wisdom of Menopause: Creating Physical and Emotional Health and Healing During the Change*. New York: Bantam, 2006.

――――. *Women's Bodies, Women's Wisdom (Revised Edition): Creating Physical and Emotional Health and Healing*. New York: Bantam, 2010.

O'Brien, Dale. Soul-Centered Astrology and Dream Tending for Living Ethically and Practically in the Here and Now. www.docchiron.com, docchiron@yahoo.com, 541-485-9772.

Oliver, Laura. Quantum Happiness Workshops. www.thestorywithin.net.

Pearson, E. Norman. *Space, Time and Self: Three Mysteries of the Universe*. Wheaton: Quest Books, 1990.

Ram Dass. *Be Here Now*. San Cristobal: Lama Foundation, 1971.

――――. *Journey of Awakening: A Meditator's Guidebook*. New York: Bantam, 1990.

Ram Dass and Stephen Levine. *Grist for the Mill: The Mellow Drama, Dying: An Opportunity for Awakening, Freeing the Mind, Karmuppance, God & Beyond*. Berkeley: Celestial Arts, 1995.

Richardson, Cheryl. *Take Time for Your Life*. New York: Broadway Books, 1999.

Robbins, James M. "The Costs of Rising Divorce Rates Across the US," Ezine Articles, www.ezinearticles.com.

Salzberg, Sharon. *Faith: Trusting Your Own Deepest Experience*. New York: Riverhead Trade, 2003.

――――. *The Kindness Handbook: A Practical Companion*. Boulder: Sounds True, Inc., 2008.

Salzberg, Sharon, and Mirabai Bush. *Voices of Insight*. Boston: Shambhala Publications, 2001.

Schneider, Sarah Yehudit. *Kabbalistic Writings on the Nature of Masculine and Feminine*. Jerusalem: A Still Small Voice, 2003. First published 2000 by Jason Aronson, Inc.

――――. *You Are What You Hate: A Spiritually Productive Approach to Enemies*. Jerusalem: A Still Small Voice, 2009.

Sarah Yehudit Schneider's books and correspondence course are available at www.astillsmallvoice.org.

Schutz, Susan Polis, ed. *The Language of Love*. Boulder: Blue Mountain Press, 1999.

Siegel, Bernie S. *Love, Magic and Mudpies: Raising Your Kids to Feel Loved, Be Kind, and Make a Difference.* New York: Rodale Press, 2006.

————. *Love, Medicine and Miracles: Lessons Learned About Self-Healing from a Surgeon's Experience with Exceptional Patients.* New York: Harper & Row, 1990.

————. *101 Exercises for the Soul: Divine Workout Plan for Body, Mind, and Spirit.* Novato: New World Library, 2005.

————. *Prescriptions for Living: Inspirational Lessons for a Joyful, Loving Life.* New York: HarperPerennial, 1999.

————. *365 Prescriptions for the Soul: Daily Messages of Inspiration, Hope and Love.* Novato: New World Library, 2003.

Singer, Michael A. *The Untethered Soul: The Journey Beyond Yourself.* Oakland: New Harbinger Publications, Inc., 2007.

Stone, Douglas, Bruce Patton, and Sheila Heen. *Difficult Conversations: How to Discuss What Matters Most.* New York: Penguin, 1999.

Stone, Hal. *Embracing Heaven and Earth.* Albion: Delos, 1985.

Stone, Hal, and Sidra Stone. "The Basic Elements of Voice Dialogue, Relationship, and the Psychology of Selves: Their Origins and Development." Voice Dialogue International, www.voicedialogue.org/reading-stone.htm.

————. *Embracing Each Other: Relationship as Teacher, Healer & Guide.* Mill Valley: New World Library, Nataraj, 1989.

————. *Embracing Our Selves: The Voice Dialogue Training Manual.* Mill Valley: New World Library, Nataraj, 1998.

————. *Embracing Your Inner Critic: Turning Self-Criticism into a Creative Asset.* San Francisco: Harper One, 1993.

————. *Partnering: A New Kind of Relationship.* Mill Valley: New World Library, Nataraj, 2000.

————. *Accessing the Spiritual Dimension*, CD.

————. *Aware Ego*, five-CD set.

————. *An Introduction to Voice Dialogue and the Psychology of Selves*, two-CD set.

————. *Making Relationships Work for You*, two-CD set.

————. *The Psychology of the Transference*, two-CD set.

Stone, Sidra. *The Shadow King: The Invisible Force That Holds Women Back.* Albion: iUniverse, 2000.

All books, videos, CDs, and a broad array of downloadable reading material by Drs. Hal and Sidra Stone are available at www.voicedialogue.org.

Also at this website is a list of Voice Dialogue Facilitators. Click on Global Resources for the resource directory.

Strueber, Mary. "The Highly Sensitive Person," InnerSource, Inc., A Center for Psychotherapy and Healing, www.innersource-inc.com. See Library for link to online HSP self-test. Mary specializes in working with the Highly Sensitive Person. Contact her at 410-269-6298, ext. 5.

Taimni, I. K. *The Science of Yoga: The Yoga-Sutras of Patanjali in Sanskrit*. Wheaton: Quest Books, 1999.

Tolle, Eckhart. *The Power of Now: A Guide to Spiritual Enlightenment*. Novato: New World Library, 1999.

Trout, Susan S. *Born to Serve: The Evolution of the Soul Through Service*. Alexandria, Va.: Three Roses Press, 1997.

Vahia, N. S. "Psychophysiological Therapy Based on the Concepts of Patanjali," American Journal of Psychotherapy 27, 557-565, 1973.

Vaughan, Frances E. *Awakening Intuition*. Harpswell: Anchor, 1978.

Weisman, Arinna, and Jean Smith. *The Beginner's Guide to Insight Meditation*. Hollingbourne, Kent: Bell Tower, 2001.

Whitfield, Charles L. *Healing The Child Within: Discovery and Recovery for Adult Children of Dysfunctional Families*. Deerfield Beach: Health Communications, Inc., 1987.

Zukav, Gary. *The Seat of the Soul*. New York: Free Press, 1990.

———. *Soul to Soul: Communications from the Heart*. New York: Free Press, 2008.

Glossary

Authentic Self: The true "Self" that exists at the core of our being that seeks expression, independent of our job, function and roles.

Aware Ego Process: The executive function of the personality, and it grows stronger each time we become aware of a self, choose to separate from that self, embrace its opposite, and make the decision that is in the best interest of the whole person. Developing an aware ego is the most important goal of Voice Dialogue. As we move forward in the consciousness process, the ego separates out from these selves and becomes a more aware ego, which allows us to make more conscious choices.*†

Awareness: A state from which we witness the "selves" without feelings or attachment to the outcome. Through awareness, we can consciously choose alternative options, creating more wholeness.*

Bonding Pattern: The re-creation in a current relationship of either positive or negative psychological or emotional interactions that we experienced in our childhood. This term is used to describe the type of feelings and emotion, that either connect or repel us in any relationship.*

The Caretaker: Usually a primary self who constantly takes care of others in our relationships because the Caretaker was role-modeled by a parental figure, or in order to gain acceptance and love.*

Conscious Communication: Involves a two-step process: (1) Become aware of the subpersonalities that are involved, and the feelings and needs of the Inner Child. and (2) Express this awareness effectively. When we use our Aware Ego to make informed choices, the mind quiets and the next level of communication incorporates the wisdom and guidance from the intuition and the Inner Self.

Conscious Relationship: Connecting with another authentically without fear of expressing our vulnerability. In a conscious relationship, there is a commitment to support the other person's personal and spiritual growth.

The Controller: Usually a primary self where the focus is to protect ourself by controlling others in the relationship through any and all means. The Master Controller says, "When it is done my way, then everything usually works out well."*

Core Sensitivity: Our essential true being, also known as the vulnerable Inner Child that resides at the center of the personality.

Cover-up: The process of covering over and negating how, at our most essential level, we are vulnerable.

Defense Mechanism: A negative pattern of behavior intended to protect against emotional distress, destructive impulses, or a threat to our self-esteem, especially by the suppression of unwanted thoughts or memories. Also referred to as a primary self, a subpersonality, or a protective mechanism.

Dialoguing: The process of talking to a self or subpersonality with the aid of a facilitator or by self-facilitating.*

Disowned Self: A part of the personality created either by experiencing or observing a behavior in our role models (most often our parents) that we were hurt by, frightened by, didn't like, or never learned. A disowned self can be created when we were criticized for exhibiting certain behaviors.

Ego: In Voice Dialogue, a combination of our operating ego and an ever-expanding Aware Ego Process.*

Energetic Linkage: A subtle, nonverbal connection that occurs within and between people, animals, places, and things. When we are conscious of our energies and how we are connecting or disconnecting, we have the ability to create relationships with ourself and others that are more harmonious and deeply intimate. When energetic linkage is lacking, relationships feel very lonely.

Faith: A belief in, devotion to, or trust in somebody or something, without logical proof.

Higher Self: The higher being that exists beyond the personality in the Transpersonal Realm of Consciousness. A bubbling fountain or "inner source" of love, wisdom, joy, peace, and strength that is within everyone. Also referred to as Inner Self.

Higher Spiritual Plane: The realm of existence beyond the personality. Also referred to as the Transpersonal Realm.

"I" Statements: A communication skill essential for using the Formula for Conscious Communication, in which we take responsibility for our experience by expressing our feelings, using sentences starting with "I feel."

Impersonal Energy: A cooler, more self-contained way of being that helps create healthy boundaries when needed.

Inner Child: Our essential true Self, which resides at the center of our personality. We have a number of inner children who play important parts in our lives, like the vulnerable Inner Child. The Vulnerable Inner Child is the focus of this book, as it is the key to our self-esteem, to intimacy, and to our intuition.

Inner Critic: A primary self, which criticizes the individual often because of feelings of anxiety. By constantly pointing out personal inadequacies, the Inner Critic tries to get us to change our behavior before other people criticize us. The rationale for this behavior by the Inner Critic is to motivate and protect us. Inner Critic messages include: "What a stupid thing to say! You are getting fat! You are too skinny. What is wrong with you? When will you ever learn?"

Inner Nurturing Parent: The caring, loving subpersonality that can take care of the vulnerable Inner Child.

Inner Self: The inner being that exists beyond the personality in the Transpersonal Realm of Consciousness. It is the radiant center of our being. A bubbling fountain or "inner source" of love, wisdom, joy, peace, and strength that is within everyone. Also referred to as Higher Self.

Intuition: Derived from the Latin word *intueri,* which means "to see within." It is the act or faculty of knowing directly without the use of rational processes that can be heard when the mind gets quiet. Also referred to as the still, small voice within.

Intuitive Channel: Connects the personality/ego/small self to the Higher Spiritual planes. Also referred to as the Inner Self, the Higher Self, Consciousness, or the Transpersonal Realm.

The Judge: The subpersonality that judges things and others that are strange, different, uncontrollable, or feared. We push away from them by judging.*

Life Lesson: The internalization of the deeper meaning of a life experience so that the experience has a profound effect, changing our consciousness and our behavior, and eventually transforming our life.

Meditation: A method for quieting the mind, and turning our attention from an outer focus to an inner awareness, opening ourselves to an experience of the spiritual realms of consciousness.

Middot: A Hebrew word for soul-traits, which we can refine through spiritual and ethical practices.

Mindful Awareness: The process of staying in the present, without becoming distracted; a state in which we are focused and fully conscious of the flow of the thoughts of the mind and the senses of the body.

Mussar: A body of ethical teachings from the Jewish tradition that guides people to examine their soul-traits or character traits and maps out a daily practice whose purpose is to build character and create possibilities for transformation. *Mussar* means "correction" or "instruction."

Negative Bonding Pattern: A relationship where the parent-child interaction of the two people has turned from positive to negative. Once it has turned negative, the two people are unable to nurture each other.*

Operating Ego: The combination or team of primary selves we think of as "I" or "me" as we live our life. It is how we operate as an individual in the world. This system consists of the primary selves (e.g., the Inner Critic, the Pusher, the Perfectionist).

Operating Selves: Usually how we identify ourselves as an individual, or how we would like to be seen by others.*

The Perfectionist: A primary self that is seeking approval and constantly strives for great and better results for any and all achievements. Usually the perfectionist self is a team member within a system of primary selves, such as the Inner Critic, the Judge, the Pusher, etc.*

Personality: A team of "selves" or subpersonalities that emerge to help us live our lives.* Also referred to as ego or self.

The Pleaser: A primary self that is seeking to gain approval, acceptance and love by meeting the needs and wants of others.*

Positive Bonding Pattern: In positive bonding patterns, each person meets the other person's needs. However, there is no room for conflict, growth, or change.*

Primary Self/Selves: The name that we give to the primary pattern of behavior, thought and emotional response that we are identified with at a particular time in our life. Examples are the Nice Guy, the Hard Worker, the Pusher, the Pleaser, the Caretaker, the Provider, the Rational Self, the Perfectionist, the Judge, the Critic, and the Responsible Father or Mother.* Also referred to as a defense mechanism or a subpersonality.

Projection: The unconscious transfer of our own impressions or feelings onto external objects or persons, for example, being frightened or disgusted by another person's anger when we have not acknowledged or recognized the angry part in ourself.*

The Protector: A self whose behaviors, thoughts, and emotions strive to protect us from anything negative.*

The Psychology of Selves: The entire theoretical framework for the Voice Dialogue Method. It includes the Aware Ego process, bonding patterns in relationships, the Consciousness model, the role of the primary selves, the role of the disowned selves, the role of judgment, and the role of the core or underlying vulnerability. Each self or subpersonality is addressed with full recognition of both its individual importance and its role as only a part of the total personality.†

Pusher: The subpersonality whose job is to gain approval for what we accomplish. It keeps us learning, striving, and achieving. The Pusher is the one that makes up the to-do lists, tries to get all the jobs done, and never lets us rest, as there is always more to do.

Responsible Self: A primary self that is linked energetically to the survival and growth of the individual's family, group, community, society, etc.*

Right Livelihood: A Buddhist term that means we are doing in the world what we are meant to do, what comes naturally to us, what we love to do, and we are making a living doing it.

Rulemaker: The first self that develops. The Rulemaker's job is to figure out, early in life, what the rules are in our particular family and/or environment to ensure the survival of the vulnerable little child.

Self/Selves: Each self is like a person who lives within our psyche and has its own perceptions, energy, beliefs, values, worldview, expressiveness, behaviors, and voice.*

Shadow: Hidden or unconscious aspects of ourself, both good and bad, which the ego has repressed or never realized. Also referred to as our disowned selves.

Soul: The part of one's being that is thought to exist within, yet separate from the body. Its nature is expansive, as it resonates with something greater. In most religious traditions, the soul is thought to be part of the Divine. Our Soul is an active force that directs our life.

Soul Hole: A wounded sense of self that occurs when childhood needs are not met at specific developmental stages.

Soul-trait: A character trait that we have developed, which is part of our spiritual curriculum that we want to correct or transform through the practice of Mussar. Also referred to as middah (singular) or middot (plural).

Soul-Wisdom: A deep knowing in the center of our being that develops from experiencing the transformational journey.

Source: Higher Power, God, Love, or whatever we feel comfortable calling this Force that is greater than we are.

Subpersonalities: The selves or parts that make up the ego or the personality. A subpersonality can be either a primary self or a disowned self.† Also referred to as self and primary self.

Teshuva: literally as "return," as in return to the Source. By practicing *teshuva*, we align with our Highest Self.

Tikkun 'Olam: A Hebrew term for healing or repairing the world by making it a better place.

Transformation: A process that results in positive, powerful change, which is irreversible.

Transpersonal: A term coined by Abraham Maslow, PhD, and Stanislav Grof, MD, which describes the capacity of a human being to transcend the personality and experience higher planes of consciousness beyond the personality.

Transpersonal Psychology: The psychological modality that goes beyond traditional and humanistic psychology and incorporates the spiritual dimension of personal growth. This alignment of the mind, body, and spirit creates a sense of wholeness that can result in lasting transformation.

Transpersonal Realm: The Higher Spiritual Planes of Consciousness where intuitions, inspirations, creations of genius, and impulses to humanitarian and heroic action occur.

Triggers: An experience that affects us negatively or positively. This experience can either be hidden, (that is, repressed or denied) or acknowledged by us. Example of a positive trigger: When I see a beautiful sunset, I feel calm and serene. Example of a negative trigger: When I hear anger, I start to feel sick to my stomach.*

Truthsayer: A subpersonality that can stand in front of the Inner Child and share the feelings of vulnerability or any "truths" from a place of strength.

Voice Dialogue, Relationship, and the Psychology of Selves: Drs. Hal and Sidra Stone's psycho-spiritual approach to consciousness. It is the basic method (along with dreams and daydreams) for entering into direct communication with our inner family of selves. Each self or subpersonality is addressed with full recognition of both its individual importance and its role as only a part of the total personality. The goal of Voice Dialogue is to move us toward an Aware Ego process.†

Vulnerability: The ability to physically or emotionally feel all emotions; being available and open to life's experiences.*

Vulnerable Inner Child: The core sensitivity that resides at the center of the personality. It is the key to our self-esteem, to intimacy, and to our intuition.*

Wise Being: The voice of our intuition; the still, small voice within. This is connected to the higher spiritual planes of consciousness, which are home to the soul.

Yoga Sutras: Part of Hindu scripture. The Yoga Sutras include aphorisms composed by Patanjali to explain the purpose of yoga, which is to turn our attention inward.

Zohar: the central work in the literature of Jewish mystical thought known as Kabbalah. It is a group of books including commentary on the mystical aspects of the Torah (the five books of Moses). It is said to have been written by Rabbi Shimon Bar Yochai, yet some ascribe its authorship to a Kabbalist named Rabbi Moses de Leon. The message of the *Zohar* is to seek spiritual truth. It is a practical guide to inner actions that one performs in order to discover deeper states of perception and sensation.

These definitions are from:

* Donna Armstrong, Armstrongs' Counselling Services, Edmonton, AB
www.voicedialogueedmonton.com, 780-444-4399,
dmarm@telusplanet.net

† The Voice Dialogue books by Drs. Hal & Sidra Stone (see Bibliography)

Appendix A

Voice Dialogue: Discovering Our Selves
by Hal Stone, PhD, and Sidra Stone, PhD

From Gary Zukav's website when Hal & Sidra Stone were his guests, 2001. This can be found at www.voicedialogue.org and is reprinted here with permission.

We each knew all the answers to most of life's questions when we met over thirty years ago. They were often opposite answers, but we were in love and this didn't seem to be a problem. Instead, we were fascinated by our differences, and, as two seasoned, mature clinical psychologists, we were curious to explore them.

As a matter of fact, we were so in love that we wanted to know everything that we could about one another. So it was that we talked about our lives, our feelings, our dreams and our imaginings. We meditated and prayed together. It was a truly profound interaction, but there were no real surprises. We each still knew what we knew, we still did not know what we did not know, and we did not move very far beyond those boundaries.

And then one day we discovered our "selves." We had been talking about vulnerability and Hal suggested that I (Sidra) move over to another part of the room and become the vulnerable child instead of talking about it. I trusted Hal and so I left the couch I'd been sitting on, sat on the floor next to the coffee table, put my head down on it and suddenly everything changed. I became absolutely quiet and experienced the world around me differently. Sounds, colors and feelings were more intense than before.

The sophisticated, rational, articulate woman with all the answers was gone and in her place was a very young child. I was extremely quiet and very sensitive to everything in my surroundings. I responded to energies rather than thoughts. I felt things I had not felt in decades, and knew things that were not known by my everyday mind. I knew, without question, the realities of my soul. After about an hour, Hal asked me to move to my original seat on the couch and I returned to my previous way of being in the world ... but my little girl was still with me and I would never lose her completely again.

This experience was a surprise to both of us! I (Hal) knew that something extremely important had just happened, that we had moved into another dimension of consciousness. I had played with talking to parts, but they were never real to me. Now they were real people. This was indeed a little girl - it wasn't a concept or a complex; she was a real person with rules of behavior, feelings, perceptions, reactions, and a history of her own.

This was the beginning of Voice Dialogue, or the dialogue with the family of selves that lives within each of us. It was conceived out of a genuine curiosity about another human being and was born in love. Embracing Our Selves: The Voice Dialogue Manual gives the details on how Voice Dialogue works.

We were very excited about our discovery. We saw that our psyches were not unitary but, instead, were made up of many selves and we set out on what has proven to be an unending journey. We went on to explore a vast multitude of selves. We spoke with pushers and critics and pleasers and perfectionists. And we spoke with beach bums, slackers, and manipulators. We spoke with feeling selves and unfeeling selves, with vulnerable, playful and magical children. We spoke with heroes and villains, matriarchs and patriarchs. We spoke with visionaries and cynics. The range of selves is amazing; it seems to be limitless.

We spoke to our "primary selves" which were very well developed. They ran our lives or, as we liked to put it, they drove our psychological cars. They were the ones that made up our personalities; the selves that "knew all the answers" when we first met. Then we went on to learn about our "disowned selves." For each primary self there were opposite disowned selves that were buried or repressed so that the primaries could keep control of our lives.

The primary selves were familiar and we were comfortable with them. It was easy to get them to talk and to tell us how cleverly and successfully they ran our lives. The disowned selves were unfamiliar and threatening to our primary selves. Each primary self felt that the disowned self on the other side was a potential destroyer of our wellbeing. For instance: "What happens if you really let go and learned to 'be' instead of 'do?' You might never want to work again!" would be the Pusher's concern.

When we talked with these disowned selves we felt as though we were living in a house with endless doors waiting to be opened with new rooms to explore. These selves carried new ways of looking at the world, new information, and creative solutions to old problems.

Then there were the areas in which one of us had a primary self that was the disowned self of the other. For example, Sidra had a strong "What will people think?" self while Hal's was the opposite: "I do what is right for me." Hal had a deeply spiritual self while Sidra's was more pragmatic. Hal was the Introvert while Sidra was the Extrovert. Sidra had a Financial Conservative while Hal had a Financial Liberal. Hal was a fearless explorer of the world within and Sidra was a fearless explorer of the world outside. And so it went.

These opposite primary selves presented a challenge. They added a new dimension to our relationship: judgment. Each of these disowned selves was one of God's little heat-seeking missiles that impacted us where it hurt the most. In our relationship! When we examined this phenomenon, we discovered that our judgments were not bad, they were simply signs that we had something to learn. Each time one of us judged the other, we were facing a disowned self.

In the past we had tried hard to avoid judging others. We felt that we were too mature and spiritually evolved for this. Now we learned to use our judgments. Each time we felt a judgment, it gave us the picture of a disowned self that needed integration. So we looked at the judgment, clarified it, and found the disowned self. For instance, Sidra might have judged Hal to be too free with money. We would look at this, determine that her primary self was a financial conservative and then work with the opposites of big spender and financial conservative in her.

We went on to discover how these selves interact in relationships. Relationships, we discovered, are the interactions of not just two people, but two groups of selves. These interactions follow simple predictable patterns. To move beyond the automatic, unconscious relating of these selves, we entered a new area of exploration and understanding.

As a way of learning about ourselves and others, Voice Dialogue is completely accepting and non-judgmental. It simply looks at what is. Some have called it a Western meditation because, as each self is explored, an awareness of that self develops. This awareness is separate from the self and acts as a witness. It carries with it a memory and an ability to recognize this self as it operates in our lives.

But that is not all that happens. Yes, it is important to have a witness that is aware of a self, but a witness just witnesses. We live in the world, however, not in an ashram. Who lives life? We saw that after we had separated from one of our primary selves, there was a qualitative change in the way we lived our lives.

In the deepest spiritual sense, we were separating from who we thought we were and allowing a new process to emerge. We named it an Aware Ego.

Voice Dialogue is about separating from the many selves that make up the human psyche and creating this Aware Ego. We do not discard anything. We embrace the selves that are already ours and we add to them those we have disowned. It is as though we were living in ancient Greece and worshipping at the shrines of all the gods and goddesses. We can have our favorites, but we take care not to neglect any of the others.

And as we embrace all that we are, we naturally become more fully human and more compassionate. We don't have to learn compassion, it just appears. After all, everything out there is within each of us.

We feel that the Aware Ego is an evolutionary step forward. This Aware Ego blends awareness with an experience of selves. It moves beyond duality by carrying the tension of opposites and, because it does so, it allows us real choices in life. It enables us to follow—safely—our unique paths.

As someone wrote to us recently: "There is something built into the method you have seeded which reminds me of a desert proverb: 'Listen to the path ... it is wiser than he who travels it'."

Delos, Inc., PO Box 604, Albion, CA 95410
Phone: (707) 937-2424 Fax: (707) 937-4119 www.VoiceDialogue.org

Appendix B

List of Subpersonalities or Selves

<u>Heavyweights</u>

Inner Critic
Judge
Perfectionist
Pleaser
Pusher

Achiever
Analytical
Assertive
Caretaker
Competent
Conformist
Controller
Daughter/Son
Disorganized
Doesn't Share Feelings
Dominating
Ethical
Flirt
Giver

Good Daughter/Son
Good Girl/Boy
Hippie
Hoarder
Hopeless
Independent
In Charge
Incompetent
Laid Back
Loner
Mother/Father
Needs to Know
Needy
Opinionated
Ordinary
Organized
Overachiever
Party Person
Patriarch
Procrastinator

Professional
Proper
Rager
Responsible
Rulemaker
Self-Centered
Sexual
Shy
Sloppy
Slow
Social Butterfly
Special
Take Control
Victim
Wall
Warrior
Wife/Husband
Wishy-Washy
Withdrawn

Appendix C

Guided Visualization to Communicate with Your Inner Child

We are going to do a guided visualization exercise, which is a tool for using your imagination to help you go inward. I will be leading you down a stairway. It is important for you to remember that the stairway is a well-lit, non-threatening place to be. If you have a difficult time visualizing a scene, don't let that stop you. Just make up something and go on. You may want to record my instructions for this visualization, so that you can close your eyes.

For ease in reading, this visualization uses feminine language, referring to the Inner Child as "her" or "she". For men, please substitute the words "him" and "he.'"

Take a few deep breaths and close your eyes. Take another deep breath and as you exhale, breathe out any tension you are holding. Continue breathing deeply. With each exhalation you will feel yourself becoming more and more relaxed, exhaling all your tensions and concerns, relaxing your body and mind. Realize that for this moment you can be free of all that may be troubling you.

Imagine a room with a closet. Go over to the closet and notice that at the back of the closet there is a door. Open the door and see a well-lit stairway that is going down. Now imagine yourself walking down the stairway. With each step you leave behind all your worldly concerns, becoming free from distractions and obligations. The deeper you go, the more in touch you are with the calm, quiet peacefulness that lies within. Take your time as you climb down each step. Take a few deep breaths as you descend the stairs and repeat the word "relax" silently to yourself. With each step you take, you are feeling more and more deeply relaxed.

As you reach the bottom of the stairs, you see a beautiful, calm, flowing river in front with a small boat waiting for you by the shore. This is a magical boat, so even if you normally get seasick, with this boat you won't. Walk over to the boat and easily step inside. Take a moment to get comfortable. The boat gently pushes off from the shore. Feel the warm sun shining down on you and the waters of the river gently rocking you as you float down the river, feeling more and more calm and peaceful. The boat is carrying you to your private sanctuary. As you come upon this setting, which for you represents peacefulness, harmony, and well being, the boat comes up to the shore and you easily step out of the boat and onto the shore of your private sanctuary. You may find that you are alone in this wonderful place, or there may be someone else there to greet you.

Now move comfortably and easily into your sanctuary. Take a moment to explore your surroundings. Be aware of the movements, the warmth, and the sounds as you enjoy the peaceful harmony that makes this your private retreat. This is a place for reflection, for serenity, for connecting with your Inner Child.

Down a path in your sanctuary you see your Inner Child. Approach the child and see if she is willing to be with you. If the child can't talk, try to feel what she is feeling. You can do the "Checking-in" process by pulling down a menu of feelings and experiencing if any of these emotions feel right—sad, happy, anxious or scared, hurt, angry, restless, excited, or any other feelings that might come up. If the child can talk, you can ask her how she is and what she is feeling. Listen with great love and respect. When your Inner Child is finished talking, or when you've gotten a sense of what she is feeling, ask her what she needs from you. Talk with the child, and if she is feeling upset, comfort her. Ask what you can do to make her feel better. You may get a direct answer, or you may not at this time. If the child will let you, you may want to pick her up, hold her in your lap, or stroke her hair, doing what is needed to let her know you are there to protect her, take care of her, and nurture her. Take a deep breath and send a flow of unconditional loving energy toward the child. Let her know that you will be there and that she can count on you for love and understanding, no matter what. Tell the child that she is safe in your private sanctuary. Give your Inner Child the choice of coming back with you or staying in the sanctuary, where she can summon you whenever she needs you. If your child wants to come back with you, you can tuck her inside your heart where she will be safe and comfortable and where you can connect any time either of you wants to be together. If your child is

226

going to stay, agree on some kind of signal that will let you know that she needs your attention. Say good-bye for now. Begin to return to the shore where the boat is waiting for you. Know that as you leave this peaceful place, you can return at any time. You see the boat off in the distance and gently continue walking the path that brought you into your sanctuary. As you do, reflect on your experience of communicating with your Inner Child. As you approach the boat you easily climb in, and the boat gently and magically pushes off. Whether or not your child is with you, relax in the boat and allow the water to rock you into a peaceful calm with the sun warming your body.

Slowly, the boat carries you back up the river. If your child is with you, take some time to share with her what she will be experiencing, allowing some time for connecting, so your Inner Child feels safe and taken care of by you. Tell your Inner Child that she will always be safe inside your heart and you will periodically "check in" with her. If she needs you, tell her to just let you know and you will be there to take care of whatever she needs.

The boat returns you to the stairway that leads up to the closet and the room where you began this journey. Get out of the boat and effortlessly climb the stairway. Remain relaxed, calm, and peaceful. At the top of the stairs, open the door that leads through your closet and into the bedroom. Sit on the bed and reflect on what you experienced in your sanctuary. How does it feel for you to take better care of your Inner Child, to be the nurturing parent for your child, now that you're an adult?

In a moment, I am going to ask you to open your eyes. If you brought your Inner Child back with you, you can put your hand on your heart, letting her know you are here for her. If you Inner Child decided to remain in your private sanctuary, reassure her that you will return there to be with her. Now take a deep breath and begin to reorient yourself. Become alert, bring your energy back to this room, and slowly open your eyes.

Take a few minutes to be with your experience. You may have gotten some insights that you might want to write down. If you didn't, don't worry. Often you might get information in a dream or later in a flash of intuition, or the next day or week when you are least expecting it.

227

Appendix D

Inner Critic Self-Test

Please place a value of 0, 1, 3 or 5 next to each question.
0 = never; 1 = rarely; 3 = about average; 5 = frequently

___1. I think about what I should or shouldn't have said or done.

___2. I have insomnia.

___3. I use alcohol or non-prescription drugs to help me relax or calm down.

___4. I'm cautious about trying anything new because I'm afraid of looking foolish or failing.

___5. I worry about what other people think of me.

___6. I worry about what's going to happen in the future.

___7. I wake up at night thinking about things I have to do.

___8. For a significant part of the day, I feel a general sense of worry and stress about some area of my life.

___9. Whenever I do something, it has to be perfect, or close to perfect.

___10. When I read over something I've just written, I'm not satisfied with it.

___11. I get anxious and self-critical when things don't come out the way I think they should.

___12. When I take a test like this, I'm sure that I don't do as well as other people.

_____ 13. I think about the mistakes I've made.

_____ 14. I feel inadequate when I compare myself to others.

_____ 15. I hear inner critical messages, which make me feel bad about myself.

_____ 16. I wonder what people would think if they really knew me.

_____ 17. I question almost everything I do.

_____ 18. When I have to deal with situations in my life that call for decision making or communicating, I don't feel confident.

_____ 19. When I say "No" I feel guilty.

_____ 20. I tend to be critical or judgmental of others.

_____ 21. I think of myself as, or others have told me I am, controlling and domineering.

_____ 22. Sometimes I get irritable, critical of others, and/or self-critical when I feel anxious.

_____ 23. I feel like there's something basically wrong with me.

_____ 24. I feel like I don't have a right to exist.

_____ 25. I have an emotional wound so deep it can't be healed.

_____ 26. My anxiety tends to make me react negatively.

_____ 27. I think no matter what I do, things won't turn out right.

_____ 28. I push myself really hard to get things done.

_____ TOTAL

Interpretation

A sum from 0 – 20 indicates no inner critic. That is usually a good thing. However, it is possible that you might be unrealistic in your assessment, or you have learned to "mask" the symptoms commonly associated with an Inner Critic. No Inner Critic could indicate that you are not self-aware, or you are detached from yourself, others, or your environment.

A sum between 21 – 40 indicates a small Inner Critic.
A sum between 41 – 60 indicates a medium Inner Critic.
A sum between 61 – 80 indicates a big Inner Critic.
A sum bigger than 80 indicates a huge Inner Critic.

A big or huge Inner Critic may be indicative of a substantial amount of anxiety or unresolved emotional issues. You may want to consult a health professional for therapy, strategies and tools, supplements, psycho-herbology or psychotropic drugs for support in managing the anxiety and the Inner Critic in your life.

Adapted and expanded from *Embracing Your Inner Critic: Turning Self-Criticism into a Creative Asset* by Drs. Hal and Sidra Stone.

Appendix E

Primary and Disowned Selves

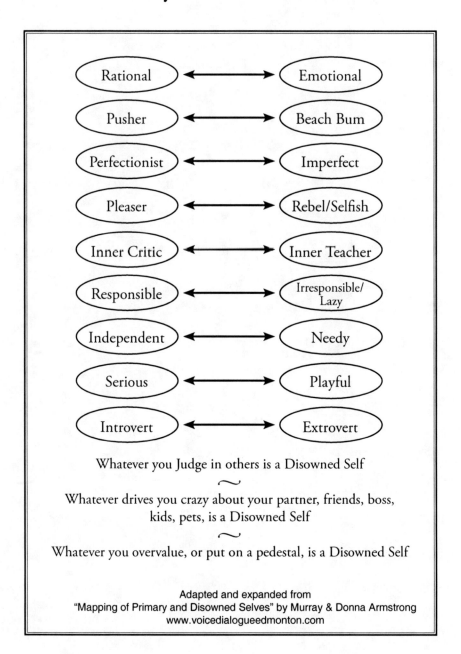

Rational ⟷ Emotional

Pusher ⟷ Beach Bum

Perfectionist ⟷ Imperfect

Pleaser ⟷ Rebel/Selfish

Inner Critic ⟷ Inner Teacher

Responsible ⟷ Irresponsible/Lazy

Independent ⟷ Needy

Serious ⟷ Playful

Introvert ⟷ Extrovert

Whatever you Judge in others is a Disowned Self

~

Whatever drives you crazy about your partner, friends, boss, kids, pets, is a Disowned Self

~

Whatever you overvalue, or put on a pedestal, is a Disowned Self

Adapted and expanded from
"Mapping of Primary and Disowned Selves" by Murray & Donna Armstrong
www.voicedialogueedmonton.com

Appendix F

Meditation Practices

Please read the "In Practice" Exercise for Chapter 9 on "Developing a Meditation Practice." It will help you prepare to try the following meditation practices.

Meditation Practice #1: Mantra Meditation

The word *mantra* is made up of two syllables. The first, *man*, means "to be aware"; the second, *tra*, means, "that which saves." So the meaning and purpose of a mantra is to cultivate an awareness that protects and saves us from the mind's negativity and the sense of separation from others. The mantra helps the mind to become steady.

Swami Muktananda has written in many of his books that the mantra is a cosmic thought that replaces all other thoughts. "It is the vibration of the Self, the true speech of the Self, and, when we immerse ourselves in it, it leads us to the place of the Self." The mantra provides a focal point for our consciousness. In *The Science of Yoga*, I. K. Taimni states that, "By producing a particular kind of vibration, it is possible to draw down a particular kind of force or to produce a particular state of consciousness." (p. 65)

Repeating a mantra clears the mind of thoughts. When our mind is quieted, we are able to experience the place of peace where the Inner Self resides.

Many traditions use repetitive prayers or phrases that actually function as mantras. Here are some examples:

Judaism: *Ain Ode Milvado,* "there is nothing but God."
                 It is a powerful statement of truth that penetrates
                 consciousness.

Catholicism: The Hail Mary.

Tibetan Buddhism: *Om Mani Padme Hum,* "All that there is, is a precious jewel in the lotus flower which blooms in my heart."

Sufism: *La ilaha illa 'llah,* "There is no Divinity except God"—an Arabic expression for the state of God consciousness. Dhikr is the formal name for this practice. Repeat *La ilaha* on the inhalation and *illa 'llah* on the exhalation.

Hinduism: *Om Namah Shivaya,* "I honor all-pervasive consciousness, the consciousness of the Inner Self." Repeat *Om Namah Shivaya* on the inhalation and again on the exhalation.

To meditate using a mantra, close your eyes and repeat the mantra silently to yourself. Whenever thoughts arise and awareness moves to focus on the thoughts, gently return your attention to the mantra.

Meditation Practice #2: Focusing on the Breath

In his book *Renewing Your Soul*, Rabbi David A. Cooper describes focusing on the breath as the object of meditation:

> The idea is to notice the body movements around every single breath. You may wish to focus on the stomach or the chest as they rise and fall on the breath, or on the total body experience from the tip of the nostrils to the base of the abdomen. The key to building concentration is to bring interest into the practice. Try to be aware of all the different qualities of each breath, and how each differs from every other. Try to be aware precisely when each expansion begins and ends, precisely when each contraction begins and ends, and what happens in between. When you are completely aware of the detailed movements around the breath, you are present in the moment. (pp. 30–31)

I'm going to guide you through a meditation using your breath. You might want to record my instructions for this exercise so you can close your eyes.

It is much easier to block out external distractions and relax the body with your eyes closed.

Get comfortable and loosen any belts or buttons that might restrict your breathing. Close your eyes and take some deep belly breaths. Begin to relax your body by scanning for any tightness you might be feeling in your feet, legs, pelvis, buttocks, stomach, chest, shoulders, arms, neck, forehead, jaws or any other place where you are holding tension. Breathe into these places, and allow them to soften, release, and relax. Take another belly breath and on the exhalation, allow any tension to flow out of your body through your fingertips and your toes. As you focus on your body, imagine a cascade of soothing white light flowing through your body, releasing, relaxing, and carrying away any tension you might be feeling. Feel your body relaxing and getting heavier, sinking into your chair or cushion as you allow yourself to be totally supported. Allow the healing, soothing white light to flow into every cell and carry away any tension or toxins.

Return your attention to your breath. Inhale through your nose and feel your chest expand and your belly extend out as you allow yourself to gently and deeply take in your breath as fully as you comfortably can. Pause for a moment and allow yourself to consciously exhale your breath through your lips, slowly drawing your belly in and collapsing your chest. Pause a moment and continue watching as your body receives the breath on the inhalation and then releases the breath on the exhalation. Continue watching your breath as you inhale, pause, exhale, and pause, throughout the duration of your meditation session. When your mind wanders (notice I say when, so don't be upset when it does), gently bring your attention back to your breath.

Meditation Practice #3: Zen Buddhist Meditation

Zen meditation uses the tool of counting the breaths to attain the state of meditation. Each inhalation and exhalation is counted as one, and the goal is to get to ten.

As you inhale deeply, allow your mind to focus on the number one, and exhale deeply. As you inhale again, focus on the number two. Continue counting each inhalation until you get to the number ten. When your mind wanders and you start thinking thoughts rather than counting your breath, gently go back to the number one and begin counting to number ten again.

It's the nature of the mind to think thoughts, so don't be upset if you can't get past counting to number two. The idea is to imagine the thoughts as clouds in the sky; just let them go by. Refocus your attention on the warmth of the sun, which you will feel as your mind focuses on counting each breath and begins to quiet.

Meditation Practice #4: Buddhist Vipassana Meditation

In Vipassana meditation, you focus on the breath while also naming everything else of which you become aware. You observe the thoughts that arise from a detached perspective.

As you are meditating, you may say to yourself, "nostrils cool, bird chirping, lower back aching," and on and on. You can also name "thought," "feeling," "pain." When you find yourself thinking thoughts, say to yourself, "thinking."

Meditation Practice #5: Pranayama—Alternate Nostril Breathing

Pranayama, a meditative component of most yogic practices, involves controlling or directing the breath. Like the above-mentioned techniques, pranayama can calm and focus the mind. At the core of pranayama practice is a belief that different methods of breathing affect the body's health and life force. One form of pranayama is called alternate nostril breathing, or *Nadi Sodhana*. The yogis consider this to be the best technique to calm the mind and the nervous system.

1. Close the right nostril with your right thumb and inhale through the left nostril. Do this to the count of four seconds.

2. Immediately close the left nostril with your right ring finger and little finger, and at the same time remove your thumb from the right nostril and exhale through this nostril. Do this to the count of eight seconds. This completes a half round.

3. Inhale through the right nostril to the count of four seconds.

4. Close the right nostril with your right thumb and exhale through the left nostril to the count of eight seconds. This completes one full round.

5. Start by doing three rounds. If you decide to take on this practice, you can add one round a week until you can do seven rounds.

Meditation Practice #6: Focusing on a Universal State That You Wish for Yourself and Others.

Metta means "loving-kindness." Buddhist metta meditation is a concentration practice that develops kindness for yourself and others. Instead of focusing on the breath as you do in mindfulness meditation, in metta you focus on the following phrases as you repeat them silently over and over again. You direct the energy of the phrases to: (1) yourself; (2) a teacher, a friend, or a benefactor, who could be someone who has helped you; (3) a neutral person; (4) a difficult person; or (5) all beings everywhere.

The formal phrases of a loving-kindness meditation follow, but you can use any phrase for universal states that you wish for yourself and others.

May I live in safety.
May I have mental happiness.
May I have physical happiness.
May I live with ease.

As you repeat these phrases, you will find that your mind will wander. Gently come back with awareness to repeating the phrases. You can do this for five, fifteen, thirty, or forty-five minutes.

As Sharon Salzberg beautifully states in *The Kindness Handbook*, "We realize through our practice that a loving heart is our natural home, and through our practice we can always find our way home."

Meditation Practice #7: Using a Candle as the Object of Meditation

Choose a comfortable seat in a darkened room where you won't be disturbed. Light a candle and place it a couple of feet in front of you. If you have a timer, set it for five minutes and increase the time at each subsequent sitting as it feels comfortable to you. Focus your eyes and your attention on the candle. If your mind wanders, put the interruptions aside and refocus your attention on the candle.

If you would like to try a more advanced candle meditation, there is a very powerful candle meditation in the central book of Kabbalah, the *Zohar*, which interestingly means brightness. In her book, *Kabbalistic Writings on the Nature of Masculine and Feminine,* Sarah Yehudit Schneider describes the *Zohar* as as "the Jewish mystical commentary on the Torah," whose intention is to explore the answer to the question, "How do I bring body, mind, and soul into perfect harmony with spiritual law?"

The *Zohar* enlightens us with this powerful candle meditation that guides us to concentrate on the different parts of the flame:

> He who desires to penetrate to the mystery of the holy unity should contemplate the flame, which rises from a burning flame or candle.
>
> Further, in the flame itself there are two lights: one white and luminous, and the other black, or blue. The white light is the higher of the two and rises steadily. The black or blue light is underneath the other, which rests on it as a pedestal. The two are inseparably connected, the white resting and being enthroned upon the black.
>
> Above the white light and surrounding it is still another light scarcely perceptible, symbolical of the supreme essence. Thus the ascending flame symbolizes the highest mysteries of wisdom. (Bereshith, Sect. 1, p. 51a)

Meditation Practice #8: Walking Meditation

A walking meditation can be an adjunct to any meditation practice. It has the benefits of developing greater concentration, which can help quiet the mind. Many of my clients describe their minds as so active they can't imagine sitting still for an extended period. The Hindu tradition calls this "monkey mind." If your mind has a tendency to jump around, making sitting meditation difficult, try a walking meditation. The idea is to spend time slowly and consciously walking, while focusing on an object of meditation. With each step you take, focus, and become aware of your breathing

One form of a walking meditation takes place in a labyrinth, which has long been used as a meditation and prayer tool. Labyrinths are often located in nature, or indoors in sacred spaces such as churches, cathedrals, or other spiritual gathering places. They combine the form of a circle and a spiral that leads the meditator on a circuitous path to the center and out again. There is only one way in and one way out. Walking the labyrinth is a vehicle to help focus thoughts, calm the mind, meditate, pray, celebrate, grieve, reflect, and connect more deeply with Spirit.

You can walk the labyrinth in silence, using the breath and your object of meditation, or silently recite a prayer or a saying; you can also contemplate a question that you would like your time walking the labyrinth to help you answer. Walking the labyrinth is a three-stage process:

1. The journey in allows you to relax, focus, and let go of the details of your life. Walk at your own pace. You may pass others and people may pass you.

2. When you reach the center, you can sit for a while and notice what you are experiencing. The center is a place of meditation, illumination, and prayer.

3. The return journey offers integration of what you received during your walk and also time to reengage with the world. When you come to the end, the place where walking the labyrinth began, take time to reflect, pausing to consider how to take what you received into your everyday life.

The labyrinth is a lovely metaphor for all spiritual meditative practices, which are designed to move you to the center of your deepest self and back out into the world with a broadened understanding of who you are.

~

I encourage you to step sincerely and happily onto the spiritual path by taking on a regular practice of one of the meditations listed in this Appendix. It will be one of the most important steps you can take for experiencing and expanding your soul's wisdom.

Appendix G

Additional Resources on Meditation

Buddhist

Aitken, Robert. *Taking the Path of Zen*. San Francisco: North Point Press, 1982.

H. H. the Dalai Lama, Tenzin Gyatso, and Nicholas Vreeland. *An Open Heart: Practicing Compassion in Everyday Life*. New York: Little, Brown and Company, 2001.

H. H. the Dalai Lama, Tenzin Gyatso, and Jeffrey Hopkins. *How to Expand Love: Widening the Circle of Loving Relationships*. New York: Atria Books, 2005.

Kabat-Zinn, Jon. *Wherever You Go, There You Are: Mindfulness Meditation in Everyday Life*. New York: Hyperion, 2005.

Kornfield, Jack. *Meditation for Beginners*. Boulder: SoundsTrue, 2008.

Nhat Hanh, Thich. *Living Buddha, Living Christ*. New York: Riverhead Books, 1995.

_____. *Transformation and Healing: Sutra on the Four Establishments of Mindfulness*. Berkeley: Parallax Press, 1990.

_____. *The Miracle of Mindfulness: A Manual on Meditation, A Zen Master's Method of Meditation, Concentration, and Relaxation*. Boston: Beacon Press, 1987.

Salzberg, Sharon, and Joseph Goldstein. *Insight Meditation: A Step-By-Step Course on How to Meditate*. Boulder: Sounds True, Inc. 2006.

Williams, Mark, John Teasdale, Zindel Segal, and Jon Kabat-Zinn. *The Mindful Way Through Depression: Freeing Yourself from Chronic Unhappiness*. New York: The Guilford Press, 2007.

Christian

Brother Roger of Taize. *Seeds of Trust: Reflecting on the Bible in Silence and Song.* Chicago: Gia Publications, 2006.

Finley, James. *Christian Meditation: Experiencing the Presence of God.* San Francisco: Harper One, 2005.

Keating, Thomas. *Open Mind Open Heart: The Contemplative Dimension of the Gospel.* London: Continuum International Publishing Group, 2002.

Merton, Thomas. *New Seeds of Contemplation.* New York: New Directions, 2007.

Teresa of Avila, Saint. *The Interior Castle.* Mineola: Dover Publications, 2007.

Steindl-Rast, Brother David. *Common Sense Spirituality: The Essential Wisdom of David Steindl-Rast.* New York: The Crossroad Publishing Company, 2008.

General Meditation

Borysenko, Joan Z. *Meditations for Courage and Compassion: Developing Resilience in Turbulent Times CD.* New York: Hay House, 2009.

_____. *The Power of the Mind to Heal.* CD. Niles: Nightingale-Conant, 2009

Dyer, Wayne. *Meditations for Manifesting: Morning and Evening Meditations to Literally Create Your Heart's Desire.* Audio CD. Carlsbad: Hay House, 1995.

Ram Dass. *Journey of Awakening: A Meditator's Guidebook.* New York: Bantam, 1990.

Tolle, Eckhart. *Practicing The Power of Now. Essential Teachings, Meditations, and Exercises from The Power of Now.* Novato: New World Library, 1999.

Hindu

Chidvilasananda, Swami. *Sadhana of the Heart: A Collection of Talks on Spiritual Life.* South Fallsburg: SYDA Foundation. 2007

Gass, Robert, & On Wings of Song. Om Namah Shivaya CD, 10th Anniversary Edition, available at www.springhillmedia.com.

_____. Kirtana: Sanskrit Kirtan Chants, available at www.springhillmedia.com.

Kempton, Sally. *Awakened Heart* Meditation CD, available at www.sallykempton.com.

Muktananda, Swami. *Meditate.* South Fallsburg: SYDA Foundation, 1991

Jewish

Shapira, Rabbi Kalonymus Kalman (trans. by Andrea Cohen-Kiener). *Conscious Community: A Guide to Inner Work.* Northvale: Jason Aronson Inc., 1999.

Cooper, Rabbi David A. *The Handbook of Jewish Meditation Practices: A Guide for Enriching the Sabbath and Other Days of Your Life.* Woodstock: Jewish Lights, 2000.

_____. *A Heart of Stillness: A Complete Guide to Learning the Art of Meditation.* Woodstock: SkyLight Paths, 1999.

Davis, Avram, ed. *Meditations from the Heart of Judaism: Today's Teachers Share Their Practices, Techniques and Faith.* Woodstock: Jewish Lights, 1999.

Gefen, Nan Fink. *Discovering Jewish Meditation: Instruction & Guidance for Learning an Ancient Spiritual Practice.* Woodstock: Jewish Lights, 1999.

Kaplan, Aryeh. *Jewish Meditation: A Practical Guide.* New York: Schocken, 1995.

_____. *Meditation and Kabbalah.* Lanham: Jason Aronson, 1995.

Lew, Alan. *Be Still and Get Going: A Jewish Meditation Practice for Real Life.* New York: Little, Brown and Company, 2005.

Schneider, Sarah Yehudit. www.astillsmallvoice.org. Sarah Yehudit Schneider offers meditation retreats, weekly conference calls, and a correspondence school called A Still Small Voice, which provides weekly teachings in classic Jewish wisdom to students around the world.

Meditation/ Spiritual Retreat Centers

There are wonderful spiritual retreat centers in every state and country that can provide you with rest, renewal, and deeper spiritual connections.

Am Kolel Sanctuary and Renewal Center, Beallsville, MD. www.sanctuaryretreatcenter.com.

Elat Chayyim Center for Jewish Spirituality, Falls Village, CT. www.isabellafreedman.org/elatchayyim.

FindtheDivine - Directory of Spiritual Retreats, Religious Retreats and Conference Centers. www.findthedivine.com.

Independent Meditation Center Guide. www.gosit.org

Insight Meditation Society, Barre, MA. www.dharma.org.

Kripalu Center for Yoga and Health, Stockbridge, MA. www.kripalu.org.

Omega Institute, Rhinebeck, NY. www.eOmega.org.

Satchidananda Ashram - Yogaville, Buckingham, VA. arc@iyiva.org.

SYDA Foundation for Siddha Yoga. www.siddhayoga.org.

Native American

Frazier, LaKotahasie. Ceremonial Teachings. Abington, VA. bluefuffalo.org

Wolf Moondance. *Rainbow Spirit Journeys: Native American Meditations & Dreams.*

Sufi

Douglas-Klotz, Neil. *The Sufi Book of Life: 99 Pathways of the Heart for the Modern Dervish.* New York: Penguin, 2005.

Khan, Pir Vilayat Inayat. *Awakening: A Sufi Experience.* New York: Jeremy Tarcher, 2000.

Mirahmadi, as-Sayyid Nurjan, and Hedieh Mirahmadi. *The Healing Power of Sufi Meditation.* Islamic Supreme Council of America, 2005.

About the Author

Abby Rosen, PhD, cofounder and director of InnerSource, Inc., is a licensed psychologist who has worked with individuals and couples for thirty-six years. Throughout her life, she has woven the threads of psychology and spirituality into a rich tapestry of professional and personal experience. She received her doctorate from California Institute of Integral Studies in 1981. Abby spent a year studying meditation and Eastern psychology in India, and helped coordinate the Seventh International Transpersonal Psychology Conference in Mumbai, India, in 1982. She was director of the Marriage Family Counseling Clinic in San Diego, has written a newspaper column called Dear Dr. Abby, and hosted a cable-TV show called "All about Women and the People in Their Lives," which addressed a variety of medical and psychological topics. Abby has given numerous workshops in the field of transpersonal psychology, the integration of psychology and spirituality. Topics include Communication for Transformation; Voice Dialogue—the Psychology of Selves; Meditation and Kabbalah; the Joys and Jolts of Relationships; Our Intuitive Wisdom; and the Power of the Mind. She lives in Annapolis, Maryland, and on many weekends can be found enjoying a walk on the beach in Delaware, where she is currently giving retreats called Tools for *LASTING Transformation*. Her hope for this book is that it inspires you on your life's journey to greater clarity, connection, consciousness, inner strength, joy, and peace. For more information, visit her website at www.abbyrosenphd.com.

About InnerSource,
A Center for Psychotherapy and Healing

InnerSource, Inc., A Center for Psychotherapy and Healing, is composed of twelve licensed professionals who share the common vision that true growth, healing, and transformation integrate the psychological, physical, spiritual, and environmental realms of awareness. The center, which opened in 1992, is located in a serene, waterfront setting in Annapolis, Maryland. The practitioners believe that within each of us lies an "InnerSource" for self-healing and wisdom. The intention of the professional staff is to facilitate this process of growth and well being, using an integrated team approach.

InnerSource services include holistic, transpersonal, and traditional brief and long-term psychotherapy for adults, children, couples, and families; holistic psychiatry; integrated internal medicine; manual physical therapy; professional organizing; massage and energy medicine; meditation; life style and business coaching; financial consulting for divorcing couples; parent education; and spiritual direction.

InnerSource also offers programs on topics relevant to the needs of the community. For more information or for a referral to a practitioner, please call 410-269-6298 ext. 1 or visit our website at www. innersource-inc.com.

LaVergne, TN USA
09 July 2010
188935LV00002B/2/P